Managing Corporate Growth

DATE DUE

Managing Corporate Growth

JORDI CANALS

OXFORD
UNIVERSITY PRESS

Great Clarendon Street, Oxford OX2 6DP

Oxford University Press is a department of the University of Oxford.
It furthers the University's objective of excellence in research, scholarship,
and education by publishing worldwide in

Oxford New York

Athens Auckland Bangkok Bogotá Buenos Aires Calcutta
Cape Town Chennai Dar es Salaam Delhi Florence Hong Kong Istanbul
Karachi Kuala Lumpur Madrid Melbourne Mexico City Mumbai
Nairobi Paris São Paulo Singapore Taipei Tokyo Toronto Warsaw

with associated companies in Berlin Ibadan

Oxford is a registered trade mark of Oxford University Press
in the UK and in certain other countries

Published in the United States
by Oxford University Press Inc., New York

© Oxford University Press 2000

British Library Cataloguing in Publication Data

Data available

Library of Congress Cataloging in Publication Data

Canals, Jordi.
Managing corporate growth/Jordi Canals.
p. cm.
Includes bibliographical references and index.
1. Corporations—Growth. 2. Corporations—Growth Case studies.
I. Title.
HD2746.C36 2000 658.4′06—dc21 99–42803
ISBN 0–19–829667–3
ISBN 0–19–829668–1 (pbk)

1 3 5 7 9 10 8 6 4 2

Typeset in Utopia
by Cambrian Typesetters, Frimley, Surrey
Printed in Great Britain
on acid-free paper by
T. J. International Ltd.
Padstow, Cornwall

PREFACE

Many Western countries show signs of fatigue: mature economies, modest GDP growth, decreasing population, flat productivity, and high unemployment. This picture reflects a languid social dynamism, and raises doubts about how the current and next generations will cope with these challenges. The solutions are complex and require deep reflection about the values and ideas that seem to dominate our societies. Nevertheless, it is clear that these countries need, among other solutions, growing firms, firms that innovate, create value, and generate new jobs.

In this context, the concern for the growth of the firm seems natural. The restructuring and re-engineering processes of the early 1990s, and the massive lay-offs they brought about have only given an additional boost to the need for growth. Corporate efficiency is indispensable, but is not a sufficient condition for corporate survival. Firms need to think about their future growth and evolution.

The purpose of this book is to contribute to a better understanding of corporate growth and its process. It deals with three basic questions. The first is the nature of the factors that influence corporate growth and how they interact. In this book we develop an integrative model that tries to explain corporate growth. Most of the recent work on the growth of the firm has followed a partial, normative approach and does not address such crucial issues as the definition of the factors that determine a company's growth and how they operate. The second question is how the decision-making process in growth decisions happens. The objective is to understand this process and improve the evaluation of growth decisions, so that they may contribute to value creation, not to wealth destruction, as so often happens with corporate diversification and reckless growth. The third question is the limits and sustainability of corporate growth. We want to explore why companies in some industries grow quicker than others, over relatively long periods of time, and why some companies seem unable to keep growing.

This book takes a General Management perspective that cuts across business functions. It seeks to place the phenomenon of corporate growth within the field of Strategy. As a matter of fact, the growth of the firm has been a topic of interest in Corporate Strategy, which includes—among other questions—the discussion of corporate diversification, vertical integration, and acquisitions. None the less, the nature and driving factors of corporate growth have rarely been studied in Strategy.

The structure of the book is as follows. Chapter 1 introduces the question of corporate growth, discusses its relevance, and outlines its connection with the field of Strategy. In Chapter 2 we present a review of the literature on the growth of the firm and a typology of growth strategies.

In Chapter 3 we present and discuss a conceptual model that seeks to explain the company's growth. This model is defined by five basic factors: the firm's internal context; the external context; the development of a business concept; its resources and capabilities; and, finally, the strategic investment decisions related to the company's future growth. Each factor and its effects on growth are analysed in depth in a separate chapter, from Chapter 4 through Chapter 8. In particular, the focus in Chapter 8 is the decision-making process of growth decisions (how growth strategies are designed and the process they seem to follow). It also includes a methodology to evaluate growth decisions.

In Chapter 9 we analyse the factors that limit and constrain the company's growth and make growth unsustainable. We distinguish between external and internal factors, in particular the absence of innovation and the potential inconsistency between the growth strategy, the firm's resources and capabilities, and the implementation of the growth plans.

This book is addressed to MBA students, professional managers, and entrepreneurs. We have tried to present solid theoretical concepts with a practical perspective. The text offers a combination of theory and business cases with a strong international flavour, and could be used in Advanced Strategy or Corporate Strategy courses.

In our research, we have studied the evolution over relatively long periods of large, well-known international companies, such as BBV, Bertelsmann, Glaxo Wellcome, Goldman Sachs, L'Oréal, Nokia, Reuters, and SAP. Nevertheless, our analysis has also included medium-size firms with intriguing growth patterns. We have examined how these companies have tackled the growth challenge, the factors that drive and block growth, the decision-making process, the role played by top management, and how these growth decisions are assessed. This examination is vital in order to ask exploratory questions, establish the initial hypotheses, and build a coherent model aimed at explaining corporate growth. The model and ideas that we present here are grounded on academic research in the field of Strategy, and are discussed with reference to the companies studied.

In the process of preparing this book I have profited from the useful and insightful advice from some colleagues. David Musson has played a key role in this work. He has encouraged the author to pursue its objective, suggested new questions to tackle, described more useful ways to address certain issues, and kept the right rhythm in the writing process. Thank you, David. My special thanks go to my colleagues at the IESE (International Graduate School of Management), José Luis Alvarez, Toni Dávila, Esteban Masifern, and Joan Enric

Ricart, for their constructive suggestions. I am very grateful to Pankaj Ghemawat. Over the past years I have learnt a lot from his ideas on Strategy and he has helped sharpen my views on some of the topics covered in this book. I am also grateful to four anonymous referees who evaluated some of the chapters and offered me numerous comments that were very helpful in refining the model, concepts, and presentation of the issues.

I have a debt of gratitude to my second-year IESE MBA students and senior managers who have attended Executive Programmes at IESE. Over the past seven years I have offered a Strategy course in which I have started to think about the issues of corporate growth. With their hard work, experience, dedication, and enthusiasm, they have taught me many lessons about corporate growth and, more importantly, about personal growth. Many managers in the companies mentioned above have offered me a unique perspective from which to contemplate how corporate growth happens. Without their help, advice, and patience the evidence of growth in those companies would not have been identified. Eulàlia Escolà and Marta Bentanachs have helped me with their efficient skills during the preparation and editing of this work, keeping their calm and professionalism even when the rhythm of events became hectic. I am also very grateful to Sarah Dobson and Hilary Walford at Oxford University Press for their outstanding editorial help.

To all of you, thank you.

Jordi Canals

Barcelona
July 1999

CONTENTS

LIST OF FIGURES

1

Corporate Growth: Is it a Relevant Issue?

1. DO FIRMS NEED GROWTH?

The firm has been the most innovative institution of the twentieth century. It has driven economic and social development, fostered the creation of new jobs, and accelerated the development of new technologies and products that have played a fundamental role in the progress of many countries. Without any doubt, firms will occupy a prominent place in any account of the social evolution in the twentieth century. Information technology, globalization, and new organizational paradigms are some of the factors that have made dramatic changes in the landscape in which firms compete (see e.g. Miles and Snow 1994; Ashkenas *et al.* 1995; Ghoshal and Bartlett 1997).

The new forms of competition are bringing about the stagnation of some legendary companies, with decades of history behind them, such as General Motors, Sears, and Digital in the USA, or Thomson, Olivetti, and Crédit Lyonnais in Europe, to mention only some of the better-known cases. The common denominator underlying these companies is the fact that at certain times during the last few decades of the twentieth century they have been leaders in their respective industries, in terms of profitability, innovation, or growth. (See Kay 1993, Drucker 1994, and Tushman and O'Reilly 1997 for a discussion of the evolution, rise, and fall of some of those companies.) In all cases, they have been exceptional companies that have seriously addressed the challenge of their survival as organizations. Some of them have successfully tackled their problems and are starting to recover, while others have not succeeded and have either disappeared—being taken over by another company—or are fighting what may be their last battle.

These companies have experienced—and in the late 1990s some of them are still experiencing—a common disease: the erosion of their competitive advantages and, as a natural outcome, the lack of growth prospects. In other words, they are big companies that no longer grow; or they may grow, but not through innovation, but through price-cutting wars, which, normally, only lead to decreasing profitability and wealth destruction. It is important to establish that we are speaking about growth and not about market share or size. We consider that the yardstick for growth should not be the increase in revenues in the short term or sheer size, but the increase in the firm's value added in the long term, which is the outcome of innovation and the development of sustainable competitive advantages. This has a clear implication: in most cases, growth is different from pursuing a bigger scale or a higher market share, although this may be necessary for growth in some cases.

Is corporate growth a goal?

The growth of the firm is not a goal *per se*. Firms are made up of people who, with the contribution of different types of resources, seek to serve customers through differentiated goods and services and create new value along the process. Growth is not, therefore, the company's key objective, nor is growth a guarantee of value creation.[1] Some firms may even need downsizing at some point in order to survive.

The problem arises when a company has not grown for many years or its growth is not financially healthy. Although the lack of growth over a long period of time does not necessarily mean decreasing profitability, it may be a signal of an inability to innovate or a firm's lack of connection with its current or prospective customers and their needs. A company that is not growing may find a ready explanation for its problem by saying that the market is flat. However, in some cases the absence of growth may point out that the company is unable to reach new customers or to design and offer new products or services that set it apart from other companies. Therefore, growth is not the key corporate goal. Growth is a means for achieving higher value added and guaranteeing the survival of the firm in the long term. However, prolonged absence of growth may be a symptom of future decline.

The need to grow is especially acute in West European countries with mature economies, modest annual GDP growth rates, and high unemployment. It seems rather clear that the solution to these problems passes through job creation, a process that can be brought about only by growing firms that have projects for the future. The stock-market valuations of public firms—which may reflect many factors—also take into account the firm's growth prospects and their effects on profitability (Geroski *et al.* 1996 observe the relationship between growth rates, expectations about future profitability, and the change in the firm's market value). The case of international companies expanding into promising—although risky—new emerging, growing markets highlights this observation, since they get the respect and interest of investors. It is also the case of Internet-based firms, whose stock prices may rise, not because of their current profitability, but for their growth prospects. On the contrary, investors seem to punish firms whose growth prospects are downgraded. The stock-market crisis in the autumn of 1998 inflicted a more severe punishment on

---

[1] The importance of corporate growth should not prevent us from recognizing both its risks and the threat of opportunistic managers seeking their own profit through growth (see Baumol 1962 and Marris 1963).

those European and US firms whose growth possibilities in emerging markets were sharply reduced, including blue-chip firms such as Gillette or Coca-Cola.

It is also worth observing that firms whose growth prospects are not that bright in the short term may prefer to reduce capital and pay investors back part of their equity, as Unilever announced in February 1999 (as a special dividend). Through this type of action, firms not only acknowledge their diminished possibilities for growth and investment, but also commit themselves to use capital more efficiently and allow their shareholders to invest in other firms with higher growth opportunities.

The new theory of economic growth also sheds some light upon the challenge of corporate growth. As Paul Romer—one of the leading scholars that has changed our view on economic growth—puts it: 'The most important lesson from this new approach is that growth takes place when companies and individuals discover and implement [new] formulas and recipes [new methods of doing things]' (Lessard et al., 1998: 9). He considers that the key factor in growth is not capital or raw materials, but soft assets such as knowledge, instructions, or ways of rearranging things. He calls this change the 'soft revolution'.

One of the many implications to be drawn from Romer's analysis is that 'there is unlimited scope for discovering new ideas, new pieces of software, new recipes', (ibid. 10). In other words, not only is corporate growth possible, but it depends on human creativity more than any other factor. This conclusion should encourage managers who operate in markets that seem to be flat.

Corporate growth, an elusive phenomenon

Nevertheless, corporate growth is still an elusive phenomenon for managers and scholars alike. As Geroski and Machin (1992) point out, corporate growth is idiosyncratic and firm specific, depending upon each firm's history and innovations. These results confirm that corporate growth can be relentlessly pursued, but it is a daunting task for managers and one of uncertain results. All this makes its study and understanding more exciting.

Moreover, corporate growth can also be a lethal medicine. Unhealthy corporate growth—from a financial viewpoint—is tremendously harmful. Reckless diversification or the pressure to increase sales or market share at whatever cost, through price wars, indiscriminate promotions, unreasonable marketing expenses, or incentives to the sales force to increase short-term revenues, is rarely a satisfactory path towards growth.

The direction of corporate growth is another subtle threat for many firms. Choosing new products, new markets, new countries, or new businesses are decisions that may lead to growth. However, each of these actions is the result of complex strategic decisions that usually absorb an enormous amount of all types of resources.

The development of a risky new product or service—such as the launch of Gillette's Mach 3—the expensive acquisition of another company that is difficult to integrate—such as the acquisition of Viacom by Blockbuster—the diversification into new businesses—like the one followed by Pepsico in the 1980s and early 1990's—or an enormously expensive globalization—such as the process followed by Ford, which culminated in the launch of Mondeo, a global car—are decisions that have an enormous impact on the company's future, in one way or another. These growth decisions normally involve great uncertainty. Nevertheless, rigour in the decision-making process and flexibility in its execution are essential, because their effects on the firms will be enormous.

Understanding corporate growth

Corporate growth seems to be an important aspect in the firm's evolution and a growing concern for managers. Nevertheless, with the exception of some authors who have argued that companies pursue growth to ensure their long-term survival (Donaldson and Lorsch 1984) or that corporate growth springs from personal goals of the top management (Marris 1963), corporate growth has not received much attention.

The most important work carried out on this subject is that of Penrose (1959), who seeks to provide a view of growth based more on processes than on goals. She claims that the use and transfer of the firm's resources—in particular, managerial resources—at a particular time are crucial for accounting for its subsequent development and growth.

In the strategy field, corporate growth has been discussed only indirectly. The work of Chandler (1962, 1990) is one of the few exceptions. This author provides an excellent historical explanation for understanding the birth and growth of certain large companies in some countries, and the factors that have accounted for their development over time. Chandler has without doubt defined the context of growth and some of the critical organizational decisions that those companies had to make. We will discuss his and Penrose's views more deeply in Chapter 2.

In the second half of the 1990s there has been an increased academic interest in corporate growth that looks very promising (see Garnsey 1998; Ghoshal *et al.* 1999). Ghoshal *et al.* (1997), based upon the observation that there seems to be a correlation between a country's economic development and the number of its large firms, highlight that management competence plays a key role in the firm's growth process. This notion is a refinement of Penrose's hypothesis on the role of resources in corporate growth and adds a new dimension to understanding corporate growth.

In the more popular management literature, some recent contributions have offered the experience of companies that have been able adequately to manage and sustain their growth (see e.g. Gertz and Baptista 1995; Baghai *et al.* 1996, 1999; Slywotzky *et al.* 1998). Their starting point is the general concern in many companies that some techniques and their emphasis on process re-engineering and restructuring have been harmful for corporate productivity. The reaction of some consulting firms has been to stress the importance of the company's growth and not just the concern for short-term efficiency. This literature is more descriptive, contains useful ideas for reflection, and, in any case, provides a beacon to remind people to think about the future and suitable ways of managing it.

Corporate growth seems to be important for firms and managers, not only because in some cases it may be good for firms, but also because it may become the prelude of failure, and there is a great interest in understanding how it happens and how it can be managed. This book takes a General Management approach, cuts across functional areas, and aims to place the subject of corporate growth and its process within the field of Strategy. In subsequent chapters we will present a model that tries to explain and integrate the factors that speed up growth, the decision-making process of corporate growth, the steps these decisions seem to follow, and the limits to corporate growth.

In the rest of this chapter we will address two introductory questions regarding corporate growth. The first is the existence of different drivers that accelerate corporate growth. They show how idiosyncratic corporate growth is, as Geroski and Machin (1992) point out. The second presents other reasons that highlight the importance of corporate growth.

2. CORPORATE GROWTH: DIFFERENT DRIVERS AND PATTERNS

If firms have to be concerned about their growth, their managers have to think about certain key issues. What mechanisms help companies to grow profitably at higher rates than competing companies? What are the principles that govern corporate growth? What are the limits to this growth process? How should growth decisions be evaluated? When is growth good and when bad? How are growth opportunities distinguished from reckless expansion?

Before proposing possible answers to these questions, we will briefly present some cases of well-known companies that have managed to sustain high growth rates. We will first try to observe certain common patterns present in these growth processes. Past growth or success is not a predictor of future growth or success. As has happened with other firms, such companies are not free from threats and their growth can slow down. Nevertheless, one can learn from their experiences in growing, consider how they did it and reflect on the underlying factors, even if one cannot draw instant recipes from them. The companies we present in this section have been growth firms for many years through different, although complementary, pathways: corporate renewal, innovation, product development, and mergers and acquisitions. Elsewhere in this book we will discuss the case of firms that have failed, in part because of the growth decisions they took.

Banco Bilbao Vizcaya (BBV): A renewal-based growth

In 1988 Banco de Bilbao and Banco de Vizcaya, the third and fifth largest banks in Spain, respectively, decided to merge, thus forming the largest Spanish banking group, Banco Bilbao Vizcaya (BBV). This bank was positioned as a medium-sized (by European standards) universal bank with a strong presence in commercial and corporate banking, a small but growing business in financial markets, and a portfolio of shareholdings in industrial or services companies beyond banking (see further Canals 1993a, 1997a, 1999). However, the instant growth provided by the merger did not deliver the desired results in terms of profitability. In fact, between 1988 and 1993, the bank's performance remained below expectations.

The crisis that the bank fell into in early 1994 was the spur it needed to pull itself out of its state of mediocrity. BBV designed and started to implement the so-called 1,000 Days Programme in 1994. This was not a classic strategic plan. It was, above all, a plan for revitalizing the bank. Its goal was to make BBV the best investment alternative for shareholders within the Spanish banking industry, using the resources and capabilities that already existed within the BBV group. This generic goal was divided into a series of clear sub-goals: to be the leader in each segment of the financial services business in Spain, to tackle all the business opportunities arising in these segments, to optimize the bank's capital structure, and to fulfil the expectations of shareholders, customers, and employees.

In order to achieve these goals, almost 100 specific action plans were defined for execution during the next 1,000 days. These plans were structured around ten key issues for the bank: corporate growth, the development of new profitable businesses, consolidation of the international strategy, the restructuring of weak businesses, adaptation to the euro, product innovation, the improvement of information technology, organizational responsiveness, the development of the BBV culture, and the consolidation of a corporate atmosphere of high commitment and high performance.

The bank's performance between 1994 and 1998 was exceptional, particularly if one considers that growth in the European banking industry as a whole was very limited in those years. Thus, in that period the group's assets more than doubled, revenues increased by 115 per cent, return on equity went up from 12.1 per cent to 21 per cent, and market capitalization increased by 353 per cent, from 750 billion pesetas (4.5 billion euros) in 1994 to 2,300 billion pesetas (13.8 billion euros) by the end of 1998, becoming one of the largest European banks in terms of market capitalization. By way of reference, the Spanish banking industry's market value increased 110 per cent during the same five-year period. These growth rates were among the highest in the world banking industry in 1998.

From a qualitative viewpoint, the strong consolidation of the bank's international strategy enabled BBV to become a leading bank in Latin America, acquiring well-positioned banks in Mexico, Peru, Colombia, Argentina, and

Venezuela, with a total investment in these countries exceeding 2.5 billion euros. These growth rates are all the more astonishing when one considers the slow growth shown by the banking industry as a whole in industrialized countries. What explanation can be given for this performance?

The answer is complex but a number of hypotheses can be put forward. The first is that the plan succeeded in awakening and dynamizing unique capabilities that were lying dormant within the BBV group owing to the lack of definition that prevailed until 1993 in the group's strategy, market positioning, and future plans. The second hypothesis is that, with this programme, BBV developed a vision about customers' needs and a way to serve them, organized a series of projects around this vision, and invested in them. In other words, BBV turned the 1,000 Days Programme into a catalyst for the bank's change and renewal.

The third hypothesis is that any growth option implies a choice between a series of alternatives. BBV decided to be stronger in the financial markets area and increase market share in Latin America and chose not to increase its presence in Europe or Asia. Such choices—which imply discarding other alternative options—are essential for understanding the processes of corporate growth.

To summarize, the case of BBV shows that, by mobilizing the organization's effort and focusing the attention of the people on key actions, firms can put into motion a change process that enables them to embark upon growth paths at rates exceeding the industry average, even in stagnant industries such as banking.

SAP AG: An innovation-driven growth process

SAP AG (an abbreviation for Systems, Applications, Programs in Data Processing), a German software company, was the leader of the enterprise information systems market at the end 1998, and also the fourth largest software maker, behind Microsoft, Oracle, and Computer Associates. Its application R/3 ran the operations of about half of the world's 500 top companies in 1998 and it had become the software standard for corporate integrated applications software.

SAP was set up by four young engineers in Walldorf, Germany, in 1972. While still working with IBM, they had an idea for an integrated software package, but their company was not interested in its development. Any description of high-growth European companies includes SAP among the leaders. Its revenues grew tenfold between 1990 and 1998, reaching 5.1 billion euros in 1998. Growth at SAP has been explosive. How has it achieved it? The explanation has to do with perceiving new corporate needs in the enterprise information systems market and the development of new products to address these needs. SAP's managers and engineers develop visions of the future in terms of new products and services and translate these visions into new products or software systems. They also count on partners to implement the products.

The ability to develop new products is related to the firm's large annual investment on R&D—about 20 to 25 per cent of total revenues—the recruitment of young and creative engineers and programmers, an intense training culture to help new engineers better understand customers's needs and SAP's vision and culture, a flat organization with very loose and informal relationships, and a rather conservative approach to financial management, with low debt.

A key and underlying theme in all the systems SAP has developed over twenty-five years is the integration of software applications to run a firm's operations. Their first product, launched in 1979, was R/2, especially designed for mainframe computers. It was a success, especially among European firms, because it addressed a pressing need of large companies that had different software programs to run their activities.

Nevertheless, the founders of SAP did not stop there. They started international operations very quickly, choosing the USA as a key market. The management of the US subsidiary was tough and rivalry very intense, but it provided a unique valuable experience for the future of SAP. When they developed the S/3, a successful new product in 1992, the US market was already well known to the firm's managers. SAP's managers also had another great idea. Some software companies were designing and improving fantastic software packages to run manufacturing, sales, or accounting, as independent functions. SAP's founders decided to design new programs destined to link all the firm's operations.

A sea-change event, which helped bring about that vision, happened in the early 1990s, with the so-called client-server revolution. These were cheaper servers that delivered information to personal computers. This technological breakthrough allowed firms to slice information and repackage it in new and different ways. SAP took advantage of this innovation and linked it up with its idea of integrating functions and activities. The outcome was the launching of R/3 in 1992, a program especially designed to work in the new server environment. The program was an instant success, selling more than $500 million that year and more than $2 billion in 1997.

The value added by the new system provided by SAP was that companies could run their operations and scrutinize their business in an integrated way, from purchasing to distribution and customer service. At the same time, the program would allow companies to discard a maze of different and incompatible software systems, each of them created to run a small part of the firm's total operations. This might seem a small step, but it was very difficult to be able to manage an international or global company without knowing the level of inventories in different countries or the manufacturing capacity available at any given point in time. In order to sell the new software globally, SAP engineers designed the new program in such a way that it could work in different languages and currencies, which was a startling advantage for multinational companies operating in different countries. For all the advantages of R/3, its implementation was complex and expensive. Around the new program, SAP had generated a new industry of high-price consultants whose expertise was to apply and implement the new software in each company. As some people put it, SAP was not just a company, it was a new industry.

When the launch of R/3 was planned in late 1991, the discussion about whether SAP should remain a product company—that is to say, a company that designs new software packages—or a consulting or solutions company was controversial. The first option—remaining a product company—would involve designing great products and selling as many copies of them as possible. The second option—a solutions company—would involve becoming a consulting company whose mission would be to help firms implement software packages. In this option, revenues would come from the services provided.

The board made the decision to remain a product company and implement it in such a way as to make R/3 the standard infrastructure for enterprise applications. One of the reasons to support this option was that the alternative would have involved hiring thousands of consultants to implement the software. This scenario was somehow beyond the capabilities of SAP at that point. On the other hand, its executive committee decided to strengthen its internal consulting group, which would operate as a unit to provide support to key customers and external consultancy firms that would enter this new market. It would assist them with the installation of the software package. The target the board set was to pursue about 20 per cent of the implementation business and leave the rest to other consultancy firms.

An essential condition for the success of this option was to encourage consultancy firms to undertake this new opportunity SAP had forged. It initiated a web of alliances with distinguished companies such as Andersen Consulting, Arthur Andersen, Price Waterhouse, or Deloitte & Touche. The philosophy of the cooperation between SAP and each of the partners was that R/3 was a great initiative that would create vast new possibilities for systems applications, and SAP would not compete with them in implementing the package. That was their business opportunity. SAP would focus exclusively on developing even better products. The basic principles of these alliances were threefold: they could not be exclusive, they had to be beneficial to both parties, and there would not be a financial tie between SAP and the partner.

SAP's approach to its industry has been very innovative, along several dimensions. The first is its conception of new software packages that could integrate different systems and functions. The second is its early international approach, which is very intriguing if one takes into account the size of the German or the West European market. The third is the way in which it observed and took advantage of the new generation of customer servers. The fourth is the option to remain focused and concentrate on designing better products, when the temptation to grow in a completely new business is very attractive. The fifth is its decision to forge alliances with consultancy firms and its approach to these alliances, which it has managed in such a way that it has maintained its partners' satisfaction with the agreement while opening up new business opportunities for them. With these experiences, SAP has proved that innovation, supported by a good organizational structure, linked up to customer service, pays off and that it can become a sustained driver of corporate growth. It also shows that European companies can be innovative when they develop a unique business concept and give their innovations an adequate organizational support.

It is true that SAP has been banking on the growth of this industry and its challenge will be to sustain the rhythm. Nevertheless, nobody doubts that, without SAP and its innovative products, this industry would not have grown so fast.

Glaxo Wellcome: A merger to improve R&D capabilities

Growing companies stand out for their flexibility. Thus, in addition to growing through internal development, they take all of the opportunities that come their way. The case of Glaxo and the acquisition of Wellcome is a good illustration of this growth pattern (see further Canals and Bardolet 1998).

In 1994 the European pharmaceutical industry was highly fragmented and there were no truly pan-European pharmaceutical companies. One of the few exceptions was Glaxo, the largest European pharmaceutical firm. Between 1981 and 1989 its revenues tripled, increasing to £2.8 billion. Five years later, in 1994, Glaxo had doubled its turnover. During the 1980s Glaxo changed the face of the industry, thanks to the vision of its CEO, Sir Paul Girolami, who encouraged research in new products such as Zantac and boosted the company's marketing efforts. Glaxo's sales were led by what was then the world's highest selling drug, a genuine blockbuster, Zantac, an anti-ulcerative drug introduced in the early 1980s.

Going against other opinions, Paul Girolami decided that Zantac should be positioned as an extremely high-quality and high-price premium drug, which would set it apart from other anti-ulcerative drugs and provide resources to finance other R&D projects. This approach proved to be right. In 1994 Zantac had achieved record sales of £2.4 billion, with a 35 per cent share of the anti-ulcerative market. Glaxo had staked a large part of its growth on this product's success and the strategy had worked out. The problem was that Zantac's patent expired in 1997. From then on, the market would be invaded by cheaper me-too generics and the sales of Glaxo's original would probably drop sharply.

In 1994 Glaxo had products in seven different treatment areas. Its managers could also boast of having succeeded in introducing eleven completely new drugs on the market between 1980 and 1994, which was a by no means insignificant achievement. All of these drugs belonged to the prescription-drug category. Glaxo did not market any products in the over-the-counter (OTC) category.

In Glaxo, the R&D and marketing policies were the firm's key success factors and were given greater priority than in other pharmaceutical companies, which were perhaps more focused on distribution. Innovation had been a key factor in the company's success and Glaxo's management had no intention of changing that approach. Glaxo's R&D achievements were based on the calibre of its scientists, their absolute commitment to the company, the spirit of team-work, a very strong research tradition, and very exacting project assessment procedures.

Thus, Glaxo's R&D and marketing strategies had been innovative and consistent and had enabled the company to achieve significant growth. Nevertheless, in 1994, Glaxo's senior management felt that the time had come to accelerate growth and started to study the possible acquisition of Wellcome. There were doubts within the pharmaceutical industry about Glaxo's ability successfully to see the merger through. All of Glaxo's growth in recent years had been internal. However, the potential benefits of the merger were considerable.

With the merger, Glaxo was pursuing not instant growth, but the scale, resources, and capabilities to strengthen its R&D and speed up new product development. Its managers were convinced that a powerful range of innovative products, in various treatment areas, would enable it to achieve significant growth in market share. The range of products that would be achieved from a merger with Wellcome would be much broader and more competitive, because it would be possible to complement areas of expertise and knowledge and the new R&D projects could be endorsed by bigger resources. Glaxo's presence in certain treatment areas that had remained untapped until then (antivirals, for example) could be increased and synergies would be found between the two companies' products. For the treatment of AIDS, for example, it had been found that Glaxo's 3TC and Wellcome's AZT could provide an effective combination. The same was true with other products.

Furthermore, with the acquisition of Wellcome, Glaxo would acquire a brand of acknowledged renown. It was often said in industry circles that patients preferred to be treated with drugs that had a well-known brand rather than with generics, even if the latter were cheaper. The Wellcome brand was highly respected in the UK and also in the USA. Another advantage was Wellcome's expertise in the OTC market. Thanks to its alliance with Warner-Lambert, Wellcome could effectively help in turning some of Glaxo's star products into products for the OTC market and thus increase the group's sales.

The changes that were in the offing in the pharmaceutical industry in 1995 (the entry of generic drugs, strong pressure on costs, OTC drugs, etc.) seemed to indicate that future growth would require larger size in order to be able to take on more costly R&D projects. In 1995 Glaxo's managers perceived the need to expedite the company's traditional growth based on innovation and new product launches, with an ambitious move—the acquisition of Wellcome—that would enable Glaxo to increase the R&D budget and make better use of the capabilities of both firms. The two companies' boards approved the merger in 1995. The new group's performance at the end of 1998 seemed to confirm the soundness of the strategy followed, and the success of the process of integrating both firms, especially if one takes into account the loss of nearly £800 million in sales of Zantac and Zovirax in 1998, owing to patent expiration.

Too often, mergers seem to be driven by cost-cutting and they pave the way for instantaneous growth, which is not always sustainable. Only when mergers allow the firms involved to combine capabilities and develop more and better products, can they become growth engines. This seems to have been the case of the new Glaxo Wellcome.

Glaxo (like BBV or SAP) shows a number of traits that seem to be present in many companies that have achieved sustainable growth. These include a sense of innovation and entrepreneurship, the ability to discover opportunities in the environment and tackle them successfully, the development of a vision about its future, and the will to renew and revitalize the company's internal processes and capabilities in the face of new challenges. In the next chapters we will discuss these dimensions and take up these cases again within a wider framework to understand better corporate growth and its risks and limits.

3. WHY IS CORPORATE GROWTH IMPORTANT?

The cases discussed in the previous section illustrate some of the mechanisms driving corporate growth, such as internal revitalization, new product development, innovation, and mergers and acquisitions oriented towards developing new capabilities and products. Among others, these cases offer a reflection: many leading companies are growing companies.

None of these cases can be used to infer unequivocal conclusions about corporate growth. These companies are not immune to competitive threats and their growth may fade away or become rather unhealthy. Nevertheless, their growth experience is here, and there is something to learn from this. The description of these cases is intended to pinpoint some of the mechanisms of growth and will help us present a more integrated model in the next chapters.

In this section we want to outline some of the reasons why healthy growth is an indispensable part of corporate life, a basic consideration in corporate strategy, and an object of ongoing reflection by a company's senior manager (see Gertz and Baptista 1995 and Europe 500 1998 for alternative views). Healthy growth—in particular, innovation-based growth—always involves risks, but zero growth might involve even higher risks. Corporate growth is critical in managing revenues and costs, developing talent, attracting capital, managing the risk of substitution, and breaking the mature-industry mindset. Moreover, a rigorous approach to corporate growth may help a lot in avoiding growth decisions that may lead to failure.

Managing revenues and costs

A company that is not growing in an industry that is not growing has only one way to survive: to reduce continually its cost structure. This has been one of the pillars of the strategy followed in recent years by Banco Popular in Spain (see Boudeguer and Ballarín 1993). The traditional retail banking industry in Europe is no longer growing. Banks such as Lloyds or BBV have been very active in looking for new customers in a low-growth market. Banco Popular has been less active.

Banco Popular's strategy was always aimed at seeking profitability above growth. Thus, it managed very well the cost of its liabilities, accurately assessed the return on its assets, and implemented an extraordinary cost-cutting effort to prevent any decline in performance. The combination of these factors enabled this bank to be exceptionally profitable for many years. However, a change in its strategy was implemented in 1996. Its goal was to achieve higher growth.

The challenge for Banco Popular was that improving profitability in the long term (return on sales or return on equity) might have required a certain level of new projects that could generate growth. The lack of growth projects aimed at attracting new customers over many years meant that revenues had remained stagnant. So long as profit levels were maintained and capital was used efficiently, this was not serious. The problem for Banco Popular was that its financial margin was decreasing, and the investments and costs involved in being a player in the banking industry were increasing so that growth in revenues might be necessary to cover them. And the answer to this problem was not a merger—which sometimes makes things worse—but new products and services that would make a difference.

Basically, Banco Popular was a well-managed bank and, looked at from this viewpoint, very fortunate, because it had been able to control its costs and investments well. But the lack of growth was threatening its profitability. Other companies, in other industries, that have ceased to grow have found that their revenues have levelled off and their expenses have started to climb dangerously. In this case, the drop in margins and profits is instant.

This is a phenomenon that affects many companies that have to undertake new investments or expenses in order to produce better, to distribute more efficiently, or to maintain sales. When these projects generate growth, there is a chance that expenses could be covered and investments recovered. However, when companies are not growing, these investments or expenses tend to squeeze margins. Stagnant revenues and increasing expenses combine to form a scissors effect that relentlessly snips away at profits.

In search of talent

Great companies are made of great people. These individuals may not be featured in the front cover of newspapers, but they are good professionals, among the best in their field, and able to develop other professionals.

No firm can achieve more than what the combination of its people and their qualities can offer. Although the empirical correlation between talent and corporate success is difficult to draw, many senior managers know from their experience that attracting, recruiting, developing, and retaining talented people are key tasks. Some consulting, manufacturing, and financial services firms know this truth very well and their senior managers spend a lot of time in dealing with and getting to know young graduates.

Nevertheless, the attention senior managers pay to this process is an indispensable factor, but not the only one. Firms should also offer (among other factors such as a friendly environment, a good career, or an attractive compensation package) interesting professional challenges and new projects—that is, projects that can have an impact on the firm, its people, and its customers, and generate growth. Firms that do not show enthusiasm about their future and the projects they have, or that do not develop new opportunities for growth, will face a more difficult obstacle when trying to recruit the talent they need to guarantee their survival.

The need to attract capital

For public companies, the need to attract capital today, to improve the prospects to attract it in the future, and to convince potential investors that the company has a future makes growth potential an important factor.

Investors weigh their decisions on the basis of a series of variables. One of these is return on investment. This variable depends on many factors, but there is no doubt that the company's ability to ensure healthy and sustained growth is one of the most important. Essentially, the added value that a company can generate in the future is a function of the new projects it tackles, both to maintain current sources of income and to revitalize them.

The considerable success that the privatization of state-owned companies has enjoyed in many European companies, particularly from the investors' viewpoint, is related to the growth prospects that these companies have offered. From British Telecom in Britain to Repsol in Spain, the vast majority of these companies have offered investors not only a change in ownership or, in some cases, a guarantee of improved management, but also a forward-looking business project resting on a more solid base.

Growth expectations are a powerful driver of stock prices, as we have discussed before in the case of Internet-based stocks or international companies with solid operations in new markets. Their decline in the autumn of 1998 was the reflection of a higher risk aversion, but also an indicator that the growth prospects of many firms—especially those with investments in emerging markets—had suddenly decreased.

Avoiding the risk of substitution and imitation

The choice many companies face is not between growth and stagnation. On the contrary, the dilemma is growth and renewal versus decline. The reason for this is that product substitution or imitation takes place in all industries and may seriously endanger the stability of the company's revenues (Ghemawat 1991). Thinking about new projects that can generate growth enables firms to tackle the challenge of substitution and imitation, by getting ahead of other firms or by becoming different.

The risk of substitution exists when a new product that is superior in quality and price appears on the market. This phenomenon may occur—but not only then—during a product's maturity phase. Companies that are already in this phase and do not generate new ideas for serving their customers may find themselves pushed out of the market because of the increased innovation or better service provided by other companies.

A classic case is IBM and its late entry into the personal-computer industry. Once they are connected in a network, personal computers are able to carry out many of the tasks of mainframe computers on which the IBM's business was based. The personal computer seems to match best the needs of small companies and, above all, reach individual customers. Leader of the computer industry, IBM was not the first company to enter into the personal-computer business. Indeed, initially it spurned this emerging industry. The result was a set of business opportunities that IBM missed because of the company's reluctance and the effects of substitution of mainframes by networked personal computers. It is not that its managers were incompetent, but rather that they could not foresee the future at that time because the uncertainty was enormous, and that they adopted a passive stance regarding that growth option.

A similar phenomenon—although of a different nature—is that of imitation. This is to be found in industries where companies, with quite a substantial deployment of resources and effort, tend to behave in a similar way. In the European car industry, companies have adopted similar capacity and product development strategies to improve their productivity. The result of this tendency to imitate competitors has been excess capacity, price wars, and poor performance. (See Canals 1997*b* for a discussion of excess capacity in global industries.) Firms that systematically explore growth opportunities may find it easier to develop them than companies that do not, and through them they may manage or offset the risks of substitution and imitation.

Managing the product's life cycle

New products and services are platforms upon which firms build their future. If they are really good, they may even allow firms to grow more quickly. Nevertheless, growth led by innovation is also important, because, whatever the length of the life cycle of the products on which a company has based its development in the past, it is nevertheless limited. The classic model of the product life cycle considers four phases: introduction, growth, maturity, and decline. Once a product has entered the maturity or stagnation phase, the possibilities of further growth—or steady revenues—are lower, unless, for example, the product is redesigned, its cost–price–value combination is changed, or an alternative approach is given to its distribution (see Day 1990).

A company that wishes to survive must not only try to prevent its product from entering into decline but also avoid the situation by which other firms make its products obsolete. Thus, the aim is not only to maintain a passive stance—prevent a product from declining—but also to develop a more active attitude to speed up growth—such as launching new products or undertaking new initiatives. Hewlett-Packard's practice of thinking about new projects that can generate growth and launching new products with the explicit goal of cannibalizing some of the company's current products is a good example of how a company can focus the renewal of its product range and, above all, create a more solid base for ensuring its continuity.

Breaking the mature-industry mindset

The concept of product maturity has been readily transposed to the industry as a whole. Thus, some people talk about mature industries—that is, industries that do not grow. This is an inappropriately used concept. Maturity, as a business concept, refers more to products than to industries. One can talk about companies or industries with mature products but not about mature companies or industries.[2] Normally, a mature company is a company that is stuck in a rut.

Porter's work (1980) contributed to underscoring the importance of industries' structural attractiveness when designing and assessing business strategies. Furthermore, his five-forces model offers a concise and rigorous way to explore an industry's features and their impact on the company's strategy. However, concentrating excessively or solely on the industry's features has led in some cases to the conclusion that there are structurally good and bad industries, and that firms cannot grow in the context of unattractive industries. These are not irreversible conditions. What is true is that there are industries that are not growing and industries that are growing, and the latter seem to be more attractive from a business viewpoint. However, although growth is one variable that contributes to configuring an industry in one way or another, it is not the only one.

A company that actively faces the future and reflects on new ways and paths for growth is a company whose approach is not confined solely to reducing size or cutting costs but also finds new ways to serve its customers, integrate employees, and offer a better return on shareholders' investment. This is the best mentality for reinventing an industry and shaking off the syndrome of so-called bad or unattractive industries.

Swatch, the Swiss watch manufacturer, offers a highly illustrative example of how to overcome this mentality by thinking about how to grow in a mature industry through new projects. The 1960s and 1970s were years of decline for Swiss watch manufacturers. Their products ceased to be innovative, they were considered expensive by many buyers, and their world market share fell against their US and Japanese competitors. By the end of the 1970s it seemed that Swiss companies were doomed to have only a minority presence in this industry, perhaps confined to the top end of the market. They were unable to penetrate

---

[2]   Baden-Fuller and Stopford's discussion (1992) on this issue is provocative. Rumelt (1991) and McGahan and Porter (1997) offer highly interesting empirical results on the importance of the industry and company-specific factors in accounting for a company's performance.

the mass-market segment—which was the segment that was growing—with typically Swiss products. Swatch's experience shows that the power of ideas is always superior to that of so-called mature industries or companies. When the Swiss watch consortium's new president, Nicolas Hayek, took office in 1982, he set out to change a trend that many considered irreversible (Taylor 1993).

Hayek laid out a new strategy based on certain basic elements. The first was to design production systems in which personnel expenses accounted for a tiny fraction of total costs. Part of the new competition for Swiss companies came from Japan, whose companies offered low-priced products, with low labour costs, that were typical of the country at that time. The second factor was to boost the Swiss watches' image for design, quality, and elegance against the new products that were coming in from Asia, including low- and medium-priced watches. The third factor was to transform the watch into a consumer product, with very attractive new designs and low prices. Until then, the watch was a product that was bought once and lasted for many years. Swatch's new marketing approach succeeded in creating in the consumer's mind a product with different varieties and attributes to suit different circumstances. This approach led the company to implement the concept of watch collections having similar designs or features, thus creating a fashion.

Thus, Swatch not only succeeded in stopping the apparent decline of the Swiss watch industry but it also transformed both its method of production and its marketing approach, to the point that Swatch watches have become sought-after collection pieces. Its growth since the mid-1980s has been spectacular.

Another example that illustrates the value of new projects to foster growth above the industry's structural factors is British Airways. When this company was privatized in 1984, it faced a twofold challenge. On the one hand, it had to restructure operations that were still stuck in another time and with inefficient management. On the other hand, it had to face the internal renewal of its strategy and culture to ready the company for weathering the new winds of fierce competition that would start to blow in the world airline industry. In the space of just a few years, this industry has gone from being a fragmented industry, dominated in the national markets by state-owned companies with a local or regional scope, to being a global industry, with global competitors, in which the operational privileges associated with state-owned companies are gradually disappearing.

Until it was privatized, British Airways had never been perceived as a flexible, innovative company offering high-quality services. Its main advantages were probably external to the company: its privileged site at Heathrow Airport and its domination of the British market. As these advantages would disappear with the progressive liberalization of the industry, British Airways was in a potentially tricky situation. However, in the mid-1980s this company embarked upon a spectacular renewal and change programme, in which all of its employees were involved, from top managers down to the maintenance teams. The result has been dramatic. In the midst of a genuinely difficult industry, where most companies have been reporting losses since the end of the 1980s, British Airways has succeeded in sustaining growth. It has emerged as one of the global companies providing a great service, has considerably increased the number of passengers and routes, has pioneered certain services, and, last but not least, has achieved a satisfactory return for its shareholders. The exploration of new opportunities to generate growth, even in apparently mature industries, may help accelerate the transformation of some mature mindsets.

4. SUMMARY

In this chapter we have introduced the subject of corporate growth, not as a firm's objective, but as a process that may be necessary for corporate survival. Growth is important because it can be good for some firms, but also a disaster for others. Growth is, indeed, a relevant issue for firms.

After presenting the cases of companies undergoing fast, sustained growth, such as BBV, SAP, and Glaxo, we have discussed some of the main reasons why growth is important. Among these, we have stressed the need to attract talent and investors, to maintain an adequate control of the threats of substitution and imitation that all companies face, and to overcome the mature-industry mindset. A careful evaluation of growth decision may also help avoid reckless corporate expansion.

The analysis of the growth process undertaken by these companies highlights the existence of numerous growth drivers and different growth pathways. There is also a need for a more comprehensive view of how growth takes place and the process it follows. We will present some corporate growth typologies in Chapter 2 and an integrated model of corporate growth and its main factors in Chapter 3.

2

Growth Strategies: Some Typologies

1. INTRODUCTION

Companies follow different growth paths, as we have discussed in Chapter 1. A significant part of the recent literature on the growth of the firm has focused on efficient ways of growing.

In this chapter we will offer some growth typologies based upon different variables. Some of them are external to the company, while others are internal and defined by the company itself. These typologies will provide a better understanding of different growth options. However, when talking about types of growth strategy, it is important to avoid the sweeping statement that certain growth paths or alternatives are superior to others. A growth path may be good for a certain company in a particular industry, but may be bad for another company operating in the same industry.

Thus, many empirical studies have shown that non-related diversification is less likely to succeed than related diversification (Rumelt 1974; Montgomery 1994). However, there are companies such as General Electric and ABB that have a unique ability to manage groups of business that are relatively unrelated with each other, in terms of resources, capabilities, products, and markets. It is also commonly stated that internationalization processes are usually more efficient ways of growing than horizontal acquisitions (Porter 1996). Again, this is a valid statement for some companies, but perhaps not for all companies. One should not forget either that a good growth decision, regardless of the procedure chosen, may succeed or fail depending on other variables, such as the firm's resources and capabilities or the evolution of the industry and the competition.

Consequently, studying alternative growth paths is useful for generating possible action alternatives and understanding them, but it cannot become a procedure for diagnosing a priori which paths are best without referring them to a particular company. Its prescriptive value is therefore low. However, its descriptive value, like that of any typology, is greater. This is the specific purpose of this chapter.

Before presenting these typologies, in the following section we will describe the main academic contributions to understanding the firm's growth. Some of them have given rise to some typologies of corporate growth, which we will discuss in Section 3. In Section 4 we will introduce a new growth typology derived from the external opportunities a company has and the resources it uses.

2. SOME VIEWS OF CORPORATE GROWTH

With some exceptions, corporate growth has not occupied an explicitly prominent position in the field of management. In this section we review the most important contributions made to its study: the microeconomic approach, the resource-based theory, the evolutionary view, and the corporate-strategy approach.

2.1. The microeconomic approach

Microeconomic theory has viewed the firm as a mere production function that the entrepreneur or senior managers seek to optimize. In this context, the firm is a mechanism that allocates resources efficiently in a similar manner to what the market does (see Coase 1937; Williamson 1975). As a consequence, this approach basically focuses on short-term static equilibrium—for example, how output changes if an input's variable cost changes. However, the treatment given by this approach to the firm's growth is a mere prolongation of the short-term analysis.

According to this approach, growth is basically nothing more than the result of the firm's adjustment to a supposed optimal size. This explanation may be correct in certain cases, but it is essentially incomplete. As we will see in Chapter 3, growth may be a reaction or an adjustment to a desired optimal size, but it is neither its main cause nor its primary explanation.

2.2. The resource-based theory

Penrose (1959) offers the first comprehensive explanation of the firm's growth process. She bases her theory of business growth on the dynamic theory of economic development formulated by Schumpeter (1934). Schumpeter describes the entrepreneur as an agent who perceives opportunities in the external context and takes advantage of them.

If the entrepreneur decides to profit from these new opportunities, he or she may have to reorganize his or her activities to use the available resources in a context that is perhaps different from the traditional one. Penrose uses this hypothesis in order to propose her theory of the firm's growth. Such a theory must provide an 'examination of the changing productive opportunity of firms'

(Penrose 1959: p. 32) and an explanation of the restrictions or limits to growth. The resource accumulation process over time explains the growth of the firm. Thus, she points out that the company is not a production function but a combination of resources. These resources' heterogeneity is what makes companies different from each other.

The main resource available behind the firm's expansion is managerial. According to Penrose, 'Managerial services are the only ones that firms should make use of' (p. 48). Indeed, they are so critical that the limitation or absence of available managerial resources is the main block to the firm's expansion process. According to Penrose, 'a firm will expand only in accordance with plans for expansion, and the extent of them will be limited by the size and the experience of the managerial group' (p. 49).

Penrose's contribution is extraordinarily important as, to date, it is the first and only one that has offered a broad view of the business growth process, and, furthermore, has provided the rationale for the so-called resource-based theory of the firm. However, there are some limitations that can be observed in her theory. The first is that managerial resources are essential in any firm. However, they are not the only resources and, sometimes, not even the decisive ones. In technology-intensive companies, knowledge is not to be found only among managers, but among the new product development teams or the sales force in close contact with customers. A second limitation to this approach is that resources are an essential growth driver but not the only one: the interaction between internal resources and the firm's industry is critical (Henderson and Mitchell 1997) and cannot be overlooked in any model offering a plausible explanation for the business growth process.

As we will point out in the model we describe in Chapter 3, corporate growth needs other explanatory variables, such as the company's internal context, its external opportunities, or its unique business concept.

2.3 The evolutionary view

Nelson and Winter (1982) set out to provide a model of the firm's evolution over time, seeking to identify and highlight those factors that contribute to and influence that evolution. This evolution is governed by routines. They consider that 'most of what is regular and predictable about business behavior is plausibly subsumed under the heading "routine", especially if we understand by that term the relatively constant disposition that shapes the approach of a firm to the non-routine problems it faces' (p. 15). These routines include recruitment policies, evaluation of investment projects, R&D, and advertising policies.

Although these authors deal with economic change and do not address directly the growth issue, they do point to it implicitly. According to this view, growth is not the adjustment of a certain output function to the size considered optimal. Growth is the result of the interaction of a firm's routines and knowledge. An important consequence of this view is that growth has limits, not so much because of the possible shortage of available resources, as Penrose pointed out, but because of the intrinsic resistance to change within a firm when routines have been effective for a long period of time. Therefore, the true limit to growth is not the scarcity of resources, rather it is routines—the way people work with the information and knowledge accumulated by the organization over time—that hamper change in the behaviour of individuals and the firm.

Nelson and Winter make an original contribution to the evolution of the firm. However, this contribution is not made with the intention of explaining corporate growth or its inducing factors. Furthermore, the central role played by routines cannot play down the people's ability to innovate and change. Their contribution complements Penrose's theory for two reasons: first, because of their emphasis on the role of routines as a way of sharing and developing new capabilities within the organization, and, secondly, because of their perception of organizations' difficulties to change and the limits to corporate growth. These limits are found not so much in the abundance or scarcity of resources as in the resistance to change in routines that have been successful over a period of time.

2.4. The corporate-strategy approach

The field of corporate strategy offers a normative view of the firm's growth. Thus, its approach departs from Penrose's tradition, which seeks to identify the factors that enable a firm to grow. On the contrary, with different shades of emphasis depending on the author (Chandler (1962, 1990) is a clear exception, as his approach is historical and longitudinal and his motivation is less prescriptive), this approach seeks to recommend to the firm the lines of growth that are most attractive on the basis of certain variables.

The origin of modern corporate strategy is to be found in the work of Chandler (1962), Christensen, Andrews, and Bower (1965), Ansoff (1965), and Andrews (1971). In his study of the growth of large US corporations during the twentieth century, Chandler describes—with an enormous wealth of detail— the importance of organizational innovations. These innovations, and, in particular, the creation of the divisional structure, with the appointment of division managers and middle managers in each division, are presented as the basic force that enabled certain companies to have certain competencies so that they could undertake an expansion that, with time, would lead them to become some of the largest companies in the world.

Chandler (1990) is concerned not so much with resources, as is Penrose, but rather with organizational capabilities and the ways of organizing activities and units within the firm, in that such ways must enable growth through a more efficient use and application of these resources. (This concept is later refined by Teece *et al.* 1997.) It is this differential factor that explains why these companies experience sustained growth over a long period of time while other rivals operating in the same industry do not grow at the same rate or even disappear.

Ansoff (1965) addresses the issue of the firm's growth by asking what business portfolio—the group of business units—a diversified company should have. In this respect, the driving force behind growth is the gap between the current business portfolio and the potential or desirable portfolio. This gap is defined with respect to two variables: the resources available to the company and the attractiveness of the industry that each business unit operates in. As can be seen, Ansoff's contribution is normative: it does not explicitly explain how companies grow or the factors that drive them, but rather points out what the future composition of a certain firm's business portfolio should be. However, this contribution is important, because it opened the door to a literature, mainly originating from the consulting industry, that had a very marked impact during the 1970s and early 1980s. (For an excellent summary of the main contributions in this area, see Hoffer and Schendel 1978 and Hax and Majluff 1984.)

The third original contribution to the field of growth from the corporate strategy viewpoint is that of Andrews (1971), which had a major precedent in Christensen, Andrews, and Bower (1965), a book that consisted of a series of notes and case studies for the course 'Business Policy' which, at that time, was offered in the first year of Harvard University's MBA Program. A crucial element of Andrews's contribution is his definition of corporate strategy: 'a pattern of major objectives, purposes or goals, and essential policies and plans for achieving those goals, stated in such a way as to define what business the company is in or is to be and the kind of company it is or is to be' (Andrews 1971: 28). This definition presents a conception of growth that is not explicit but rather implicit in the definition of each company's corporate strategy. Thus, if the company is to grow, it is essential to choose clear goals and to define policies that are in line with them.

A particularly interesting question that is barely raised in this literature (except by Penrose) is to explore the limits to the firm's growth. Indeed, the above authors do question which businesses the company should be in, but they do not explicitly ask what the limits to the number of businesses are, nor the types of business in which it should operate.

Rumelt (1974) sheds some light on this issue in studying the performance of diversification strategies. The option to enter businesses that are related with those previously developed by the firm seems to show superior results to entry into non-related businesses (see Montgomery 1994 for an overview). The limits to growth in terms of diversification decisions seem to be determined by the relatedness between the firms. Relatedness is important because it points out the possibilities for sharing resources and capabilities among business units. In this respect, Prahalad and Hamel's (1990) key concept of core competence stresses the view that growth strategies are healthy as far as firms stretch and leverage their current core competencies. Nevertheless, they do not aim at developing a model of the growth of the firm.

In an attempt to synthesize some recent strategy concepts with classical contributions better to understand corporate growth, Ghoshal, Hahn and Moran (1997) propose a model that relates firm growth and management competence. By management competence, these authors refer to the combination of two concepts that go beyond the use and transfer of resources: entrepreneurial judgement and organizational capability. By entrepreneurial judgement they define the managers' ability to generate new solutions, discover new opportunities, and develop new knowledge about a problem. On the other hand, organizational capability embodies the need to change the firm's internal context to implement the entrepreneur's point of view.

Ghoshal, Hahn, and Moran use these two concepts to propose a model of the growth of the firm. In it, they conceive firm growth as an iterative process that is driven by the interaction between organizational capability and entrepreneurial judgement. Their contribution is important for several reasons, not least, because they move the debate beyond the importance of resources and they highlight how critical the internal context is for growth, as we will see in detail in Chapter 4.

3. CORPORATE GROWTH PATHWAYS

In this section we will briefly review some of the most useful approaches for classifying the pathways companies might follow in their growth. In his historical study, Chandler (1962) observes three major stages in the growth of large US companies during the twentieth century. The first stage is concentration on a single type of business in the home market. The second stage starts when companies make vertical integration decisions upwards or downwards to improve production or distribution efficiency. The third stage consists of diversifying into other businesses and countries. Chandler proposes this succession of stages not as steps that firms must follow inexorably, like a kind of historical law, but rather as a general rule that he has observed in the firms included in his study.

Hax and Majluff (1991), when introducing their approach to corporate strategy, propose a conceptual framework based on the specific directions followed by growth (see Fig. 2.1.). The first and most basic distinction made is between expansion in existing businesses and diversification. Expansion in existing businesses offers three main alternatives: changes in the firm's product, in the geographical mix, and in the degree of vertical integration.

Let us start with the changes in the product mix and geographical scope. In this respect, the firm has three main alternatives: growth with the same products in the same markets, growth with the same products in new markets, or development of new products for the same markets. As for vertical-integration decisions, these offer two generic alternatives: vertical integration upwards, in which the firm becomes a manufacturer of some of the raw materials or

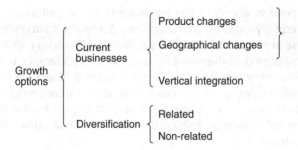

Fig. 2.1. Growth alternatives

intermediate products it uses; and vertical integration downwards, in which a new stage of the production process is added or the firm gains control of downstream distribution.

Diversification into new businesses can be subdivided into two categories. The first is diversification towards related businesses. These are businesses that share resources and capabilities with the firm's current businesses and that can be transferred, with a greater or lesser degree of complexity, to new businesses. The second category consists of the expansion of the firm towards non-related businesses. This type of decision includes those that give rise to conglomerates, where the cohesive forces are a management team or an internal capital market that decides how resources are allocated among the businesses that compete for them.

Gertz and Baptista (1995) present another growth typology based on the analysis and diagnosis of the firm's growth possibilities. Their discussion is focused more on single-business companies than on diversified companies. The three levers for growth they propose are the following. The first is growth driven by the firm's present customers, through increased added value, the identification of possible market niches for related products, access to channels for certain groups of customers, and reformulation of the pricing strategy. The second lever consists of improving the firm's economic structure. This option is not in itself a clear growth option. As a matter of fact, it could be considered as a basic element, a necessary condition, for undertaking future growth with greater possibilities of success. The third option consists of improving execution so that the firm's operations support and foster growth. Within this option, the authors identify improvements in the different processes that are directly or indirectly related to customers, such as the process by which value is delivered to customers or the processes by which information about customers is obtained.

Baghai, Coley, and White (1996), within the framework of a survey of high-growth companies carried out by McKinsey, detail the stages, or different successive steps, of growth, to use their terminology. This growth typology is the result of a combination of the short- and long-term options available to a company. One positive aspect of this approach is that it underscores that not all options are equally valid for all companies. From their survey of selected companies, these authors conclude that a company has seven growth options. None of them excludes the others and the use of one in preference to the others must be based on considerations that are not universal. These options are the following: maximize sales to current customers, attract new customers, innovation in products or services, innovation in distribution methods, acquisitions, expand towards new geographical markets, and, finally, diversify towards new fields of business.

In the following section we will offer a new taxonomy of growth options and strategies that combines both an external and an internal dimension of firms.

4. A NEW GROWTH TYPOLOGY: A DUAL APPROACH

In this section we describe a typology of growth options that combines two perspectives: the firm's external context and the origin of the resources used for growth.

We will briefly analyse the external context. A firm has some options or avenues for growth when it considers its external context: growth with current or prospective customers, growth with new products, growth in new markets (geographical scope), and, finally, growth in new businesses (business scope) (see Fig. 2.2.). These four dimensions are not pure. Rather, a consideration of any one of them should, in turn, take into account its combination with the others. Thus, Fig. 2.2 should not be seen as a series of differential, mutually exclusive alternatives, but as possible avenues for the company's expansion in the future that can be combined with the others at a given time.

Growth with current or prospective customers requires an appropriate assessment of the current positioning of the company and its products, the effectiveness of the pricing policy, distribution channels, product portfolio,

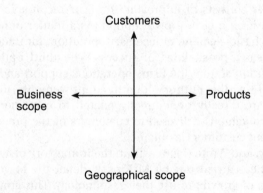

Fig. 2.2. Growth options according to external criteria

and market segmentation. Some of the possible outcomes of this analysis may include improving old products or launching new products to the same customers or new customers, changing the pricing policy, or improving the company's product portfolio. Product-driven growth requires reappraising the company's product portfolio, considering the opportunities for cross-selling to the same customers, or developing and launching new products that will provide a basis for sustainable growth in the future. Growth based on new markets involves a geographical diversification of the company and, in many cases, expansion abroad. Expansion abroad, in turn, may require reformulating the product portfolio or the type of customer targeted by the company, and a fundamental change in the way a firm operates. Finally, entry into different businesses implies looking for growth opportunities in other industries. It is the classic case of business diversification. It is not correct to say a priori that any one of these growth paths is superior to the others. Any assessment must be made on a case-by-case basis, taking into account the company's resources and capabilities, its competitive position in the industry in which it operates, and the specific growth possibilities offered by the industry.

The other dimension that we will consider in this typology is the origin of the resources the firm uses for growth. We will distinguish just two options: internal and external resources. This second case occurs when the firm establishes an alliance or merges with another firm.

The typology we present here is based on these two factors just discussed: the external context and the origin of the resources firms use, which can be internal or external. Their combination offers four growth options, which we will briefly discuss below (see Fig. 2.3).

| | | **External context** | |
		Same business	**Different business**
Resources used	**Internal**	**Market penetration** • Market share • New customers	**Resource deployment** • New product development • New business development
	External	**Market expansion** • International expansion • Horizontal expansion: alliances, mergers, and acquisitions	**Shared diversification** • Mergers and acquisitions • Alliances

Fig. 2.3. Growth options: A dual approach

4.1. Market penetration

A first growth option is to look for ways of fostering penetration in the same market, either by increasing sales to current or prospective customers, by offering them the company's classic products or services, or by improving the product portfolio by adding new related products that can foster growth. A special type of penetration consists of a sales strategy based on achieving a higher market share through, for example, lower prices. A new pricing policy that is in line with customers' needs and expectations and implemented without prior warning may have a significant effect on the company's growth.

The case of Banco Santander in the Spanish banking industry in the late 1980s, with the launch of checking accounts with a competitive interest rate, is a very clear case of the advantage of first-movers. However, the sustainability of the results achieved with this type of action is directly proportionate to the speed (or lack of it) with which competitors react. If competitors decide to react immediately with a price war, the fall in margins is immediate for all companies. However, if competitors are slow in reacting, the company starting the offensive may achieve significant results.

This growth option can also take the form of repositioning some of its products or services, improving the conditions associated with a product or service, or developing and launching new products or services. Accor, a French multinational firm that competes in the hotel industry, frequently changes the positioning of the different types of hotel it has in order to attract new customers looking for a special niche in the market to keep growth alive.

A key assumption of this strategy is that the company wishes to operate in its current markets and with those products it knows best and with which it has developed distinctive competencies over time. What is more, the company is not considering developing or acquiring new resources: it simply seeks to make better use of the resources it already has.

4.2. Resource deployment

The second growth strategy, resource deployment, consists of using existing resources and capabilities, and seeking to enter new businesses through them, without resorting to external resources.

This growth option is based on the availability of internal resources, normally technology and financial resources generated in mature businesses, that require a low level of investment and offer relatively high rates of return. The availability of resources drives firms to look for new ways to grow, as was the case of firms such as Daimler-Benz, General Electric, ABB, or Deutsche Bank.

New product development can offer the opportunity to enter into new business. Nevertheless, diversification and new business development are more common when a firm wants to widen its business scope. The diversification strategy is geared towards creating conglomerates—that is, groups of companies that contain very different business units. While the number of large conglomerates has decreased in the West, they are still common in emerging economies such as South Korea, India, or Mexico (see Khanna and Palepu 1992).

One of the reasons for the existence of conglomerates is that internal capital markets can occasionally be more efficient than the organized capital markets (Canals 1997a). This fact has at least two consequences. The first is that it is not easy for these companies to raise capital on organized capital markets and, therefore, they prefer to finance growth from their own resources. The second is that the return offered by the financial system is lower than that offered by a real investment in a business, which induces companies to invest, not in the financial system, but in companies.

The basic problem with financial conglomerates is organizational (see the excellent work by Goold *et al.* 1994 and Collis and Montgomery 1997 on this subject). In economies with high growth rates that are closed to outside competition, conglomerates can survive. However, when an economy is opened to outside competition and the growth rate falls, unless the conglomerates' management can add value to each of the companies in the group, the final outcome is stagnation or decline in some business units.

Indeed, the normal trend—save for very rare exceptions—in Western countries is for the conglomerates to disappear or focus their activity on a few businesses. With more efficient capital markets, the discipline imposed by investors, lower growth rates, and a higher degree of rivalry, conglomerates become a business phenomenon that it is very unappealing to emulate.

4.3. Market expansion

The third growth strategy is market expansion and consists of widening the geographical scope of the firm or its size, but remaining in the same business. The difference between this and the market penetration option is that, in the latter case, the resources used to increase the company's presence are solely those generated from within the company, while in this option the company also uses external resources through alliances, mergers, or acquisitions.

In this case, we can distinguish between two types of actions. The first is the internationalization of the company. A company with certain resources and capabilities and certain products has an immediate growth path: offer the same products or services in different geographical markets. This has been the traditional strategy of European and US firms such as Ikea, Ford, Citibank, and Marks & Spencer in their international growth process. However, internationalization requires something more than deploying resources and capabilities in other markets (Bartlett and Ghoshal 1989; Canals 1994). The difficulties that this process entails are enormous, as so many international companies have found out for themselves, particularly in high-growth, emerging markets. In addition to the normal risks of operating in a market, internationalization entails a higher financial risk (arising from the problem of the exchange rate and its variability) and, sometimes, also an important political risk. Alliances to enter into new markets aim at reducing some of the risks associated with internationalization.

Nevertheless, internationalization can be considered a feasible way of growing because the company deploys in the new areas resources and capabilities that it has already acquired. In addition, internationalization increases market diversification, may help the company gain access to economies of scale by operating with higher volumes, and, finally, enables the company to learn from a context of different customers, rivals, and suppliers and, later on, share this experience in other geographical areas. This learning objective can be an explicit and very important goal in international alliances, such as the joint venture in Japan between Fuji and Xerox that has been alive for many years.

The second option is horizontal expansion in the same industry through mergers and acquisitions. Recent mergers in banking, oil, and telecommunications in Europe and the USA are clear examples of this type of strategy. These movements follow a twofold rationale. On the one hand, there is the possibility of restructuring the industry by reducing the number of companies operating in it. On the other hand, expansion can achieve higher levels of efficiency, either because it helps reduce costs or because the larger size of the company enables it to benefit from economies of scale in certain expenses. Sometimes, there is a third rationale, more difficult to achieve in practice, which arises from the fact that the resulting company has a larger customer base to which it can offer new products.

4.4. Shared diversification

The final growth strategy is shared diversification, which has some common factors with the resource-deployment option (see Section 4.2). Its distinctive factor is that the company not only deploys its own resources but also shares resources with other companies to achieve growth in new business.

Two typical cases of such decisions are the acquisition of other companies to penetrate industries in which the company does not operate (or in which it does not have extensive experience), and the formation of alliances to develop new technologies and products. The acquisition of Yahoo! by AOL is a clear case of this category of growth.

In the case of shared diversification, it is important to note that, in addition to the costs normally associated with alliances or acquisitions, particularly in terms of their management and organization, we now have a further dimension to consider. Diversification invariably involves a unique risk and, consequently, increases the inherent risks of acquisitions and alliances. However, within this context, both acquisitions and alliances have one clear advantage:

they can mitigate or reduce the volume of resources required to enable the company to expand its activities into new businesses. Furthermore, when the chosen partner has experience in the new business, the cost of operating in it may be lower.

5. SOME CLOSING REMARKS

In this chapter we have discussed certain typologies of the forms and paths for growth that a company may consider. The main feature of these typologies is the fact that they are descriptive. A normative approach to growth paths may lead managers mistakenly to think that the growth process follows a preset model that is dependent on a given set of variables. Indeed, the growth typology we have presented in this chapter shuns such automatism and considers more the company's background, the resources and capabilities that have been developed over time, the opportunities offered by the environment, and the type of specific growth decisions made.

In Section 4 we presented a new typology based on a dual approach that combines the scope of the business in which the firm plans to grow and the resources available to attain such growth. We should stress that such typologies can do no more than offer a description to assist in evaluating the advantages and disadvantages of certain options. By no means is it our intention to take a prescriptive stance or state that a particular option is good or bad in general. As we have pointed out, such assessments must be made on a case-by-case basis, taking into account the company concerned, its resources and capabilities, and its external and internal context.

Understanding Corporate Growth and its Process: An Explanatory Model

1. INTRODUCTION

With the exception of Penrose (1959), who provides a comprehensive theory of the growth of the firm based on resources, most of the work on corporate growth has followed a partial, normative approach that does not address a critical question: what are the factors that lead to healthy and sustainable corporate growth and shape its process?

In this chapter we present a conceptual model that seeks to explain the growth of the firm and provide an answer to that question.[1] This model consists of five basic factors (see Fig. 3.1.): the firm's internal context; its external context; the development of a business concept; its resources and capabilities; and the strategic investment decisions related to the firm's future growth.

This model considers the role of resources in corporate growth introduced by Penrose (1959), as discussed in Chapter 2, and which is by far the best contribution to this topic.[2] However, the model we introduce in the chapter tries to move the question forward in some dimensions. This model considers that corporate growth and the growth process itself are dependent simultaneously on the five variables we have presented earlier, one of which is resources and capabilities. Resources are essential, but so are the firm's internal context that explains the process by which resources are accumulated, the external opportunities that exist to deploy the company's resources and capabilities, the firm's business concept, and the decision to allocate resources to opportunities. The exclusive focus on resources could lead to a limited interpretation of the growth process.

---

[1] The model we present here does not set out to account for the size a company has at a given time although size is the natural outcome of the company's growth. Neither does it seek to evaluate the advantages of one growth option over other options, as is the case, for example, of transaction-cost theory when it assesses diversification decisions.

[2] Penrose highlights the importance of managerial resources. However, over–emphasizing their importance would be similar to underlining the overriding importance of the heart in the human body and forgetting the essential, indispensable contribution of other critical organs such as the brain or the lungs.

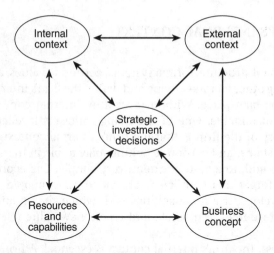

Fig. 3.1. A model of the growth of the firm

Take, as an example, the growth of a company such as Walt Disney. This cannot be understood solely from the viewpoint of the resources available at a particular time. Walt Disney's resources have been accumulated and shaped over a certain historical process. In addition, its managers have perceived growth opportunities in the environment. Subsequently, they have developed a business concept about how to meet customers' needs. Finally, they have evaluated options and made some strategic decisions that have set the company's growth course towards the future. It is the combination of these factors that has enabled Walt Disney to grow the way it has and not just the resources which it had at a certain time in its history.

We could also look at the case of Saatchi & Saatchi. Its growth in the 1980s shows a starting point that, in a way, was not that different from Walt Disney's. Saatchi & Saatchi, too, had access to a set of extremely valuable resources and capabilities. However, the final outcome of its growth in the 1980s was very different from Walt Disney's.

If both companies had a set of more or less abundant and unique resources, what was it that made them different, apart from operating in highly different industries? When we look at other factors, we see that the companies' history was very different and had given rise to different capabilities and internal contexts, different growth opportunities perceived differently by their managers, a unique business concept that shaped the way to organize activities and serve customers, and, finally, some specific growth decisions—within the context of perceived opportunities.

In the following sections we will present and briefly discuss each of the factors of the model. Each will be analysed in depth in the following chapters.

2. THE FIRM'S INTERNAL CONTEXT

The organizational structure, formal systems, corporate values, and corporate culture—among other factors—shape and define the firm's internal context in which decisions take place. Without a healthy internal context, corporate growth is not sustainable. One of the main criticisms levelled against the economic theory of the firm is that the firm's internal context, its organization, control systems, and corporate culture, play a role in that theory that is partial, limited, and, to a certain extent, very simple. The economic view of firms tends to forget that companies are made up of people who, through their work, develop certain capabilities with which they manage, use, and allocate some resources and assets and create new value (cf. Ghoshal and Bartlett 1997).

In this process, the firm's internal context is essential. A firm creates value and grows in a sustainable way when it enjoys certain competitive advantages that it can deploy in new markets. These advantages, in turn, are the result of resources and capabilities that the organization has developed over the years in a particular internal context.[3] The internal context is also essential for the generation of both tacit and explicit new knowledge (Nonaka and Takeuchi 1995).[4]

The firm's internal context is also a decisive element in the strategic decision-making process. Since the pioneer study of Bower (1970) on the resource-allocation process in large firms and the contribution to corporate innovation made by Burgelman (1983), the role of the internal context in some key strategic choices has been absolutely critical (see Noda and Bower 1996). The decision on growth is one of these key choices.

2.1. Some key factors

What are the factors that shape the firm's internal context? In the companies we have analysed, we have observed four influential forces: structure and formal systems, the sense of purpose in the organization, corporate culture and values shared by its members, and the role of the top management. These factors influence the growth of the firm by shaping individual behaviour and the firm's decision-making process. We will study them in detail in Chapter 4, but let us introduce them briefly now.

Structure and formal systems are the architecture of any organization (see e.g. Mintzberg 1979). They deal not only with the problem of how to split up

---

[3] In this sense, mention must be made of North's (1990) study on the interaction between history, the development of institutions, and organizational performance.

[4] This approach to the effects of the internal context on the development of the company has been considered in part in Penrose's work (1959) on resource-based growth, and in the tradition of the theory of the firm based on evolutionary processes (Normann 1977; Nelson and Winter 1982).

tasks, but also with the allocation of decision rights, budgeting systems, coordination among units, process design, measurement systems, and incentives. The structure and formal systems provide a reference and a set of constraints and incentives to the organizations' members that may contribute to shaping their behaviour, although in a limited and partial way. For instance, the partnership system at Goldman Sachs (until 1999) had a direct impact on its organizational structure, enforced teamwork and accountability, and related compensation with the overall firm performance.

The second factor is purpose. The firm's purpose defines and encapsulates the organization's reason for being and for developing certain activities. It helps inspire people to assume their responsibilities within the firm. A company like Glaxo Wellcome exists to improve the standard of living of individuals by developing better pharmaceutical products. Hewlett-Packard's purpose consists in making technical contributions for the benefit of individuals and corporations. The role of purpose in any organization is to inspire, give support and focus people's activities towards some objectives, so that it provides them with a deeper sense and understanding of their efforts and initiatives.

The third factor that helps shape a firm's internal context for growth is its corporate culture and values. They are principles of the organization that describe what the firm stands for, such as encouraging individual initiative, providing service to the customer above all else, developing a corporate social responsibility, paying attention to quality and excellence, aiming for continuous self-improvement, and developing a trust-based community of stakeholders. As Collins and Porras (1995) point out, corporate values have an intrinsic power and they do not require justification to the organization's members, nor to other stakeholders. Corporate culture and values make a strong contribution to shape the informal structure of any company, and may even have more influence on the growth and evolution of the firm than the structure and formal systems. When both are aligned, their combination emerges as a formidable platform for corporate growth.

Among these values, innovation and entrepreneurship within a firm stand out (see Burgelman and Sayles 1986; Baden-Fuller and Stopford 1992). The firms analysed in this study show a great sense of innovation, which turns out to be a critical factor in explaining their growth and its process. Innovation can be considered as an outcome of the formal structure, systems, and values of the firm. This is true, in the sense that they may contribute to shape an individual's behaviour. Nevertheless, it is more than just an outcome. Innovation embodies an attitude that drives the organization's action and people's activities. It is at the heart of the development of new products, new technologies, new delivery systems, and new business concepts. Innovation is one of the engines of growth. It is shaped by the firm's structure, systems, and values, but also influences them, so that they can constantly activate and renovate the firm's purpose.

The internal factors we have just described can be—and indeed are—influenced by the top management. In fact, senior managers not only make their own decisions, but also influence other people's decisions by shaping the internal context, either its formal dimension (structure and systems) or its informal dimension. The role of top managers in promoting corporate growth in the companies observed is critical, not just because of the strategic choices they face. The sense of continuous improvement, innovation, and entrepreneurship cannot be improvised and needs the care and guidance of the firm's top managers. As Ghoshal and Bartlett (1997) have so eloquently described in their vision of the individualized corporation, top managers need to rethink how they add value. Sustainable corporate growth demands a similar attitude from the firm's top managers.

To sum up this discussion, the firm's organizational structure and formal systems, purpose, corporate values, and top management shape and define the firm's internal context. We will review these factors in Chapter 4. In the next section we will briefly describe the importance of some of them in the evolution of Reuters.

2.2. The transformation of Reuters

Purpose and a sense of innovation have defined Reuters' internal context and been key drivers of its evolution and growth. As will be seen with the other cases in this chapter, Reuters has also benefited from the other factors included in our model of corporate growth. Here we focus on just one of them, but it is important not to miss the others. From its foundation in 1851 until 1964, Reuters was a news agency. However, in the early 1960s the slow growth in this industry and the increased rivalry led Reuters to reconsider the company's future. After exploring the opportunities offered by the industry and assessing the capabilities developed by the organization, Reuters' managers took the view that information related to financial markets would become increasingly important in the future.

Its values, purpose, sense of innovation, and a flat and entrepreneurial organization spurred a rapid change process. It was not the existence of an external threat that stirred change, but an internal context deeply rooted in innovation. Thus, in 1964, Reuters entered the business of transmitting financial data between the world's leading financial institutions and markets with its Stockmaster system, and, in 1981, the Reuters Monitor. This was the first system to offer real-time news access to the various agents operating on financial markets. At the same time, Reuters created a private information transmission network that the system's customers could use to carry out some of their transactions on the bond, equity, and currency markets. This was a revolutionary innovation that changed the way financial markets operated, pushing back once again the frontiers of the financial information industry.

Another product that had an enormous impact was the Reuters 2000 Series, which was launched on the market in 1987. The services offered by this new series were segmented according to the different financial markets and were offered to customers either as a bundle of services or separately. Again, this product marked a quantum jump in the industry and consolidated Reuters' position as a market leader.

In 1995 the company took another major leap forward. Over the previous few years, rivalry had become more intense, and other firms, such as Bloomberg or Dow Jones, were offering more innovative products in certain market segments that were not adequately covered by Reuters' products. But Reuters' purpose and values helped the firm recover and put it back on the right track. In this context, Reuters decided to launch its 3000 Series. Unlike the 2000 Series, this new series combined real-time information and the analysis of this information as two interacting, integrated products. The new series also added powerful innovations in graphic design and configuration of the financial information that could be readily adapted to the customer's individual requirements.

Since 1964, the year when Reuters decided to enter the financial information business, bringing with it a series of innovative products, this company has created a new industry that until then was non-existent and that will provide the basis for its future growth. Thus, in 1998, products related with this business accounted for about 65 per cent of the company's total revenues. Rivalry had become more intense, but Reuters still held an estimated 50 per cent share of the world market.

In this diversification process and the creation of new growth platforms, the internal context of Reuters, its purpose and innovation, and the willingness to offer customers the very best systems and the most accurate information, have been decisive. In this respect, Reuters' experience shows the importance not only of exploiting growth opportunities, but also the key role of the internal context in fostering the growth process.

Reuters did not have a good year in 1998. Revenues grew by only 5 per cent. Competition was increasing and Reuters felt the pain of the turmoil in international markets and the devaluation of local currencies with which it was operating. All this shows that even great companies that have grown for many years may lose their magic. Nevertheless, Reuters' internal context and sense of innovation are solid pillars upon which this firm can base and sustain growth in the future. Without them, growth would be an ephemeral event.

3. THE FIRM'S EXTERNAL CONTEXT

Corporate growth decisions and the growth path followed by a firm are influenced by the external context and the opportunities that its industry offers. In fact, some authors conceive growth as being essentially related to the company's external opportunities—new customers, products, or markets—or as a reaction to these opportunities (see Ansoff 1965; Abell 1980). Thus, the external context—the industry a firm operates in—and opportunities that managers perceive in their industries or in other industries appear as forces driving the company's growth. However, these opportunities are not its only determinant factor. It is precisely the interaction between these opportunities, the company's internal context, the resources and capabilities that the company has been able to develop over time, and some strategic decisions that marks the company's growth path in the future. Penrose's emphasis on the role of resources—particularly managerial resources—in the company's growth process, playing down the role of external opportunities, is similar to the almost exclusive emphasis given to the role of outside opportunities as a driving force for growth. Both contexts are critical, closely related, and, together with the other factors, shape the company's future evolution (Henderson and Mitchell 1997).

3.1. Growth opportunities: The expansion of Telefonica

In the growth process, the discovery and exploitation of external opportunities play a unique role. A company with discrete capabilities but some opportunities for growth may use these opportunities to improve its capabilities, perhaps profiting from being the first to enter a particular market. The case of Telefonica is particularly significant in this context (see Knief *et al.* 1995).

For many decades, Telefonica de España was a monopoly protected from both foreign and domestic competition, as was the case in many other countries where the telephone service had been state owned and competition free virtually since its creation. In the late 1980s, Telefonica's senior managers perceived the need to implement profound changes in the company. There were several reasons for this change. On the one hand, there would be increased rivalry with the liberalization of the telecommunications industry imposed by the European Union. On the other hand, once the company had been privatized, it would be necessary to offer private shareholders a reasonable return. It was unlikely that such a return could be obtained in the context of a small market such as Spain, whose natural growth was not going to be very high during the next few years and where the activities of rival companies could seriously erode Telefonica's position. There was another factor that also had significant importance: the investment that would be required to continue being a significant player in the industry would increase considerably in the future and only companies of a certain size would be able to take on the challenge successfully.

The deregulation and liberalization of the telecommunications industry in Latin America provided an excellent opportunity for dynamizing Telefonica's growth process, enabling the company to enter new markets with enormous growth potential. The growth process in Latin America started in 1989, when it invested in the Chilean company Entel. In 1990 it acquired a holding in Telefonica Argentina. In 1991, in alliance with AT&T and GTE, it acquired a stake in CANTV, the Venezuelan telecommunications company. In 1994 Telefonica was awarded the mobile telephony licence in Colombia and won the privatization bids for Entel in Chile and CPT, the Peruvian telephone company. Two years later, it won the privatization bid for CRT, the telephone company covering the Brazilian state of Rio Grande do Sul. In 1996 it acquired other local companies in Brazil, and it became the priority market for Telefonica in Latin America.

By the end of 1998, Telefonica had invested more than $9 billion in the region and its international operations accounted for almost one-third of the company's revenues. However, leaving to one side its immediate impact on the income statement, Telefonica's expansion in Latin America is a highly illustrative case of the importance of detecting expansion opportunities in its industry to guarantee the possibility of future growth. If it had not been for its expansion in Latin America, Telefonica's future would have been very doubtful. The Spanish market was growing, the new services demanded by customers offered significant potential, but the competitive pressure of new competitors and other telecommunications companies larger than Telefonica posed a constant threat to the company's existing profitability and future growth. For Telefonica, Latin America had become a vital platform for growth.

It is also very interesting to consider in this case the interaction between external opportunities and internal resources and capabilities. When it started its expansion in Latin America, Telefonica was not the world's most technologically advanced company. Other companies with clear interests in Latin America, such as GTE, AT&T, British Telecom, and MCI, were much more advanced than Telefonica in some technology, marketing, and service dimensions. They were also companies that had already been through the liberalization processes of their respective countries' telecommunications industries. However, superior technological or marketing capabilities, or the abundance of other resources, were not enough to forestall Telefonica's actions, which has become the region's leading telephone operator.

Thus, the role of resources and capabilities is critical in corporate-growth processes. However, acting with speed and agility to detect and perceive opportunities and tackle them is extremely valuable for putting a company on a growth track and guaranteeing its long-term survival. The lesson is very clear: Telefonica's future with its Latin American investments will not be easy, but it exists. Without that investment in Latin America, Telefonica's future would be very uncertain.

3.2. Some dimensions of the external context

The study of the external context in Strategic Management is sometimes limited to industry analysis. Michael Porter's model (Porter 1980) has become the standard tool to evaluate the industry's attractiveness. Nevertheless, to understand growth opportunities managers have to move a step forward and consider the following dimensions.

The first dimension of the external context is industry change: the transformation processes and changes in the industry's value chain among manufacturers, between manufacturers and distributors, or between manufacturers, distributors, and customers. These changes transform the value creation process in an industry and the role played by each firm. Industry changes may be caused by exogenous factors outside the company, such as deregulation, or by endogenous factors caused by the firms themselves, such as a new technology, a new product, or a new business concept.

The external changes that have taken place in the 1980s and 1990s in industries such as utilities, banking, and telecommunications have been mostly caused by deregulation, globalization, and the introduction of information technologies. However, endogenous factors—such as the development of a new technology or a new organizational model—have historically had an enormous impact. Imaging technology and computerization in medical diagnosis products, digitization in communications, or the development of mini-mills in the steel industry have been factors that have revolutionized each of these industries and have led to enormous changes both in the creation of value and in its distribution among the various participants, speeding up the growth rate of some of these firms.

Industry changes shape the pattern of corporate growth and development, paving the way for models such as the product's life cycle. This model predicts that a company's products follow a particular life cycle that influences the company's own life cycle. However, the diversity of exogenous and endogenous change factors, the varying nature of each industry, and the differences among companies in terms of resources and capabilities make it almost impossible to define homogeneous development cycles for different companies.

The second dimension is the firm's perception of new customers' needs. Microsoft's decision to enter the Internet business was postponed on several occasions because of the scepticism prevailing within the company regarding the future of the Internet and the possible threat that it could pose to Microsoft. Once the Internet had become a burgeoning growth market and Microsoft had detected both its threat and its potential, it decided to enter it with the specific aim of satisfying the users' needs that were not fully satisfied by other products.

The third dimension is also customer related. Customers may become obstacles to growth or change. Indeed, it has been documented in certain industries that innovative companies that offer new products or services are not the industry leaders but rather new companies that enter the industry without any prior experience (Hamel and Prahalad 1994; Christensen 1997). Thus, the competitive dynamics between established companies and new entrants seems to tip the balance in favour of the latter in many cases.

What can this pattern be attributed to? What are the obstacles that a leading company hits that prevent it from changing and leading further innovation in the industry? Accumulated knowledge and internal routines and policies seem to be part of the explanation, as Nelson and Winter (1982) or Rumelt (1995) suggest, among others.

Christensen and Bower (1996) point out a second and completely different customer-related cause. It is a fact that the leading companies in a market usually show a preference for serving their present customers well. This outlook encourages them not to pursue innovations that might be too expensive for those customers but rather to implement incremental innovations. Consequently, new technologies or new products tend to be introduced by new companies that do not have the advantage of an extensive customer base. They have the freedom of not depending on traditional customers and can therefore consider ways of operating or develop new products and services to be offered that are truly revolutionary. Thus, current customers play a very important role in the assessment of a company's growth possibilities.[5]

The fourth dimension of the external context corresponds to competitor actions. Growth opportunities are determined both by what competitors do and what they do not do. During the 1980s, the US shaving products market was influenced by the inexorable rise of disposable razors, led by Bic. Gillette, the industry's leading company, competed on product quality, not on price. The growth of disposable products developed by some competitors forced Gillette to play in the same field until it succeeded in developing and launching a much superior product in 1990 that enabled it to slow down the growth of disposable razors. Competitors are a source of learning for the company, both on what it is advisable to do and what it is preferable to avoid. In this way, the actions of competing companies determine the learning's external context.

However, the behaviour of competitors is not readily observed. A company's actions on the market are only the tip of the iceberg of a series of internal factors—capabilities, resources handled by people, informal relationships— that an outside observer is unlikely to be able to comprehend in their entirety. As a result, what a company may learn from competitors' actions is extremely limited and imitating competitors becomes extremely complex, as Lippman and Rumelt (1982) or Barney (1995) point out.

The role of competitors is not confined to underscoring learning opportunities; competitors also shape a certain context within which a company must operate. Rival companies may point towards new quality standards for its products, introduce more cost-effective production processes or distribution methods, compete on costs, or launch new products. In short, rivals contribute to defining the competitive context within which companies deploy their resources and capabilities. In this sense, competitors have had an influence on the company's present competitive position.

Certain developments in the automobile industry may illustrate this factor. One of the most important revolutions that has taken place in this industry was led by the Japanese companies in the 1980s. On the one hand, their design and manufacturing practices had contributed to an increase in quality and

---

[5] A similar argument is postulated by Arora and Gambarella (1997). These authors put forward an interesting hypothesis about how customer demand favours certain patterns of capability development. In their study, they show that a specialized demand tends to develop specialized capabilities. On the other hand, a generic demand leads to the development of generic capabilities.

reliability, improving their performance and reducing their costs. On the other hand, their strong penetration, first of the US market and subsequently of the European market, has drawn a very different competitive map of the industry.

The improvement in automobile manufacturing processes has been extensively studied and imitated by US and European manufacturers. In this imitation process, companies have seen that, although it may be simple to imitate certain parts of the process, it is extremely complex to imitate the Japanese companies' business concept as a whole. However, Japanese companies have not only triggered an imitation and learning process among Western companies, but have also drawn a new competitive map of the industry. Not only has Japan acted as a more or less aggressive automobile exporter; its companies have also invested in Europe and the USA, thus competing very directly with local companies.

The industry's history in the USA and Europe would not have been what it is without Japanese direct investment, on the one hand, and without the management philosophy of the Japanese companies, on the other hand. Both have shaped and stimulated learning processes within Western companies and have contributed to changing the industry.

The current competitive position of a European automobile manufacturer like Volkswagen has been affected by the industry's history—in which the actions made by Japanese companies have been decisive—and by the learning process from Japanese practices. In turn, if Volkswagen's competitive position today influences its development and growth in the next few years, we can conclude that the industry's competitive dynamics in its recent past has a clear influence on the growth possibilities and the specific growth path that Volkswagen may follow in the future.

A fifth dimension of the external context in certain industries is determined, in part, by the role of complementary products. When a product combines hardware and software, for example, the development of one of the elements conditions the growth of the other. The consumer electronics industry has played a vital role in the growth of the music and film industries in the 1980s and 1990s.

In the personal-computer industry, the development of new computers and operating systems by Microsoft and Apple has boosted the world demand for microprocessors. In turn, the microprocessors' continually increasing capacity has stimulated the software development companies to design new applications.

Thus, the role of complementary products in a company's growth is decisive. As Bradenburger and Nalebuff (1996) point out, a company does not depend only on the companies that manufacture complementary products to see how the demand grows. A company may influence the development and strategy of the companies that market these complementary products. Therefore, the close interrelationship between complementary products suggests parallel growth paths for both.

All in all, the external context and opportunities are decisive in corporate growth. Porter's model provides a good starting point to explore the external context for growth. Nevertheless, the dynamics of growth requires us to take into account other dimensions that we have just highlighted. We will explore them in Chapter 5.

4. THE BUSINESS CONCEPT

Banking in advanced countries is usually considered as a mature industry in the process of consolidation, with shrinking margins and continuous price wars (Canals 1993*a*). It seems to be virtually impossible to develop sustainable competitive advantages in it.

Cases of banks that have fallen into difficulties or lost the favour of customers or shareholders in the 1990s readily come to mind. Names such as Crédit Lyonnais, NatWest, or Banesto, each one with different problems, remind us of the difficulties that some banks with a solid history have had to face in the 1990s. The problem with these banks, as with many companies in other industries, is that they have lost not only revenues, but also customers. Losing customers is like an elastic band that has lost its properties of stretching and contracting. Once it has become a shapeless piece of rubber, it is very difficult to restore its elasticity. A similar situation arises in a company that is starting to lose customers. Recovery is a very difficult task and the effort to win new customers is even more so.

Thus, an organization's decline is not only disastrous because of its effects on the income statement but also, just like the elastic band, because it causes a loss of elasticity, a loss of the capacity to continue to attract new customers or to retain existing customers with better products and services. In other words, these companies are demolishing what is clearly one of the keystones of the capacity for growth.

However, both in the USA and in Europe, we can point to banks that, in the context of an apparently not very attractive industry, have been able to weather the storm and have achieved significant growth rates and improvements in their profitability. In the USA, banks such as Nations Bank or Banc One[6] have developed a growth strategy based on a careful selection of savings products for individuals and firms, a choice of geographical scope for their operations that has countered the drive to be global at any price, and a highly efficient internal operations system that has enabled them to offer customers a superior quality service at a lower cost than other banks. In Europe, we can also identify banks that have succeeded in rejuvenating their organizations and attaining significant growth rates. ABN AMRO Bank, BBV and Lloyds are good examples of this dramatic transformation.

Banks that have experienced high growth and return rates share one feature

---

[6] In April 1998, Nations Bank merged with Bank America and Banc One with First Chicago.

that is a basic factor in the growth of the firm: the development of a new business concept. The business concept is the view that a firm has about how to deliver customer value. It encompasses a specific vision about customers' future needs, the role of the firm in serving them, the strategic choices the firm has to make for that purpose, and the unique organization of the different activities in the firm's value chain. So, the notion of business concept considers not only industry foresight (Hamel and Prahalad 1994), a theory of the business (Drucker 1994), or strategy innovation (Hamel 1998), but also the strategic choices and organizational reconfiguration necessary to meet customers' needs.

4.1. Beyond innovation

The development of a new business concept requires something more than just innovation (see the framework suggested by Markides 1997). Experiences in the area of innovation reveal some interesting results. Innovative companies are not always those that end up becoming leaders. In 1971, EMI, a British company specializing in the music and industrial electronics businesses, developed the first computerized scanner. But a few years later, after an initial success that surpassed even the most optimistic forecasts, its medical unit had disappeared. Ampex, the US company that developed the first video tape player for domestic use in the 1950s, stopped mass production of domestic video players in the early 1970s, shortly before the market started to explode, to the benefit of companies such as JVC or Sony. Both EMI and Ampex could be rated, without any doubt, as innovative companies, pioneering products that have had a marked impact on our society. However, neither EMI nor Ampex plays any role in their respective industries today, in spite of their innovativeness and the fact that, for a certain time, not only were they leaders but they had virtual monopolies in their markets.

We will not discuss here the fundamental reasons for corporate decline. Rather, we want to point out the importance for any company of developing new business concepts. In the final analysis, EMI and Ampex ceased to lead their industries, not because they were pioneers or innovative, nor because they did not have a point of view about the future, but because they were not innovative enough in their business concept, the choices they had to make, and the configuration of the value chain. That is to say, other companies succeeded in developing a more successful business concept. It is evident that not any innovative business concept is valid. Unfortunately, only some of them happen to be right. There are firms with strong visions that at some point failed to adjust to the new realities. Nevertheless, a firm needs to develop its business concept. Otherwise, it will have one anyway, but it may be the outcome of routine, not of strategic reflection.

A business concept includes a vision about customers' future needs, how the firm will serve them, what the industry could be like in the next few years, the strategic choices it has to make, and the way to organize its activities in order to make the future happen. There is a risk that a firm may be wrong with a certain business concept. Nevertheless, without a business concept, the company will wander aimlessly, without any direction, and, in such conditions, it is impossible to give a superior service to customers or become an organization able to attract and retain the best professionals.

Although the development of a strategic vision is necessary and indispensable, it is not sufficient. The corporate world does not move just on ideas; these ideas must be followed by actions. Thus, generating new visions would be a pointless exercise if companies were not able to transform these ideas into tangible realities through some strategic choices and new ways to organize their activities, which are essential elements in the business concept. In the next section we will discuss the notion of the business concept and its role in the expansion of Nokia. We will analyse it in more detail in Chapter 6.

4.2. The experience of Nokia

The case of Nokia, the Finnish conglomerate that has become the world leader in mobile phones, and has challenged Motorola—the traditional leader in this industry—shows the relevance of developing a unique and innovative business concept.

Nokia was founded in 1865 in the town of Nokia (Finland). The bulk of activities until the 1970s were in wood and paper products. By 1987 Nokia had already been transformed into an industrial conglomerate with an important presence in consumer electronics and telecommunications. One of those divisions was Nokia Mobile Phones (NMP), which was considered the jewel of the crown. It became the world's leading mobile phone manufacturer in 1998, with sales of 40.8 million mobile phones and an estimated global market share of 25 per cent. Its growth rate in 1998 was 74 per cent.

NMP accelerated its growth in the second half of the 1980s with new product launches and some capacity expansion decisions. It proved to be a skilful player in the game of alliances, mounting joint ventures with Alcatel, to design new cellular systems for a potential European network, and AT&T, to develop its own semi-conductors. Nevertheless, the position of the Finnish firm in these different businesses was far from clear, being steamrollered by the US and Japanese competitors.

Jorma Olilla, the head of the cellular phone division at that time, realized that Europe would have a digital standard for mobile phones, a condition for that industry's growth. In turn, that would provide a vast, standardized market. If Nokia were present there as a strong supplier, it could become one of the leaders. His major problem was the lack of resources in his division, in particular, when compared with Motorola or Ericsson.

His opportunity arrived in 1992, when the board of directors named him as the firm's new CEO. With that appointment, the board also made clear that it was endorsing Olilla's business concept and his vision about the future of the mobile phone industry, and of Nokia in particular. Among his first decisions in his new job, three stand out: the additional resources committed to back up research in new products, the partnerships forged with key suppliers in order to improve quality and expand capacity (which could easily become a bottle-neck if the market grew too quickly) and the divestments of some business units he proposed, unloading computer and TV factories.

Nokia was also very lucky, because the efforts of Olilla and his team coin-cided with GSM, the new digital phone standard that took off in Europe. The standardization process allowed Nokia to concentrate its efforts on a few models that could easily be adapted to the varying frequencies around the world. Nokia and its direct European rival, Ericsson, could ride the wave of the digital phone explosion in Europe and focus their R&D efforts on it. At the opposite extreme, Motorola, the market leader, had to struggle with a frag-mented US market—at least, from a standard's point of view—and got stuck in the old analogue standard in the second half of the 1990s.

Some observers may claim that Nokia was lucky and Motorola was not. Nevertheless, Nokia developed a new business concept that was backed up by a large commitment of resources. Eventually that concept happened to be successful. Without this unique business concept, Nokia would not have been able to profit from luck.

4.3. The role of opportunity gaps

As in Nokia's case, developing new business concepts involves devising new ways of doing things, and organizing activities and serving customers differ-ently. It entails the discovery of opportunity gaps. Opportunity gaps are poten-tial areas for the firm's expansion and include the anticipation of customers' future needs, the discovery that customers' current needs are not well served, the repositioning of some existing products and services to bridge the expecta-tions gap, or the development of more efficient operational processes. Those concepts will be discussed at length in Chapter 6.

The role of opportunity gaps is particularly interesting in the case of those companies that have held leading positions in an industry for many years. Leading companies usually excel in managing incremental changes but are usually less good at generating more dramatic changes in their business concepts. The recent problems of such well-known companies as IBM, Kodak, General Motors, or Digital are good examples of this phenomenon. They have got stuck with an old business concept that has become obsolete.

It is not easy for managers—accustomed to operating successfully in certain environments for long periods of time—to throw their assumptions about their company or industry out of the window and reformulate them from scratch. This is especially true the more successful the company is. If the company has done well so far, why should it change? The ability of companies such as Nokia, SAP, and L'Oréal to anticipate the need for change, reorganize operations, and speed up the launch of new products at a breakneck speed, sometimes with the enormous cost of cannibalizing their present products, is striking. To operate any other way, their managers say, would be to opt for the organization's decline—which is harder to detect the slower it is—or a lower growth rate in the future.

Underlying this way of operating is the assumption that, unless an organization stimulates and legitimizes innovation and encourages the challenge of conventional ideas with new ones that may lead to new business concepts, it will be difficult to see how a company can continue to be truly innovative.

Creating new business concepts to approach the future is a task that, to a certain extent, needs a scientific approach, in that it requires the systematic search and evaluation of different options. However, it is above all a capability that helps managers continually to reflect on new and different ways of serving their customers. Thus, creating new business concepts is a matter of combining creativity with rigorous analysis and realism so that the dreams may come true. We will discuss those issues in more detail in Chapter 6.

5. RESOURCES AND CAPABILITIES

5.1. Their role in the growth process

The cases of Walt Disney and Saatchi & Saatchi discussed briefly at the beginning of this chapter offer a contrasting view about the importance of resources and capabilities in explaining the growth of the firm.

Resources and capabilities related to producing and releasing successful movies, managing the Disney brand name, and launching and delivering new consumer products (such as plush toys, watches, or ice creams with the Disney name) are essential factors that have driven Walt Disney's growth since the mid-1980s. Failures of companies with an abundance of resources (like Saatchi & Saatchi) cannot downplay the importance of resources and capabilities in explaining the growth of the firm.

Resources are comprised of the firm's tangible assets (such as capital or patents) and intangible assets (such as reputation or brand name). Resources alone are not productive, with some exceptions. They need to be combined and deployed to productive uses by managers. Capabilities, such as manufacturing, marketing, and financial acumen, are the capacities that people in an organization have developed over time in combining and deploying resources and defining organizational processes—that is, certain ways of doing things. Core capabilities allow a firm to develop certain activities, such as marketing or manufacturing, with a high level of competence.[7]

---

[7] For alternative views, see Wernerfelt (1984), Prahalad and Hamel (1990), Amit and Schoemaker (1993), Barney (1995) or Collis and Montgomery (1995). Selznick (1957) uses the concept of 'distinctive competence' to refer to those activities that a firm does very well relative to its rivals.

Penrose (1959) provides a good starting point for understanding the role played by resources in the growth process. She points out that the firm should be viewed as a collection of resources able to carry out its purpose. In this context, growth appears as a process for applying the resources available to the company's new projects. The resources available offer expansion possibilities from which the company can benefit. Among the resources required for growth, Penrose points out the importance of managerial resources. They drive growth opportunities and set the limits to expansion.

Penrose's contribution has been of key importance in placing the theory of the growth of the firm on a more solid basis. The main limitations of Penrose's model—which we have already outlined at the start of this chapter—are that it does not explicitly consider how the internal or external contexts influence the resources and capabilities that the company has managed to accumulate over time. Neither does it discuss the role of decisions and the decision-making process in the company's future growth path.

Although the contributions made in recent years to the theory of the firm and the discussion of the resource-based view of strategy have not explicitly addressed the issue of growth, they have developed some of the concepts and notions put forward by Penrose (for a summary, see Collis and Montgomery 1997). Thus, for example, it has been stressed that, for certain resources to become sources of competitive advantage for a company, they must be combined in a way that enables the development of capabilities that are essential for the organization's future.

We will present and discuss these issues in Chapter 7. In the next section we would like to highlight the importance of resources and capabilities in the expansion of L'Oréal, the world leader in some segments of the cosmetics industry.

5.2. The case of L'Oréal

The development of capabilities that finally become true differential competencies is a complex process, related to the knowledge and learning that take place within organizations. The case of L'Oréal highlights these factors. This French company has been the leader of the cosmetics industry for many years. Its products have been consistently on the cutting edge.

Its growth process has some unique features reflected in double-digit growth rates in profits and revenues between 1980 and 1998. L'Oréal started in 1907. Until the 1970s it was a company centred around hair care, a small segment in which it was the world leader, with a strong home platform in the French market. In 1997, after the acquisition of Maybelline, a US cosmetics manufacturer, L'Oréal became the leader in the US cosmetics market, with a 34 per cent market share.

Unlike other cosmetics firms whose main strength is their marketing capability, L'Oréal puts a special emphasis on R&D. Its R&D budget was about $280 million in 1997, almost nine times the budget of Revlon, its most direct competitor in the USA. It registered 295 patents in 1996, one of the highest in the French economy. The sheer size of its R&D budget gives L'Oréal a tremendous advantage over any other competitor.

But size alone is not the only key factor. L'Oréal's success in new product development lies in the strong relationship between the research and marketing departments. The French firm is well known in its industry for the close collaboration between both departments. In this respect, product development is a two-way street, with new initiatives coming from both ends. Although collaboration among both departments starts at the stage of product development, it does not stop there. Once a new product is about to be introduced, the marketing process has to be carefully managed. Since the new product is going to bring about some innovation, it may not only replace a former product within a certain category, but also undercut some products in a higher category. Coordination to manage the cannibalization is of the highest importance.

L'Oréal has also embraced a philosophy of moving away from being a French-centred health-care manufacturer to become a global firm. That process has involved the development of new capabilities outside those needed in the French market and a radical change in its culture. In the early 1990s Western Europe generated about 85 per cent of the total revenues of the firm. In 1997 that figure was about 58 per cent and decreasing. A decisive step in this process was the acquisition of the Maybelline brand in 1996, which allowed L'Oréal not only to double its presence in the US market, but also to increase its awareness about new market trends. Maybelline was also chosen in 1997 as the brand to penetrate the Chinese market.

The continuous transformation of this French company can be attributed to many success factors. Nevertheless, the careful management of resources and capabilities stands out as the engine of its extraordinary development over the years.

The experience of L'Oréal also highlights the importance of some of these factors and their impact on its growth. The first is that L'Oréal has constantly applied its capabilities in research and marketing to new products, new segments in the cosmetics industry, and new markets (lately, the USA and the Asian region). The second factor is that managerial resources have been very important in this process, although not exclusive. L'Oréal's R&D and marketing capabilities at the laboratory and market levels, respectively, have been essential. The third factor is that a stand-alone capability may not be the most successful platform to compete from in the future. L'Oréal shows that it is the combination of several of them (R&D, marketing, brand management, etc.) that can explain more accurately its evolution. This combination of capabilities spurs new product development; eventually, some of the new products become market leaders, consolidating L'Oréal's previous position.

6. STRATEGIC INVESTMENT DECISIONS

The company's internal context, competitive position, external opportunities, business concept, and stock of resources and capabilities available define some options or opportunities that a company has before it at any particular time. However, neither this company's growth path nor its growth rate is completely determined by such scenarios. It is the decisions as to what growth alternatives are chosen and the process by which these decisions are made and implemented that eventually trigger the company's future growth. Of course, these decisions are closely related with the prior development of a business concept and depend upon the firm's internal and external context, and its resources and capabilities.

6.1. Choices that make the future happen: Volkswagen and Bertelsmann

Strategic decision-making was an essential ingredient of Volkswagen's growth in the second half of the 1980s, helping it become the largest European car manufacturer at the end of the 1980s. It was also decisive in its recovery in the mid-1990s (see further Canals and Giménez 1994).

In the late 1980s Volkswagen decided that its future would depend on expanding globally, working better with suppliers, concentrating the number of its platforms, and building new manufacturing plants in lower-cost platforms. The implementation of this business concept led the German company to invest in one of its largest investments ever, a state-of-the-art manufacturing and assembly plant in Martorell (near Barcelona, Spain), through Seat, its Spanish subsidiary. The new plant had a capacity of about 320,000 automobiles a year, with an expected productivity of sixty-five automobiles per employee a year, and a total cost of 2,800 million euros. Volkswagen had other options, such as investing in new plants in Latin America or reshaping its largest factory in Germany. Instead, it chose at that point to invest in Seat.

The crisis that hit the European automobile industry in the early 1990s seriously threatened the future of Seat. Nevertheless, once the new plant had adjusted to the market needs and had been adapted to operate at full capacity, Seat became a good platform to manufacture low-cost cars with a Mediterranean design, filling a gap in Volkswagen's product portfolio. This highly irreversible strategic decision was the key to its strategy of global expansion, cost-cutting, and component sharing across a range of products.

Strategy consists of making choices among options that are apparently conflicting or mutually exclusive (see Ghemawat 1991; Porter 1996). Strategy does not consist of achieving an improvement in operational efficiency. This is useful and necessary but under no circumstances can it replace strategy. In fact, merely improving operational efficiency is not a source of sustainable advantage. The role of strategic choices is essential not only in developing competitive advantages, but also in corporate growth, as Bertelsmann's evolution and growth show. In 1998 the German conglomerate was the third largest media company in the world, with about $16 billion in revenues, behind Time Warner and Disney.

Founded in 1835 by Carl Bertelsmann, a printer, Bertelsmann became a regional publisher of religious books. Reinhard Mohn, Carl Bertelsmann's great-grandson, took the helm of the firm after the Second World War. During his tenure as the firm's CEO, he and his management team made some important strategic decisions, that shaped the evolution of the German publisher.

The first was Bertelsmann's creation of book clubs, first in Germany and later on in the rest of Europe and the USA. Its purpose was to expand the firm by offering readers the chance to build personal libraries, with both classic and modern books. The business concept was clear and unique and the strategic decision was coherent. For many years, the book clubs were very profitable and the main source of Bertelsmann's growth. Without this decision, Bertelsmann's expansion would not have been that important. In 1998, the book clubs world-wide had more than 26 million members. The second decision was the push to diversify activities beyond book publishing. Bertelsmann entered into printing operations, magazine publishing (with Gruner + Jahr, a Hamburg-based division)—and the music business (with Arista Record).

The early presence in these industries was very decisive in the early 1990s when the firm's strategy was to become a large, decentralized, media company. Had Mohn not taken Bertelsmann into the book clubs, its evolution and growth as a publisher would have been slower. Moreover, this division provided the additional resources to invest and allowed the German firm eventually to have a major presence in other segments of the media industry, like music, and, later on, multimedia. The importance of some strategic decisions in the growth process is clear.

6.2. Some views on the role of the firm's strategic decisions

The role of strategic decisions is not new in the field of management. Barnard (1936) discusses the firm's decision-making process, focusing on certain critical decisions, and on senior management's leadership in this process, as essential factors in the company's development.

In his study of the growth of certain US companies, Chandler (1962) empha-sizes the choice of some organizational innovations as a basic component for guaranteeing the company's long-term growth. The birth of the multidivisional firm seems to lie at the heart of the impressive growth of companies such as General Motors or DuPont. In a comparative study between Germany, the US and Britain, Chandler (1990) completed his initial explanation of corporate growth. He stresses that the growth of US and German companies—as opposed to the relative backwardness of British companies—was due to a combination of three types of strategic decision: investment in manufacturing, investment in global distribution and marketing infrastructure, and, finally, the implemen-tation of efficient organizational forms that facilitated these companies' growth at that time.

The unique role played by investment decisions in business strategy is highlighted and analysed in detail by Ghemawat (1991). He shows that a business strategy must concentrate on examining in depth those irreversible strategic decisions that will clearly mark the company's future development. These are decisions that involve a significant commitment of resources (a new production plant, the introduction of a new technology, launching a new product, entering a new business, etc.) and whose nature makes them highly irreversible, that is, the company cannot readily undo them without a cost.

The commitment of resources contributes to steering the company's capabilities in a particular direction. It therefore involves choosing between several options. The investment decision itself and the volume of resources involved in this decision mean that such decisions cannot readily be imitated. Consequently, these decisions can be a source of significant competitive advantage for the company.

Simon (1993), in a synthesis of some of his previous work, stresses the importance of the company's decision-making process in determining the organization's future and the possible nature of its competitive advantages. Simon points out that the decision-making process has three essential components. The first is to anticipate the future. The second is to generate alternative actions that will be the organization's response to this future. Finally, the third component is making the choice and implementing it. The empirical importance of the specific characteristics of some strategic decisions in their success seems to be very high (see Papadakis *et al.* 1998). Although Simon's model may seem somewhat simple in this context, its interest lies in the fact that, once again, it stresses the importance of certain strategic decisions in determining the company's growth process in the future.

Strategic decisions and choices can be approached in a variety of ways. The external-control school supports environmental determinism and considers strategic decisions as mere reactions to external threats and opportunities, playing down the role of managers. Nevertheless, the hypothesis that managers and their decisions matter seems to have some empirical evidence (see e.g. Bourgeois and Eisenhardt 1988, or Hitt and Tyler 1991).

In the companies whose growth we have analysed one can observe that the strategic choices they make to stimulate growth share some basic subprocesses: the perception of internal or external opportunities, the emergence of a business idea, the definition of the project, the deliberation, the decision itself, and its implementation. The sub-processes we have observed share some similarities with the ones portrayed by Bower (1970) regarding resource allocation decisions, or Burgelman (1983) regarding new ventures within established firms, but also present some important differences.

The view of strategy and, ultimately, of corporate growth as a choice between different options has a natural connection with the other components of the model we have described. As we explained before, in all the cases discussed in this chapter, the five factors of our growth model are present, even if for the purpose of simplicity we focus on one of them in each section. The relationship with the company's internal context is straightforward: the company can implement strategic decisions successfully only when they are aligned with the internal context (organizational design, corporate culture, etc.).

The development of a business concept also shows a direct relationship with strategic decisions. These are assessed and implemented with an implicit or explicit vision of what customers' future needs will be and how the company can serve them. Bertelsmann's strategic choices described above entailed a business concept (the book clubs), that was indispensable for committing resources to new activities.

The relationship with resources and capabilities is also straightforward. These are not limiting factors, but they do mark certain opportunities for action and the possibilities of success that a particular action may have. Thus, the decision to diversify has to look, not only at the other company's businesses from the market viewpoint, but also at the possibility of deploying in the new business resources and capabilities that the company previously used in other businesses. Again, the Bertelsmann's case offers some insights in this respect. The capabilities developed in both book publishing and printing were indispensable in its entry into magazine publishing and printing.

There is a clear relationship between strategic decisions and the firm's external context. On the one hand, the industry, the external context, has contributed to shaping the company's competitive position at a certain time, through the interaction process we have previously described. On the other hand, the external context, at a certain point in the company's history, opens up new possibilities. The decision finally made by the company, the way it is implemented, and the interaction with the external context may turn a risky opportunity into a success story or a relatively safe opportunity into a resounding failure. However, the opportunities offered by the external context and that entrepreneurs are able to perceive lead to a set of options for the future growth and development of the company that managers cannot disregard. Reinhard Mohn, at the head of Bertelsmann, also illustrates this concept. He and his team developed a business concept that included a strategic vision of the future, and were willing to commit resources to it. Nevertheless, they were not ignorant or oblivious of the possibilities those markets were offering, even with an important level of uncertainty.

7. SOME FINAL IDEAS

In this chapter we have presented a conceptual model that seeks to explain the growth of the firm and its process. This model tries to provide an answer to a basic question: what are the factors that influence the company's growth? Implicitly, it also helps explain why there are some companies in an industry that are growing and others, in the same industry, that are not. This model

Internal context	External context	Business concept	Resources and capabilities	Strategic investment decisions
Corporate culture	Mature traditional market	Universal bank	Managerial talent	Adopt 1,000 Days Programme
Slow decision-making process until 1993	Increasing rivalry in Spain and the rest of Europe	Customer-based value chain	Capital	Acquire controlling shareholdings in non-financial firms
Experience with mergers	New competitors	Cross-selling of financial services	Brand name	Acquire banks in Latin America
Top managers' turnover	Opportunities in Latin America	Capitalize brand name	Branch network	Hire key people to strengthen some weak business units
	Advent of the European single currency			

Fig. 3.2. The corporate growth process: BBV, 1994–1998

Internal context	External context	Business concept	Resources and capabilities	Strategic investment decisions
Quick decision-making process	Systems integration	Cooperate with partners: special design of the value chain	People's talent	Invest in R/3
Entrepreneurial culture	Operations integration		Capital	Develop global presence
Product innovation	US market	Link all company's activities	Systems integration	Develop consulting capabilities
Customer service	Other growing markets	Remain a product company	Reputation for top-notch quality in software	Enter the US market
Flat organization	Consulting and professional services	Turn R/3 into the business platform	Marketing to large customers	Move into the middle market

Fig. 3.3. The corporate growth process: SAP, 1980–1998

consists of five basic components. As a summary of the role those factors play in corporate growth, Figs. 3.2 and 3.3 provide an overview of how this model helps explain the growth process of BBV and SAP, both of which were discussed briefly in Chapter 1.

The first factor is the company's internal context: its structure and formal systems, purpose, corporate culture and values, and the role of top management. The second factor influencing growth is the external context and the opportunities that the company has, either because it seeks them out deliberately or because its customers, suppliers, or competitors force it to follow them.

The development of an innovative business concept is the third factor. Growth is possible and sustainable when the company conceives a future, organizes its activities to serve customers' needs, makes decisions consistent with that perspective, and tries to shape the industry it competes according to that perspective.

The fourth factor of the model we have presented is the set of unique resources and capabilities that a company has accumulated and developed over time. The resources and capabilities available to the company at any given time condition or expand its growth possibilities, and the growth path it decides to follow.

Finally, the fifth factor consists of the strategic investment or decisions that, by virtue of their size and impact, shape the company's future. These decisions often involve a choice among certain options (for example, competing in one or several countries), show a certain degree of irreversibility, and commit a significant volume of resources in the organization. How these decisions are evaluated and made will have a crucial effect on the company's future growth.

In the next five chapters, we will discuss in detail each of these basic factors that influence a company's growth, as well as the process it follows.

4

The Firm's Internal Context: The Soul of Corporate Growth

1. CHANGE AT BRITISH AIRWAYS

British Airways' transformation in the 1980s and the spectacular growth that followed that change may help us understand better the importance of the firm's internal context in its growth process.

In 1982 British Airways was a state-owned company whose financial performance in recent years had been disastrous and whose quality of service was criticized by its customers. Mediocre financial performance and poor service made for a dreary atmosphere within the company. When the British government decided to privatize the company, it implemented a restructuring plan and a programme to raise private capital. However, even more importantly, an internal renewal process that would be decisive for the company's future was put into motion.

The top management immediately understood the need to change the mentality of the approximately 40,000 employees who worked with the company if it was to survive the regulatory changes and the new competitors that would appear on the market. How should such a change be approached? A company like British Airways could not start from scratch and recruit new employees uncontaminated by the bureaucratic mentality and the attitudes to customer service accumulated over so many years.

The answer attacked the problem on two fronts. On the one hand, the company started to change the internal management systems. In particular, the performance assessment system (starting to measure not just the results but also the way they were achieved), the compensation system (introducing a pay system with a variable performance-linked component), and the career development path within the company (changing the previous promotion system) were transformed. Such steps were necessary but insufficient to change an organization the size of British Airways. For this reason, the company's top management decided to send another signal to all its employees: the development of a training programme aimed at encouraging all employees to reflect on the new challenges that were on the horizon and accelerating a change of attitude to the problems that would arise and the way to solve them. Ultimately, British Airways' managers sought a change in the employees' attitude that, backed by a profound change in the company's formal structures, would help increase loyalty and commitment to the company and, ultimately, improve customer service and financial performance.

British Airways' managers used this training programme to communicate and facilitate assimilation of the new emerging corporate values of the company's philosophy. The programmes' names were suggestive. The first one, a two-day programme targeting all of the company's employees, was called 'Putting People First'. The second programme, directed at more than 1,000 managers, was called 'Managing People First'. These programmes catalysed a major change in the quality of work and service as perceived by British Airways' customers.

The impact of these programmes on the organization was enormous over the next fifteen years in terms of growth and return on equity. The outcome has encouraged the company to continue in its effort to improve the level of training and the quality of service offered by this company. Without doubt, this aspect has been decisive in enabling British Airways, for many years considered a bureaucratic, slow-moving company that looked down on its customers, to transform itself into one of the world's most profitable airlines, one of the fastest growing in the industry and the one preferred by many airline customers.

British Airways' recovery and growth are not only to be attributed to a series of timely strategic decisions made by its management, nor even to an external context of growth in air traffic. Although these factors may well have contributed to the company's recovery and growth, the enormous change experienced by the company, which placed it on a sustained growth path, was primarily possible thanks to one critical factor: the change in the company's internal context. The airline industry is becoming more competitive every day. To sustain its past performance and growth, British Airways will have to keep working on how to make further improvements in its internal context.

In this chapter we will analyse the internal context and its main factors.

2. THE INTERNAL CONTEXT AND ITS FACTORS

The internal context of the company's growth consists of those firm-specific factors, different from the growth strategic decisions (like launching a new product or entering into a new market), that influence these decisions and the growth process itself. The internal context is defined by a set of factors that have a major impact on the generation of new ideas (for example, the development of a new product), the translation of these ideas into concrete projects, the assessment of these projects at different levels in the company (from engineering to senior management and passing through the various departments involved in the process), the final decision-making processes regarding these projects, and, finally, their execution. Without a supportive internal context, corporate growth will not last.

In a world of perfect rationality (see Allison 1971; Eisenhardt and Zbaracki 1992), managers study some of opportunities existing in their environment, assess each one in accordance with certain preset criteria, and make a decision. (Simon 1993 provides a very good summary of this view of the decision-making process.) However, decision-making processes in real life have complexities that are not addressed in those models. Not only is the agents' rationality limited but also the process of defining a new idea, its translation into a project, and the project evaluation within the organization make the decision-making process more complex.

Among those factors that shape the internal context, we can mention the company's internal organization structure, with the distribution of tasks and responsibilities between the different departments or units and among the people working in these departments; management systems such as control mechanisms (what is measured and how) or compensation systems (what is paid and what variables are used to calculate the compensation); internal promotion systems; and, lastly, the procedures (administrative practices and routines) used to assess and make decisions about certain questions, like investment decisions.

Bower's (1970) pioneering study on the resource allocation process among competing investment projects in large companies has stressed the importance of the company's internal context in some key strategic decisions.[1] Discussing investment projects, Bower states that the internal context epitomizes the organizational forces that influence the project's definition process and the decision made by a senior manager to support it (this is the stage that Bower calls impetus). Bower distinguishes between the structural context, defined by factors such as the organizational structure or the process for defining and approving investment projects, and the situational context, defined by those internal short-term factors that may influence the decision-making process at a given moment. In this discussion, Bower goes beyond Penrose's notion of administrative organization that enables growth. In short, the internal context influences the decision-making process from the definition of a new idea to its final approval or rejection. It seems to have an important effect on those strategic decisions that Bower discusses and the growth processes that we study here.

It should be highlighted at this point that certain growth decisions may not involve investment in the short term. For example, a decision made by a clothing firm to expand by distributing through mass merchandisers, in addition to

---

[1] Bower's work has provided the rationale for a series of papers on the decision-making process in different contexts. For example, Burgelman (1983) and Burgelman and Sayles (1986) on entrepreneurial capabilities within an organization; Doz (1996) on alliances; and Noda and Bower (1996) on decision-making processes in companies operating in the same industry, with similar external opportunities, but which end up making different decisions.

its own stores or traditional retail outlets, may perhaps not require an investment in increased production capacity in the short term. However, many
growth decisions (such as the launch of a new product, the acquisition of
another company, or an alliance to manufacture or sell jointly) entail investment decisions. In this sense, this type of decision concurs with those studied
by Bower. In this case, the internal context invariably ends up influencing
growth and the process by which growth decisions are made. In the following
pages, we will briefly discuss some of the major factors that contribute to defining the company's internal context and that influence its growth process (see
Fig. 4.1.).

2.1. Structure and formal systems: organizational design, control systems, and compensation systems

The structure and formal systems of a firm are the first factor that shapes the
internal context. These systems include the organization's design (the division of responsibilities between different departments or units, the mechanisms for internal coordination, specific responsibilities and tasks, etc.); the
control systems (what is measured, how it is measured, who measures it,
etc.); and the compensation systems (how is the salary calculated, what
components it has, what non-monetary items are included, etc.). (See further
Galbraith 1977 on organizational design and Simons 1994, 1995, on control
systems.)

A second factor that influences the internal context is the set of rules and
administrative procedures used by a company in the course of the formal
decision-making process, in particular, those that are related with decisions

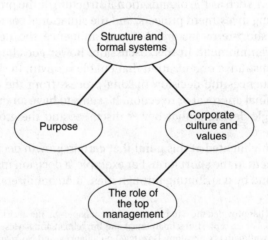

Fig. 4.1. The internal context of corporate growth

that require a major investment or a change in the firm's strategy. These rules include aspects such as how the study of the project is prepared, which people should be involved in the study, what criteria should be taken into account in designing it, who should review it, and, finally, who approves the corresponding decision and who implements it.

Each stage in the decision-making process is enormously important. Some ideas may be shelved and never turn into projects—even if they are brilliant and highly promising—simply because they do not manage to get through a certain administrative filter, which perhaps is not applicable to that particular idea anyway. Bureaucracy, originally conceived to facilitate and standardize certain decision-making processes, may cause the early demise of many growth ideas. Other ideas may progress and become projects. However, the weight of certain departments and people in the project's study may generate a disproportionate support in some cases, or a certain disinclination in others, to examine the project in greater depth. The approaches used by the professionals who work in the R&D, sales, and finance departments help shed light on the various ingredients of a particular project. However, if in this process one of the departments predominates over the others—whether formally through who makes the decision or what arguments have greatest weight, or informally through the implicit weight held by a particular department within the organization—the decision may be seriously unbalanced in its study and approval process right from the outset.

These factors determine the company's formal systems. These systems are public and known—or, at least, they should be—by all of an organization's members and have an important function: they affect these people's personal and professional behaviour, both positively (encouraging actions expressly recommended by the senior management) and negatively (discouraging certain behaviour or actions).

The private partnership structure of Goldman Sachs has been a specific organizational arrangement recognized as essential to that legendary Wall Street investment bank. In sharp contrast with other distinguished US investment banks, Goldman Sachs has operated as a private firm. Early in 1999—after a failed attempt in 1998—the partners decided that the firm should go public. The key reason why Goldman Sachs looked down on going public for so many years was the connection between partnership and business decisions, including those that had an impact on the firm's growth. The partners, as owners of the firm, were risking their own money with their decisions. This context meant a very disciplined decision-making process. An intrinsic element in the life of Goldman Sachs is accountability, not only to shareholders or the executive committee, but to the rest of employees as well. Young professionals in the trading room have to be ready to offer an explanation for their performance, not only to their bosses, but also to their peers.

Partnership also strengthens the importance of coordination, collaboration, and teamwork. The most profitable investment banking operations tend to involve different units, like equity trading, research and mergers and acquisitions.

Unless those teams work cooperatively and keep the customer's interest ahead of their own interest the deal won't be pulled off. Nevertheless, Goldman Sachs is also famous among young graduates for the collaborative atmosphere in special places, like the trading rooms. Recruitment is also dependent on the partnership structure. The bank puts an enormous effort into screening, selecting, developing, and promoting professionals. The aim is always to select the new generation of managers within the firm.

The partnership approach does not solve all the organizational problems—as the top-management crisis of January 1999 showed—and will be broken after Goldman Sachs has gone public. The need to raise more capital and the capacity to provide financing on a larger scale are important factors in the decision, apart from the windfall many partners will receive. Nevertheless, the bank wants to preserve part of its magic, even under a new capital structure. This will be another test on just how much partnership has meant for the banks' performance.

Formal systems have enormous advantages when they are properly designed and are in line with the company's strategy. They show relatively clear action paths to be followed in different circumstances and, if they are applied correctly, set a uniform level of expectations for the entire organization. However, formal systems also have significant limitations; for the moment, we will point out two. The first is that formal systems may induce adverse effects that are not specifically desired by the organization. The recent case of a multinational consumer products company that adopted certain compensation policies to increase sales and foster growth may help us understand this problem.

Driven by a desire to grow more quickly and increase its share price on the stock market, this company's senior management approved a compensation system for the various units' sales managers that was linked to sales made, even though sales had not actually been collected. The internal pressure to increase sales was so enormous that, in some countries, sales managers implemented an absurd practice: they filled the distributors' warehouses with product at the end of the month—before closing the monthly sales report—and then allowed the distributors to return the goods, if they had not managed to sell them, after sixty days.

Over a period of several months, sales in these countries increased. With the increased sales and earnings prospects, the company's share price also increased. It took the company's internal control system about a year to discover the procedure. The final outcome was not only a severe correction by the capital markets and the removal of certain managers who had been involved in the practices, but also a fall in the company's morale and loss of trust as these practices became known and communicated among different people at different levels in the organization. Furthermore, it was some time before relationships with the distributors were restored to previous levels. The company's reputation with them and the customers was severely tarnished from the process. This may indeed be an extreme case. However, it is very illustrative of the effects that a particular incentive system, designed and implemented with very specific goals, may have in an organization.

A second problem with formal systems is that, although they are necessary, they are not enough. People in organizations usually work with the desire to do things well and comply with the established procedures. However, their motivation is often not confined to compliance for its own sake or to get a significant financial compensation.

People are motivated by different factors. Many people work for something more than money, even though money is an important factor. Following Pérez López (1993), we can distinguish three types of motivation in decision-making processes: extrinsic motivation (determined by the formal compensation system), intrinsic motivation (determined by the effects of the action or decision on the agent—for example, in terms of professional or personal development, or satisfaction with having done one's duty), and transcendent motivation (determined by the impact that an action or decision has on other people).[2]

The existence of different levels of motivation shows the insufficiency of formal systems in an organization, which may modulate the level of extrinsic motivation and, perhaps, have a certain impact on the intrinsic motivation, but are unlikely to influence transcendent motivation. In other words, the structure and formal systems comprise the basic architecture of an organization's foundations but are insufficient for the construction and growth of the organization itself. Other factors are needed, such as the organization's implicit purpose or values, which will be the subject of the following sections.

2.2. Purpose

A firm's purpose is defined as the essential reason why it exists and carries out its activities. Obviously, in this case, the explanation that a company exists to make money is inaccurate and incomplete. A firm must create and add value in the course of its activities to offer a return on capital, once the various expenses that the company must incur have been covered. However, the goal of making money does not define its purpose.

Each company is unique in the way it defines its purpose, even though the similarities are often enormous. Thus, Federal Express defines its purpose as 'People, Service and Profit'. Merck defines its purpose as improving the quality of life for people and society through ongoing improvement in the treatment of disease. Hewlett-Packard defines it as the search for innovative technological solutions that help solve complex computing problems. Collins and Porras (1994) have compiled a collection of the purpose of numerous well-known and

---

[2] Pérez López's distinction between these levels of motivation is original, particularly his discussion of intrinsic and transcendent motivation. Transcendent motivation has been discussed indirectly by some authors who have written on trust or reputation as essential elements of corporate culture and values, but they come short of Pérez López's approach.

admired companies, expressed in very similar terms to these examples. David Packard, founder of Hewlett-Packard, expressed the relationship between financial goals and purpose in an organization in the following terms: 'I think many people assume, wrongly, that a company exists solely to make money. While this is an important result of a company's existence, we have to go deeper and find the real reasons for our being'(Collins and Porras 1994: 38).

The firm's purpose contains certain ingredients—not in themselves strictly rational—that inspire an organization's members and help them identify with it, dedicating time and effort beyond that required by the financial compensation they get. It is reasonable to think that the purpose has a direct effect on the organization's growth decisions. Not only does it increase the members' level of commitment and concern; it also imbues in them an additional sense, helping them to perceive those options and growth opportunities that may be valid for the company, and to reject those that would not contribute to the purpose by which the company exists. The process by which the purpose influences the decisions made within an organization is complex and varied. The firm's purpose can also have different meanings for different people within the organization. However, the purpose is a constant reminder of what gives meaning to all that the organization and, more importantly, its members do.

Glaxo Wellcome's mission statement highlights that it is 'a research-based company whose people are committed to fighting disease by bringing innovative medicines and services to patients throughout the world and to the health-care providers who serve them'. It sums up its purpose by declaring that 'disease has no greater enemy than Glaxo Wellcome'. Glaxo Wellcome wants to be recognized as the world's premier health-care firm. To achieve this goal, Glaxo Wellcome has defined a set of corporate strategies: to sustain long-term investment in science and technology, to develop the skills of employees, to focus on the needs of patients to help them live healthier, more productive, and longer lives, and to maintain cost efficiency and productivity improvement programmes.

This set of strategies is translated into the different divisions and functions of the firm. One of the most notable is R&D. It is absolutely vital to the purpose of Glaxo Wellcome. The objective of its research is to discover and develop novel compounds that will offer a significant progress over other medical treatments. As a result of its R&D policy, between 1990 to 1997 Glaxo Wellcome launched twenty-four new products, which accounted for about 38 per cent of its revenues in 1997, which is a high rate in the pharmaceutical industry. Glaxo Wellcome's case shows how a clear purpose (fighting disease with innovative medicines) can be translated into specific goals, strategies, and R&D policies. It constantly guides the efforts of its scientists in their new discoveries and shapes the capital-allocation process among the different therapeutic areas.

Reuters also offers us some clues about how the firm's purpose has an effect on some strategic decisions. Since 1849, when Paul Julius Reuter used carrier pigeons to bridge a gap in European telegraph lines, Reuters has been a leader in delivering news and information quicker than other competitors. Reuters products are known by their global coverage, accuracy, and speed. To develop and deliver them, the firm uses the latest technology. In 1999 Reuters was operating the world's largest private communications network with satellites beaming information around the world to almost half a million computer screens.

In the mid-1990s Reuters faced a challenge, as its main information product was falling behind The Bloomberg, another financial information system offered by Bloomberg. Its features, especially in terms of data analysis, were considered superior to Reuters' series 2000. The leader, Reuters, had been caught up by the follower. But its reaction was formidable. The new series 3000, which was supposed to speed up the growth of Reuters in the years to come, was also superior in many ways to The Bloomberg. As its CEO put it, Reuters' action was prompted by the need both to answer a competitor's move, but also to abide by the purpose of offering systems that would deliver financial information with the highest accuracy and speed.

2.3. Corporate culture and values

Corporate values are those explicit or implicit principles that predominate in any organization. Normally, they are basic, universal principles, such as respect for other employees, the endeavour to perform a task as well as one can, or the commitment to give customers the best possible service. However, the fact that they are universally known does not mean that they provide specific guidelines for action for all an organization's members. Hence, many companies wish to formalize and specify those values that form part of a particular corporate culture, in order to facilitate their implementation by employees and their rapid assimilation by people who join the organization. These explicit or implicit values have an enormous impact on people within the organization and shape their behaviour—although they do not determine it completely. They are unlikely to override individual freedom, but they certainly contribute to guiding individuals' actions in one direction or another.

Corporate values and organizational culture have been studied extensively and have become very popular subjects in recent years (see e.g. Kotter and Heskett 1992; Collins and Porras 1994, 1996; Tushman and O'Reilly 1997). However, I do not intend to discuss the components of corporate culture in depth, or the process by which it is shaped; rather I wish to highlight its contribution to and influence on the company's growth. (See also Barney (1986), who highlights the role of corporate culture as a source of competitive advantages for a company.)

The connection between values, corporate culture, and corporate growth has many dimensions. However, at this point, we would like to single out just two: the organization's entrepreneurial spirit and its innovative capacity, which are influenced by the formal systems but which can also form part of its core values.

In Chapter 1 we discussed the growth process followed by companies such as BBV, SAP, and Glaxo. In that chapter we saw the importance of innovation, the desire to offer better products to provide a better solution to certain problems (related with health, financial services, or information systems), and the existence of a sense of entrepreneurship at all levels of the organization. It seems logical to think that those companies where innovation is fostered at different levels will allow and stimulate the generation of ideas and projects at a higher rate than the industry in general. An environment that facilitates innovation tends to avoid stagnation and may help the company benefit from the external opportunities that facilitate its growth.

Among the values that foster innovation and entrepreneurship, we would like to highlight two. The first is the permanent existence of positive challenges within the organization. People grow professionally if they are able to take on new challenges, or readdress those they already had with a new, more stimulating, and more enriching approach. The desire to improve continually, to work better, to take on new challenges, to find more imaginative, better, and cheaper solutions, and to develop a new product that is more efficient for the final customer is an aspiration shared by people in all types of organization. When these desires are supported by corporate values that accept, institutionalize, and reward them, a virtuous circle is created between the aspirations of good professionals and the values and culture prevailing in an organization. In this sense, it is vital that internal aspirations and corporate values move in the same direction. A significant degree of discrepancy would be very demotivating for the organization's members. Equally important is the consistency between corporate values and formal systems. Corporate values (for example, a high level of excellence in customer service) that were not mirrored in formal systems would immediately damage the organization's credibility. Consequently, a critical task of a company's senior management is to seek ongoing challenges for all those who work in it, encouraging them both to improve current activities and to undertake new projects, creating a permanent sense of aspiration and improvement.[3]

A second component of corporate culture that has an undeniable impact on growth decisions—and on other decisions, in general—is the existence of an environment favouring the personal and professional development of each individual who works in the organization. This type of environment pursues several goals. The first and most obvious is to facilitate the integration of each person in the company and to enable him or her to contribute, thereby fulfilling both parties' expectations. Another goal is to spur ongoing personal and professional improvement, so that each individual is able to respond to the challenges that face him or her and to assimilate the changes that the organization must make.

---

[3]   Hamel and Prahalad (1989) refer to a similar concept as 'strategic intent'. This is an organization-wide goal that motivates its members and helps them adequately focus their effort. However, here we are referring not so much to this predominant organization-wide goal as to the challenge of continuous improvement that all of an organization's members should have. In this sense, we use an idea that is closer to the concept of 'stretch' described by Ghoshal and Bartlett (1997).

One aspect of this environment that is particularly important in growth decisions is the existence of a certain degree of tolerance in risk-taking and errors. When one walks, one has to lift first one leg and then the other. This movement entails a certain risk of losing one's balance that most people are able to control. However, if one did not take this risk, nobody would be able to move. A similar situation exists in organizations. Without the many decisions that are made—some important, others less so—organizations would grind to a halt. A company that prevented its people from taking new risks could possibly find that its capacity to innovate decreased in the long term. It is not enough to say that a company has prospered doing things in a certain way for many years. The business world is complex and changing. Companies must find a balance between retaining what is essential and innovating. If innovation stops, the company's long-term growth may be compromised.

To help understand better the impact of the corporate culture and values on a company's growth and evolution, we will briefly discuss the history of Ikea and its growth process (see also Bartlett and Nanda 1990). Ikea started its activities in furniture manufacturing and distribution in Sweden in the early 1950s. The product concept created by the company's founder was different from that of its competitors. The idea was to produce and sell simple, practical items of furniture that were easy to install. The products would be distributed through mass merchandising outlets owned by Ikea, which buyers would go to. There they would buy and take home the different pieces of furniture, which they could install directly, without any technical help. In the early 1970s Ikea embarked on an expansion process in continental Europe and, several years later, in Canada and the USA.

Ikea's most distinctive feature is the unique vision of its founder, Ingvard Kamprad, whose dream was to contribute to improving the daily quality of life for a broad spectrum of the public through better furniture. Kamprad was considered a visionary, someone who was able to glimpse the changes that were taking place in the industry and the new patterns of demand that were developing among consumers. He translated this vision into new business opportunities for the company.

However, Kamprad's vision was not confined to a product concept but also encompassed numerous details throughout the organization. The company had a relaxed atmosphere and, at the same time, there was an enormous concern for reducing costs, simplifying operations, and offering a better customer service. In cost-reduction initiatives, the company acknowledged the workers' efforts to avoid squandering resources and kept this philosophy alive with specific policies; for example, as a general rule, luxury hotels and first-class plane tickets were avoided. Employees were also encouraged to think of solutions that would enable the company's resources to be used more efficiently. As a result of one of these initiatives, the 'self-service' concept was introduced in furniture sale: having chosen the model they wished to purchase, the buyers themselves went to the warehouse to collect it. One of the consequences of this corporate philosophy was the existence of an anti-bureaucratic mentality and the relegation of formal authority to the absolute minimum. Thus, all of Ikea's managers regularly spent a certain amount of time working in one of the stores so that they would not forget the key to the company's business.

Ikea's growth was quite spectacular during the 1970s and 1980s, thanks to a strategy based on offering products with a certain quality level at a relatively low cost. In order to achieve this, the company had established three types of policy, all of them interrelated, that were the practical result of the founder's vision. The first was a concern to buy quality raw materials at low prices, replacing more expensive materials with cheaper ones with a similar quality. The second, closely related to the first, was to develop long-term relationships with the suppliers of these materials. To help in this, Ikea provided its suppliers with information on the specifications of the materials it required, helping them improve their production processes. A third policy—a direct consequence of the second—was to maintain a relatively constant order level throughout the year, enabling continuous production in the suppliers' factories and, in some cases, the achievement of certain economies of scale. All of this had a positive impact on Ikea, which managed to obtain its raw materials at consistantly low prices.

However, the concern for maintaining low cost levels did not mean a lack of concern for quality. On the contrary, as Ikea's market position consolidated, the products' quality improved, particularly when the company entered the US market in the early 1980s. American buyers demanded higher quality furniture, which forced Ikea to improve its products even more. Most importantly, the company was able to provide a flexible response to changes in the patterns of demand. To account for this phenomenon, one must look both to its personnel's extraordinary willingness to learn and improve and to the existence of a basic, simple philosophy that gave consistency to the company's actions and helped employees think and act responsibly, without requiring a complicated set of rules that indicated in each case what should be done.

Ikea shows that a company's culture and values have a marked influence on the internal context and this, in turn, has a clear effect on creativity, innovation, successful development, and the implementation of the growth opportunities available to the company.

2.4. The role of the top management

The factors briefly discussed in the previous sections have a clear impact in shaping the internal context, each one influencing a specific aspect. One feature that these factors (formal systems, purpose, and corporate culture and values) share in common is that they can be directly influenced by what the company's senior managers do or do not do. Indeed, not only senior managers can change the formal control systems or the organization's culture, but, through these changes, they can also enhance or diminish the role of the organization's purpose.

Senior managers, therefore, have a very special responsibility, not only in the final decisions—the ones with the greatest impact—made by an organization, but also in shaping the context within which these decisions emerge, and in defining the climate for innovation and improvement existing in an organization.

Thus, senior managers' mission in contemporary organizations is changing. Ghoshal and Bartlett (1997), to quote one of the most brilliant and compelling contributions to the new role of senior managers, discuss three new dimensions in managerial action. The first is to go beyond strategy formulation to reaffirm the organization's sense of purpose. The second is to go beyond mere formal structures to advance in shaping the company as a portfolio of processes aimed at solving problems and rendering a better service to the customer. Finally, there is a third dimension that goes beyond mere formal systems and stresses the development of the people who work in the organization. The importance of the evolution that these authors propose, and the degree to which structure and formal systems, for example, must be abandoned in favour of new management benchmarks, are debatable issues. However, it is clear that they are enormously important and complement the role of formal systems.

Top managers must perform on three essential dimensions (see Pérez López 1993): the executive dimension (or the ability to solve problems), the strategic dimension (or the ability to think about the company and its relationships with customers, suppliers, and competitors in the long term), and the leadership dimension (or the ability to address the company's institutional structure, including both its formal mechanisms and its informal systems). These dimensions underscore the critical role played by senior managers in the decisions they make and the types of environment they shape, including the impact on the organization's growth decisions.

The internal context can either facilitate the stability of the current situation or induce change by undertaking new challenges. The delicate balance between preservation and transformation that is characteristic of any organization is enormously fragile. Senior managers have a direct role to play in designing an environment that strikes a balance between these two options. In the final analysis, these points of equilibrium will determine whether the company is able to continue growing, taking advantage of current opportunities, or whether it is able to generate new opportunities. Senior managers can also play an extraordinarily active role in the process, not only to shape an internal context moving in a particular direction but also personally to promote a project and accept its possible risks.

In Chapter 1 we briefly described Glaxo's decision to acquire Wellcome. With this decision, Glaxo's top management took an enormous risk. The logical uncertainty about the final outcome, a common factor in any merger, was compounded by Glaxo's tradition to expand through the development of new products and its lack of experience with merger processes. Nevertheless, the integration plan, that included a distribution of some key responsibilities in the new firm, the creation of joint teams of managers from both companies, and the general cooperative atmosphere that the top management team tried to create, were key factors in the integration of Wellcome.

Bertelsmann's entry into electronic media also sheds some light on this point. Mark Wossner was the CEO of Bertelsmann between 1983 and 1997, during which period the German media firm grew at about 12 per cent per year. Wossner took over a firm shaped by Reinhard Mohn, Carl Bertelsmann's great-grandson, who had founded the company in 1835. Mohn had had a clear vision about the sense of decentralization and entrepreneurship that Bertelsmann's managers had to develop in order to make the company grow. He was the driver of the most important growth engine the German company had until the early 1990s: the book clubs that enabled Germans (and later other European citizens) to build personal libraries at a low cost.

In the early 1990s Bertelsmann was weak in the US market (the largest media market) and the new emerging business: electronic media. Aware of the impending risk for Bertelsmann, Wossner and his colleagues led the company though a number of risky bets. The most remarkable were a fully fledged entry into the US market with the acquisition of Doubleday and Random House (the largest US trade book publisher), the acquisition of RCA Records from General Electric (that was later combined with Arista Records to form BMG, the Bertelsmann Music Group), and the acquisition of a $50 million stake in America On Line (AOL).

Not only did Wossner convince managers about those decisions and lead Bertelsmann into the new digital era. He also organized his succession when he was about to retire, giving his full support to Thomas Middelhoff, whom the board named as CEO-designate on 4 July 1997. Middlehoff was the head of strategic planning and multimedia, and the person who had struck the AOL deal. His plan was for Bertelsmann to launch online services in Europe with the help of AOL. So Wossner left behind an heir who really understood the need to be a key player in the fastest media market: the electronic media in the US market.

The role of top management in shaping the internal context can be observed, not only in large companies like Bertelsmann, but also in small or medium-sized firms. One of them is Ficosa International, a Spanish manufacturer of car components, described by the *Financial Times* as a 'pocket multinational' (see Canals and Fernández 1995). With annual revenues of about 400 million euros in 1998, manufacturing plants, and R&D centres in Europe, the USA, Latin America, and Asia, its growth in the 1990s has been tantalizing, with annual rates of 20–25 per cent. What baffles observers is that Ficosa was in a very weak position in the late 1980s, focused on the local market and with a narrow product range.

In 1985, Josep M. Pujol, founder and CEO of the firm, realized that the future of his company depended on three actions: developing managers for the new challenges, establishing close links with car manufacturers, and international-izing operations and sales. His determination to make those things happen was clear: several times he rejected attractive offers to sell the firm to large, multi-national competitors. The effort over the 1990s has been enormous, but Ficosa is growing at an incredible pace. Its success, in a very tough industry, can be attributed to many factors. One of them is its corporate culture of quality and service, its genuine interest in the development of people working at Ficosa, its policy of decentralization of responsibilities, and the impetuous sense of initia-tive that permeates the whole organization. Behind these factors one can recognize the hard work, dedication, and professionalism of its CEO and his group of top managers, not only in pushing new projects and setting new targets, but also in developing managers and shaping the internal context of Ficosa's growth.

3. THE FIRM'S HISTORY AND ITS EFFECTS ON THE INTERNAL CONTEXT

At any given time, the company's history has significant effects on the configu-ration of its internal context, both through the organizational structure and procedures chosen in the past and through the experience that its members have acquired in the process. Consequently, the company's history has an impact on the future.

Some experts in decision theory have shown the importance of studying organizations' decision-making processes in a historical context. Thus, Neustadt and May (1986) have proposed the concept of 'thinking in time' to indicate the enormous relevance of the historical context in evaluating deci-sions. The firm's history is also important in considering and choosing the hypotheses upon which decisions are based and determining the foreseeable future consequences that could derive from these decisions.

The role of history in the evolution of the company has been completely forgotten in the neoclassic models of the firm, except for certain variables that help explain the interaction between competitors on the market. The reputa-tion that a company has acquired or the culture it has developed may be deci-sive for understanding its policies. However, these models do not explain the process by which that reputation is formed or the mechanisms that shape and modulate its impact. Models of firms based on the neoclassic tradition are useful for thinking in terms of strategic interaction (see e.g. Shapiro 1989; Kreps 1990; Saloner 1991), but they are limited when it comes to accounting for busi-ness growth processes, such as the entry into new businesses, new product development, or expansion abroad. In the end, the conception of history implicit in these models is very limited.

In the field of management, there have been some contributions to explain-ing the role of history. The first is that of Penrose (1959). Her discussion on the importance of resources to account for the company's growth introduces a dynamic view in the analysis of this phenomenon that implicitly highlights the role of history, at least in the resource accumulation and development process. However, Penrose does not address the issue directly (Dierickx and Cool 1989 deal with it more explicitly).

Nelson and Winter (1982) have also provided another contribution to understanding the impact of the company's history. The evolutionary theory proposed by these authors is based, among other ingredients, on the routines—the way to do things—that the company is able to develop over time. The configuration of these routines is influenced by a large number of factors and, in particular, by their configuration and interaction with each other during the course of the company's history. Routines affect, on the one hand, the relationships among people within the organization and, on the other hand, the relationships between the organization and its customers, suppliers, or rivals. Routines and procedures are determined both by the organization's formal system (such as control mechanisms or compensation systems) and by its informal system (mainly the organization's culture).

Companies whose growth is driven by new products develop routines that are different from those developed by companies whose growth relies on continuously revitalizing old products or entering new geographical markets. Consequently, routines—shaped by experience and time—reflect a unique historical evolution that influences the company's subsequent growth. Organizational capabilities and knowledge also have a historical dimension. Firms grow when they develop some solid competitive advantages, which, in turn, are the result of resources and capabilities that firms have developed over the years in a particular institutional context. In this sense, North's (1990) study on the interaction between institutions' history and development, of which the company is a special case, is particularly important. The passing of time is essential for accumulating know-how and generating new tacit and explicit knowledge (Nonaka and Takeuchi 1995).

The observation of the role of history stresses that a company's present and future position on the market is a function of the course followed by the company before. This course involves several factors, of which we will highlight three.

First, there are the strategic choices faced by the firm in the past. The decisions shaping a company's present include certain strategic choices that have determined the company's course of action during a relatively long period of time. The decisions about the future made by a company's managers at a certain point, together with the resources accumulated, the capabilities available, and the external context (interaction with customers, suppliers, and competitors), help push the company towards one path in preference to another. If one were to analyse the reasons for the company's competitive position at a certain point on this path, the answer should include these factors, among others.

The second factor is the existence of increasing returns. Increasing returns are a mechanism implicit in some industries by which the firm that is ahead gets further ahead (Arthur 1994). Indeed, in the case of industries with increasing returns, the path followed by the company tends to consolidate the original decision made. This would be the case of the personal-computer industry, where the existence of an installed base of computers with a certain technology (for example, the PC) tends to favour the development of programs for this type of computer and not for others, like Macintosh. Therefore, the path and, hence, the history of companies that manufacture and sell PCs are consolidated by this factor. The fact that the path is reinforced is not unequivocally positive. In the short term—even during a relatively long period of time—this may be so. However, as we will see later on, promoting a certain path may turn out to be a serious obstacle when redirecting the company's future or focusing on the business in a different way. In other words, a path that is favoured by increasing returns, as we have seen in the case of the personal-computer industry, has positive effects for the company until the fateful moment arrives when a revolutionary innovation demands new ways of competing and makes the old ones obsolete.

A third critical factor that influences the course followed by a company over time is the learning developed by its people and the knowledge accumulated by this means. Knowledge refers not only to R&D, but to the routine or non-routine activities that an organization carries out over time to design, produce, or sell goods or services to its customers (but see the alternative classifications suggested by Nonaka and Takeuchi (1995).

The evolution of Marks & Spencer provides some reflections about the role of history in a firm's evolution and growth, in particular, its past policies and the learning ingrained in the firm. A British institution venerated almost as much as the royal family, Marks & Spencer performed impressively for some thirty years. Its shares systematically outperformed the market. To get a job with Marks & Spencer would mean a job for life in one of the most admired European firms.

At the heart of Marks & Spencer's success there was a unique combination of factors. The first was its culture, kept under constant care from Baker Street, its corporate centre. This culture involved a very effective formal and informal communication flow within the company, a close connection between the corporate centre and the shops, a permanent 'dissatisfaction' and willingness to improve, and an obsession about quality and customer's reaction.

As with any quality retailer, product selection was a central ingredient in the spectacular growth of the firm. The classical business role of 'Buyer' had been replaced by four different functions. The first was that of the merchandiser, who had responsibility for the operational and control duties for the merchandise, including store stocks. The second was that of the selector, whose responsibilities included the creation of new product ranges and new product selection. The third function was that of the designer, who analysed and forecast fashion trends, through a powerful database on customers' tastes. The fourth function was technology. This was covered by a group of people who kept Marks & Spencer in constant contact with its suppliers and maintained contact among the stores. A close network of suppliers had been developed by Marks & Spencer to provide the merchandise needed. This network was in many ways a natural extension of the purchasing department. The integration between Marks & Spencer and its suppliers was backed up by a range of formal and informal, but regular meetings, and a close electronic connection. Marks & Spencer always considered these relationships as long-term commitments.

Marks & Spencer's growth was based upon the values and policies that had served it so well for so many years. Its achievements were a springboard for new challenges. However, in 1999 Marks & Spencer was facing challenges that seemed to require approaches that were different from the ones the firm had executed so well in the past. As the British retailer faced the reality of a mature market at home, with stagnating retail sales, it had to reconsider wholeheartedly its timid and so far not very successful—international expansion.

Marks & Spencer was overwhelmingly dependent on the home market, and only a few of the international ventures in the retailing industry had been successful. A more aggressive international expansion would mean that some of the experiences, values, and policies that had been so successful in the past in the British market would have to change. The British retailer would have to forgo some of its most cherished practices to adapt to a new world—among them its branding 'Buy British', its buying policies, its network of British suppliers, and its strong centralization around the corporate centre at Baker Street.

In a nutshell, Marks & Spencer's trouble in 1999 shows how history has helped Marks & Spencer's managers develop a sense about key success factors in this business and provided them and the whole company with an incomparable set of learning and knowledge in retailing. But, in a changing world, the factors that history had proved to be so successful seemed to be stopping the firm's progress.

4. SOME CONCLUSIONS

In this chapter we have discussed the importance of the company's internal context for corporate growth. Generally speaking, an organization's internal context conditions, shapes, and influences its members' behaviour in various ways. In particular, this context has a significant influence on investment or growth decisions, as we have observed in companies such as British Airways, Goldman Sachs, Bertelsmann, Ficosa International, and Marks & Spencer.

We have argued that the context not only determines growth decisions, but also an organization's capacity to perceive and tackle opportunities, discover new ideas, turn these ideas into projects, make decisions with respect to these projects, and, finally, implement them. The effects of the internal context, however, are not irreversible, because people are not totally conditioned by the context in the decision-making process, even though it can be very influential.

The crucial element of personal freedom subsists, no matter how adverse the environmental conditions may be.

Another reason why the context is not deterministic or irreversible is that the companies studied show that other factors, such as the external context, the business concept, the resources and capabilities accumulated over time, and strategic investment decisions also seem to play a decisive role in their growth. We will consider these points in the next chapters.

The Firm's External Context: Opportunities that Speed Up Growth

1. INTRODUCTION

The company's evolution over time and its growth patterns are closely related with its external context—that is, the opportunities that an industry offers its firms. These opportunities do not totally limit its growth potential, but they undoubtedly have a notable effect on the growth process.

The external context may be a serious impediment for some companies, while for others it may be the driver that stimulates innovation and the development of new products or services. The European automobile industry provides an example of such a situation. The stagnation of demand in the early 1990s and high production costs have been a major block to the growth of some car-makers. However, for firms like Volkswagen, the external context has been a springboard for innovation that has driven it to offer new models and to improve manufacturing and design capabilities.

In the field of Strategic Management, enormous importance has been given to the industry in which the company carries out its activity as a factor that shapes a company's strategy (Porter 1980). In fact, the application of the primary paradigm of Industrial Economics (that the industry's structure influences strategy and strategy influences business performance) to Strategic Management has meant an unquestioned acceptance of the decisive role played by the industry (or the external context, in general) in strategic decisions.

In the firms we have analysed, the external context of the industry provides a reference and a stimulus to corporate growth, although it does not seem to determine the growth possibilities of many of these innovative firms. The reason seems to be that the companies analysed exploit the opportunities they discover in the industry and position themselves within it. For growth firms, the way they take advantage of these opportunities and the positioning chosen seem to be more important than the external context. Nevertheless, the external context has an influence in the positioning chosen by firms, as we will see in Section 3.

In this chapter we will present a conceptual model for evaluating the company's external context and its effect on corporate growth.

2. A FIRST APPROACH: THE INDUSTRY'S VALUE CHAIN

The evaluation of the external context can start with a consideration of the attractiveness of the industry. Porter (1980), with his 'five-forces' framework, provides a model to assess the long-run average industry profitability. Those forces include the nature and degree of rivalry, the threat of substitution, buyer power, supplier power, and the threat of new entry. As a first approach, the industry's attractiveness, expressed as the long-term average profitability, is an indicator not only of the current profitability, but also of growth potential. Nevertheless, it is not possible to assume that growth opportunities arise only in attractive industries. Many industries are attractive because of the growth potential they have, but there are also growth opportunities in less attractive industries, because of the firm's positioning.

The industry's value chain (Porter 1985) offers a complementary view of the external context and a way to analyse the external opportunities that a company may have and how it can use them to foster growth. By an industry's value chain, we understand the different stages in the creation of economic value in the industry by the agents operating in it and by the interrelations among those agents. The model we present here has some similarities with the value-net framework developed by Brandenburger and Nalebuff (1996). The major difference is that the industry's value chain focuses the attention on the whole industry, not just the company. This concept provides a useful model for seeing how value is generated in an industry and its growth potential. Moreover, the industry's value chain may help understand better the impact of the changes on each of the agents that operate in it, and, therefore, on the company's growth opportunities. It also helps explain some growth decisions, such as vertical or horizontal integration, including some types of mergers and acquisitions.

The industry's value chain considers a certain company, its competitors, companies that offer complementary or substitute products, suppliers, wholesalers, retailers, customers, and the government. Fig. 5.1 shows the value chain's components.

To help us understand better the nature of the industry's value chain, we will use it to analyse the personal-computer industry. Our benchmark will be Compaq (the world leader in PC sales) and its growth since 1987 (see Fig. 5.2). In 1987 Compaq was the world's third largest PC manufacturer, behind IBM and Apple. At that time, rivalry was growing but less intense than it would be a few years later.

Both IBM and Apple competed with highly differentiated products, basing their strategy on a strong technological reputation and the support of two brands that were already very popular among computer users. However,

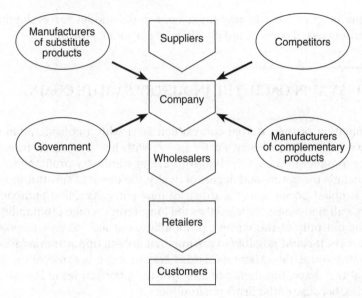

Fig. 5.1. The industry's value chain

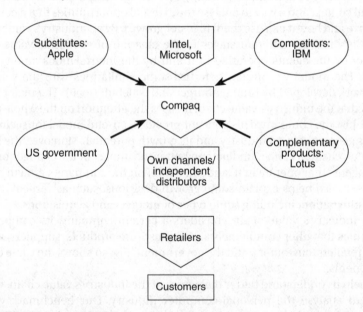

Fig. 5.2. The PC industry in 1987

competition between these two companies was not direct, for several reasons. First, IBM mainly competed in the corporate market. Apple, for its part, was very well positioned in the professional market (universities, research centres, publishing, etc.). Secondly, both companies had different operating systems. Apple's system was very appropriate for professionals, who looked above all for a high degree of user-friendliness. IBM, for its part, had positioned itself as the company that could provide an interface with other sophisticated computers and the servers used in large organizations.

In this context, Compaq targeted the corporate market with a positioning that was different from Apple's. It sought to offer quality products at lower prices. Its products were compatible with the IBM system. Therefore, Compaq's direct competitor was not Apple but IBM, and, indirectly, any company that manufactured computers that were compatible with IBM's operating system. Apple offered a substitute product for Compaq. Compaq did not compete with IBM in high-end products and it did very well—at lower prices—in low and mid-range products. Compaq could offer lower prices because its production, R&D, and overhead costs were lower than IBM's.

Compaq's suppliers—mainly Intel in microprocessors and Microsoft for the operating system—offered standard products on the market. Compaq was able to design a strategy in distribution channels that consisted of offering distributors fast deliveries, training, and good payment terms. Given its relatively inflexible distribution policies, IBM was unable to match this strategy.

In the eyes of the end customers, Compaq had won the trust of a growing segment of the market, thanks to its policy of providing trouble-free products, using software that was broadly available on the market, low prices, and a commitment to offer support and service to the distribution channel.

Compaq's main complementary product was the software that customers could use. With the growing availability of programs written for the IBM system (like Lotus), this factor did not raise any particular problem for Compaq.

Finally, the US government had historically played a minor role in this industry and this factor had barely affected Compaq, although it has recently been in the spotlight with the Microsoft and Intel cases. In other industries (such as telecommunications or airlines, for example) the role played by the government has been crucial and its regulatory policies may have an enormous effect on some of its agents.

In the context of a growing industry, PC manufacturers had a significant bargaining power with respect to distributors, customers, and suppliers. Furthermore, the rivalry among manufacturers was not as intense as it has become since then, and, moreover, each manufacturer had a slightly different market positioning, which meant that the rivalry was not particularly aggressive.

In terms of the industry's value chain, PC manufacturers and distributors generated economic value for their customers. It can be said that, with minor variations, each agent's policy was to generate greater value rather than to try to take away value contributed by the other parties. For their part, among computer manufacturers, there was no serious fighting for market share, for, as we have already seen, each manufacturer's market positioning was different from that of the other manufacturers.

A few years later the industry's situation was very different. In early 1999 the rivalry in this industry was very fierce. Traditional companies such as IBM or

Compaq had been joined by other companies such as Hewlett-Packard and Dell, which had managed to develop a reputation for fast service, low cost, and alternative forms of distribution—for example, using a telephone service and the Internet. For its part, Apple was no longer a classic substitute product. Instead, after an alliance with IBM and Motorola to develop a new micro-processor, the Power PC, Apple computers were compatible with those of IBM and other manufacturers. Without doubt, rivalry in the industry had increased enormously (see Fig. 5.3).

There had also been changes with respect to complementary products. Programs written for PCs predominated. Apple had not succeeded in persuad-ing the independent software companies to write a sufficient number of programs for its machines. IBM-compatible PCs had clearly won the game and this was one of the reasons for Apple's decline. The novelty was that some soft-ware companies had become industry stars. Some, in particular, stood out for the uniqueness of their products. One of them was Lotus, a pioneering company in the software industry. In the early 1990s this company developed and started to market a new product, Lotus Notes, which improved intercon-nectivity among computers and was particularly useful for large organizations, where communication among their people was critical. It was a widely held opinion that the industry's future lay in developing networks of computers that were able to interconnect and work jointly on different projects. Lotus' software was crucial for this. Aware of this product's importance, IBM finally bought Lotus in 1995 for $8 billion.

In the mid-1990s Intuit was a rising star. It had developed very simple finan-cial and tax planning and management software, with many possibilities for subsequent upgrading to the needs of users that required a higher degree of sophistication. Intuit had achieved enormous success with its products. The

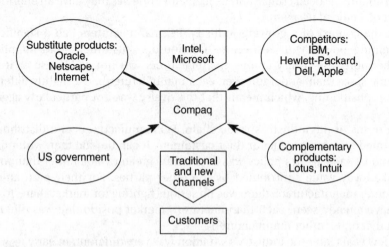

Fig. 5.3. The PC industry in 1999

difficulty in replicating or surpassing these successful products in a short period of time soon made it a target for acquisition by other companies operating in the industry. Microsoft bought Intuit in 1995.

Consequently, on the horizontal dimension of the industry's value chain, value appropriation was becoming a complicated process. On the one hand, rivalry among companies was growing and the emergence of star products meant that the added value was to be found not so much in the computer itself as in having software with special applications.

What was happening in the vertical section of the value chain? Relationships were also becoming more complex. The suppliers' position was now stronger. Intel and Microsoft were the companies in the industry with the highest market value, above that of any of the manufacturers. Experts and users also point out that the industry's intellectual leadership was also held by these companies and not by the manufacturers. Pentium, Intel's microprocessor, and the new operating system Windows 95 had been the most spectacular developments in recent years. Both belonged to suppliers who, logically, were forcing manufacturers to dance to the tune they were playing.

From the distribution viewpoint, things were not looking too good for manufacturers such as Compaq either. The increasing supply was giving rise to wars for space in the distributors' stores or was forcing manufacturers to create their own distribution network. In both cases, margins were squeezed and any particular distributor's value added was not very different from that of any other distributor.

Finally, the emergence of the Internet raised enormous uncertainties for the PC industry. If the dream of companies such as Netscape (the developer of Navigator, until 1996 the most widely sold software to surf the Internet) or Sun came true, the computer would become increasingly a box that would use programs designed by companies such as Netscape or Sun to run operating systems and programs available on servers located in the Internet. In this context, the value added by computer manufacturers could become increasingly endangered if they were not able to react to these threats.

In this context, the growth possibilities for a company like Compaq depended on improving its operating efficiency, on the one hand, but also on reinventing the rules of the game played in the industry. Its acquisition of Digital in 1998 seemed to be a move in this direction. However, it is not clear that defining the rules of the game consists merely of acquiring other companies.

To summarize, the use of the industry's value chain model provides a rapid overview of the company's external context and its growth potential: how value is generated in the industry, which steps it follows, how much value is generated by the various agents; which growth possibilities each agent has; or which strategic alternatives within the industry firms have (like vertical integration, or horizontal diversification). It is, therefore, a model that helps us understand better the company's external context and its effects on the company's growth possibilities. In turn, the changes in the value chain give rise to significant changes in each company's options of future growth. Nevertheless, corporate growth depends not so much on the industry as on the use that the company makes of the opportunities offered by the industry through its specific positioning, as we will discuss in the next section.

3. POSITIONING THE COMPANY TO GROW

The external context offered by an industry to its firms depends on the industry's intrinsic attractiveness, but also on how each firm positions itself in that industry. Hence, we observe companies with high growth and high return in unattractive industries, and, conversely, attractive industries and companies in them with low profitability. The difference between industry and firm performance must be attributed to company-specific factors. A company's positioning includes some dimensions and attributes that enable it to be viewed by its customers in a very particular way. The essence of strategy is to find a positioning in an industry that makes the company different from other companies in aspects that are truly important for its customers. It is not the purpose of this section to discuss the elements of the company's positioning, but rather its meaning in the context of the industry's value chain and its effects on the firm's growth.

We can distinguish between three cases of growth-driven positioning in different external contexts. The first is that of an external context of industry stagnation. This would be the case of the European banking industry. The revitalization strategy implemented by BBV (discussed in Chapter 1) shows the possibilities for adapting to such a context. The second case is that of an external context with incipient growth possibilities. The positioning pursued by Telefonica in Latin America (discussed in Chapter 3) is an illustration of a strong growth strategy in a context that stimulates growth. The third case is slightly different: an external context in rapid change and with enormous uncertainty. We will discuss how the positioning in this third context can accelerate growth.

The US pharmaceutical industry in the 1990s is a clear example of this situation. To understand better the positioning possibilities in this industry, we will discuss Merck's strategy and its change of positioning in 1993, after the purchase of Medco, a drug distributor, and the effect this had on its subsequent development. Its contrast with Glaxo's strategy, discussed in Chapter 1, is also revealing.

In 1993 Merck was the largest pharmaceutical company in the USA in sales (see Nichols 1994). This position was the result of a combination of factors that had made Merck one of the industry's leaders during the 1980s and 1990s. In this discussion, we will highlight some of these factors.

First, it had a research capability for discovering revolutionary medicines ('blockbusters' to use the industry's terminology—that is, drugs able to achieve a high sales volume) that was far superior to that of other pharmaceutical companies. This capability was a direct consequence of its high expenditure in R&D, amounting to about 11 per cent of its total sales in 1993. As a result of this enormous effort, between 1983 and 1993 Merck was able to launch a genuinely revolutionary product on the market each year. Two of the most outstanding developments were Vasotec, a medicine for the treatment of high blood pressure, and Mevacor, a drug to reduce cholesterol levels. These products, and others that had a major impact in various fields of medicine, were significant contributors to Merck's bottom line.

Merck's second distinctive capability was marketing. The company was reputed to be one of the industry's most efficient in communicating directly with prescribing doctors, specialists, researchers, and health-care firms. For many years, pharmaceutical companies had focused their efforts on research and manufacturing. The effort spent on these tasks was totally out of proportion with the effort spent on marketing. Together with Glaxo, Merck was one of the few companies that saw the need for a change in the marketing approach. This change came about not only for obvious reasons related with the need to sell, but also because of the advantages associated with a close connection with doctors, prescribers, and researchers. Indeed, as a result of this interaction, certain pharmaceutical companies succeeded in focusing their research activities with greater effectiveness and improving the efficiency of the new drug R&D processes.

Both Merck's differential approach to R&D and its superior marketing capability were related with a third, highly important capability: Merck was reputed to be one of the pharmaceutical industry's best-managed companies. For many years, many pharmaceutical companies viewed themselves as businesses that were in a separate category, where the discovery and development of medicines seemed to release them from other obligations. As a result of this conception, some of these companies ceased to be attractive to prospective shareholders. Furthermore, inefficient management and the difficulties in attracting new capital seriously damaged the potential for some of these companies to obtain exceptional R&D results. In other words, they were companies with a mediocre management. Merck understood that it needed to improve its management in the 1970s. The company's new CEO, Roy Vagelos, imprinted a new style with a singular view of achieving excellence in the development and sale of drugs with a high impact on society. Vagelos restructured the company, creating a team of professional managers who were able to work with teams of scientists who would develop these drugs. The impact of the company's new focus was extremely visible a few years later: Merck had become one of the industry's leaders, with an enormous capacity for generating innovative drugs.

Merck's positioning in the industry was clear. It offered unique drugs that had a high value for patients because there were no others that offered a similar level of curative or palliative efficacy. This had been the result of the enormous resources devoted to R&D, which were managed with exceptional efficiency. The nature of these drugs enabled the company to charge high prices that gave a good return. In addition, the drug patenting system in industrial countries offered Merck a long period during which the company enjoyed a veritable monopoly on the market. Merck also implemented an aggressive policy for launching generic drugs based on its star products shortly after the expiration of the drug's patent. By this means, it was able to capitalize for its own benefit the product imitation process that would start as soon as the patent expired. Within a traditionally profitable industry as was the pharmaceutical industry, with annual average returns on shareholders' equity in the USA exceeding 20 per cent, Merck had managed to surpass even these figures.

However, by the early 1990s, the pharmaceutical industry found itself in a context of intense change. There were two main forces driving this change. The first consisted of the growing importance of generic drugs as a means for obtaining cost savings in the USA, whose health system was considered very expensive by any international comparison. This trend seemed to weaken companies such as Merck that based their strategy on blockbuster products whose patent would last for many years. The authorities would be more inclined to shorten the patents' period of validity.

The second trend was the emergence of PBM (Prescription Benefits Management) companies. Through an ambitious research programme, these companies sought to promote the use of drugs that were more efficient for the patient, the progressive substitution of branded drugs by generic drugs, and the establishment of an information system on the patient's health and evolution. This approach was immediately welcomed and had an enormous impact on pharmaceutical companies, which, obviously, wished to have their products on the list of drugs recommended by those organizations. These PBM companies basically specialized in purchasing generic products, which they would then distribute among their customers, such as large hospitals, medical partnerships, or insurance companies. They therefore kept in close contact with prescribing doctors to advise them of the most suitable products. As a result, these companies were able not only to influence the price but also the type of drug that was considered suitable for the treatment of a particular disease. This, in turn, could contribute to eroding or strengthening a drug's value over time.

The emergence of these factors had two immediate consequences. First, a reappraisal of the concept of the generic drug, which strengthened the first of the above-mentioned trends—and which could therefore erode Merck's positioning in the future. The second consequence was the appearance of a new force in the industry's value chain, PBMs, which took part in choosing the most suitable products and contributed to reducing their price (see Fig. 5.4). Until then, distribution channels—the pharmacies—had played a very minor role in the industry. The new PBMs were going to change the balance of bargaining power between manufacturers and distributors.

These industry changes led to a transformation in the industry's value chain and Merck's external context. In response to these changes, the company

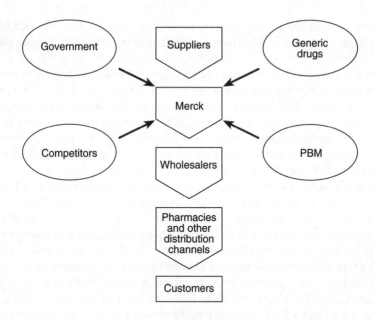

Fig. 5.4. The pharmaceutical industry's value chain

proposed the acquisition of Medco Containment Services in July 1993. Medco was one of the largest PBM companies and ran the largest US mail-order pharmacy. The price offered by Merck was $6.6 billion, considered by some to be too high as it was equivalent to almost fifty times Medco's net income in 1992.

In 1992 Medco ran a network of about 48,000 pharmacies and its membership amounted to 38 million patients. This was somewhat below the industry's largest company, PCS Health Systems, which had about 45 million member patients. Medco had an excellent reputation for highly efficient management of databases with the patients' medical profiles, the treatment patterns followed, and the drugs' impact on the patients' subsequent recovery.

Medco also had a major advantage over other similar companies: the direct sale system. This was the largest system of its kind in the USA and enabled it to establish direct contact with the patient and, by this means, increase its database.

What was the positioning that Merck wished to achieve with this acquisition? Did it make sense to carry through an acquisition that forced Merck towards vertical integration when the trend in so many industries seemed to be towards deintegrating in order to gain greater flexibility?

In the early 1990s Merck's management acknowledged that its competitive situation in the pharmaceutical industry might not be sustainable, because of the trends that were forcing a change towards generic drugs and new forms of distribution, as well as an increased pressure on prices. The reasoning was very clear: the rationale that had driven the company's growth in previous years, based on a positioning consisting of revolutionary drugs, was still right, but it was no longer enough to ride successfully the changes that were taking place in the industry.

The acquisition of Medco sought to improve Merck's future growth possibilities and its competitive position along several dimensions. The first dimension was distribution. The industry was changing; the distributors' bargaining power—which until then had been virtually non-existent—was increasing and would continue to increase over the next few years. Faced with the possible loss of value to the distributors, Merck chose to buy one of these distributors and internalize this value, which, otherwise, it could lose.

The second dimension of Merck's new positioning consisted of redefining its role as a leader in the development of revolutionary new drugs. The industry's R&D process itself was going to be changed dramatically as a result of the emergence of companies such as Medco, which, owing to the business's intrinsic requirements, had developed enormous databases on patients and the course of their diseases during and after treatment. Companies such as Merck considered that this information was extremely valuable for a more efficient management of the pharmaceutical laboratories' research processes and, in general, for a more effective management of new product development.

Thirdly, the acquisition of Medco would provide Merck with an outlet for the generic products that it would have to offer if it was to gain a significant market share in this emerging segment. The way to increase market share was by ensuring a good access for distribution of these products. Companies such as Medco were the best positioned to offer this service to Merck.

Finally, Medco would enable Merck to broaden its access to end patients through the direct-sale service. This business would undergo enormous growth in forthcoming years, particularly in generic products. By this means, Merck would be able to expand its customer base through access to new forms of distribution that had previously been unavailable to it.

To summarize, Merck's decision to acquire Medco was a response to the change in the company's external context—which was going to affect its future—and was aimed at improving Merck's competitive position in several directions and strengthen its growth potential: improve the new product development process, reduce development costs, and gain access to new distribution channels and new customers. Even in industries with such a high level of uncertainty and decreasing average returns, a firm can adjust to it and exploit that context to foster growth through a new strategic positioning.

4. SOME FINAL IDEAS

In this chapter we have discussed the role of the external context in the company's growth process. We have evaluated the external opportunities through the industry's value chain, as a model that helps understand how value is generated in an industry (and who appropriates it), where growth opportunities are, and the effects that changes in the industry have on the external context.

Finally, we have discussed the effect of the external context on the company's positioning in its industry by using the industry's value chain. This is a key aspect, because it shows how the company is capable not only of making use of external opportunities but also of creating them through its positioning and some strategic decisions. Thus, the acquisition of Medco by Merck was not only a reaction by Merck to the changes in the pharmaceutical industry's external context, but also a decision to take advantage of these changes and guarantee the firm's future growth through an improved product development process and a better management of distribution channels.

6

The Business Concept: The Heart of Growth

1. THE NOTION OF THE BUSINESS CONCEPT

In Chapter 3 we have analysed the recent evolution of Nokia, the Finnish conglomerate that has become the world leader in mobile phones and has challenged Motorola, the traditional leader in the industry. In the early 1990s Jorma Olilla, Nokia's CEO, developed a business concept that included his view about the customers' future needs and Nokia's approach to meet those needs, a special way of organizing Nokia's activities, and a commitment of resources to support that business concept. In this chapter we will introduce the notion of the business concept and will discuss its dimensions and implications for corporate growth.

The business concept is the view that the firm has about how to deliver customer value, the specific organization of the firm's activities (purchasing, R&D, manufacturing, marketing, distribution, etc.), and the choices it has to make in order to achieve it. It springs from a vision that the firm and its managers have about the future needs of its customers, the evolution of rivalry, and the role of the firm in the industry.

Any firm has an implicit or explicit business concept. The business concept is founded on the vision that managers are able to develop about their customers, suppliers, and rivals, and the unique positioning of the firm in the industry. According to that view, managers decide about the configuration of the company's different activities, its value chain, and the strategic choices associated with it. As we have seen in the case of Nokia, a good business concept leads to a combination of the company's activities in a unique way, different from what other competitors do, in order to create higher value for customers. The combination of activities should be consistent with the firm's vision.

The term innovative tends to be used only for those companies that are able to create and market novel products, with a higher value added, superior to that of other alternative products. Companies such as Honda, SAP, or Sony stand out for their ability to develop and market new products that are superior to many others available on the market. However, in recent years, companies such as Ikea, Dell, BBV, or Accor have come up with new ideas that can, without doubt, be considered innovative. Their secret has consisted not only of launching new products, but also of improving existing ones (either in price or in added value), thanks to a radically different understanding of customers' needs and a new conception of the company's operations, how they should be combined, and how products or services are delivered. Porter (1985) started to discuss some of these issues through the notion of the value chain. Markides (1997) offers a practical framework on how to think about innovation and the value chain.

The notion of the business concept that we present here shares some elements with other Strategy concepts, although, as we will try to show, it has some unique features. Among those concepts, we highlight the following. Drucker (1994) has proposed the idea of the theory of the business, which encompasses the assumptions that a firm has about its environment, mission and core competencies. Hamel and Prahalad (1994) have introduced the concept of industry foresight, which defines a point of view about the future of the industry and how the firm can shape it. They complement the concept of industry foresight with the notion of strategic architecture, which offers a view on which benefits the firm will offer its customers in the future and the new core competencies that the firm needs to develop to be able to do it. (See also Hamel 1998, who introduces the concept of strategy innovation.) Slywotzky (1996) has introduced the notion of business design, which is a way of organizing the firm's business system that includes four elements: customer selection, value capture, strategic control, and scope of activities.

The notion of business concept that we introduce here shares some elements with these concepts. Nevertheless, as we will see later, the notion of business concept is slightly different. It combines and integrates a strategic vision, the perception of customers' future needs, a specific perspective on rivals, suppliers, and substitutes, a unique organization of the firm's activities, and the strategic choices associated with them.

2. THE DEFINITION OF NEW BUSINESS CONCEPTS

The case of Accor illustrates not only the essence of the business concept, but also how it helps to speed up growth through the definition of new business concepts.

Accor, a French hotel and catering company, offers a number of experiences that may help illustrate this concept. This company started business with a hotel in Lille, which was bought in 1967. It rapidly transformed into a chain of hotels called Novotel. The goal of the company's founders, Paul Dubrule and Gérard Pélisson, was to open a new hotel every year over the next ten years.

This company's experience is interesting, not only because of the business concept on which it is based but also because of the spectacular growth it has shown during its more than thirty years of existence. In 1981—fourteen years after its formation—its turnover was about 5 billion French francs (763 million euros). In 1997 its turnover was almost 30 billion French francs (4.58 billion euros). Another interesting fact is the geographical diversity of the sources of revenue. In 1997 less than half the revenue came from France. The rest came from the US and Western Europe.

Accor's initial positioning was as a medium-quality hotel with a mix of European-level customer service and cuisine quality, and a design and service functionality that was more akin to US chains such as Holiday Inn. In particular, the company's owners considered that the catering business should be a basic part of the hotels' operations, thus breaking with the US tradition, which viewed it as a marginal activity. Accor grew very fast, achieving the goal of ten hotels in just seven years. The company's founders perceived the risk of saturating the French market in a few years and, therefore, started to think about alternative ways of growing in the future.

The first growth path was opened in 1973, with the definition of a new business concept and the creation of a new chain of two-star hotels, called Ibis. The aim was to attract lower-income customers who thought that the Novotel hotels were too expensive and luxurious for their needs.

Accor also started its expansion abroad in 1976, opening hotels in regions visited by French tourists, such as the Middle East, Africa, and Latin America. In 1979 it opened its first hotel in the USA. With later acquisitions, Accor sought to gain a significant presence in the US market, which was enjoying a higher growth rate, with the intention of repeating the success achieved in Europe.

During the 1970s Accor had also entered the catering business, with the acquisition of a very popular restaurant chain known as Courte Paille. Later, in 1983, the founders acquired the Jacques Borel International restaurant chain and its affiliated companies. This acquisition proved to be decisive in consolidating the company's presence in the catering industry. A few years earlier, in 1980, Accor had acquired the luxury hotel chain Sofitel from Jacques Borel. With this acquisition, the group completed its range of hotel services with a network of superior quality hotels.

In the early 1980s Accor had thus become one of the few companies operating in the hotel industry with a real presence in three distinct segments: the high-end segment with Sofitel, the mid-range segment with Novotel, and the Ibis chain that was a link between the mid-range segment and the low-end segment. Directly contradicting a widely held opinion in the industry, Accor had achieved a significant market share in the three segments.

Accor founders had thought that the low-end segment was a future growth opportunity that was not being covered in an efficient way by other hotel chains. Consequently, with the aim of filling this gap, in 1985 it defined a new business concept that led to the launch of the motel chain Formula 1. The business concept behind these establishments was very clear: minimum investment, good basic services, quality, and cleanness. The financial invest-ment was accompanied by fast construction, which enabled a quick expan-sion. In fact, the motels were built using prefabricated units that were assembled at great speed on-site. The motels' design was also standardized, which enabled large volumes of prefabricated units to be purchased. In just five years, the company had managed to open about 10,000 rooms of this type in France, with an average occupancy rate of 77 per cent, which was consid-ered a notable achievement.

Accor founders developed successive business concepts and managed the group's growth by combining three types of lever. First, there were external levers aimed at seeking a market position by satisfying traditional or emerging needs that were insufficiently covered by traditional establishments. This was the case of Novotel, which offered very good value for money to customers, compared with other hotels.

The second lever was internal and consisted of a unique organizational culture, based on what the founders called the three constituencies, which were like three columns supporting the organization: customers, employees, and shareholders. The three columns had to be balanced, otherwise the company's future would be unstable. The relationship between the three parties was defined by Accor in the following manner. Employee satisfaction led to a better service and a satisfied customer. Satisfied customers became loyal users of the hotel, giving stability and growth. This growth provided the basis for an adequate compensation for the company's investors, which, in turn, provided increased opportunities for raising capital for future invest-ments.

Finally, the third lever was the specific value chain that sustained the busi-ness concept that they had defined. Faced with an industry that was tending towards specialization, Accor's managers pursued very clear vertical integra-tion and horizontal diversification strategies.

However, the integration concept went much further. Indeed, the company had developed a notable capability in real estate development—identification of desirable locations, property purchasing, project financing, and hotel construction—as well as a recognized reputation in the field of hotel manage-ment.

This was how Accor's founders reacted to the trend towards specialization in the industry. Their outlook, which justified these actions, was that the customers' future needs would be met, not by specialized firms, but by firms with a better knowledge and management of each of the activities that led up to the final service, because of the close interrelations among them: function-ality, service, and cost for the customer. According to them, the separation of these activities and overspecialization could ruin a company.

Accor's managers also thought that, given the cyclical nature of the hotel industry, it was wise to diversify operations in related areas. Only the compa-nies that achieved long-term financial solvency would survive the shake-ups that had been a historical feature of the industry.

The successive notions of innovative business concepts have not only enabled Accor to achieve extraordinary growth since the early 1970s but continuously and successfully to search for new ways to offer a unique service in markets at times considered flat or uninteresting, such as the low-end hotels with Formula 1 or the Motel 6 chain. Accor has also been a pioneer in internationalizing the hotel industry, with a significant growth abroad that has enabled it to diversify its sources of revenues. In this expansion, the constant search for new business concepts has been essential.

3. THE CORE ELEMENTS

Accor's evolution and business concepts help us examine the elements that a business concept must have if it is to create an innovative, growth-driving model (see Fig. 6.1.).

The first element of the business concept is the strategic vision. It captures an aspiration about how to have an impact on customers and society (like Henry Ford's desire of putting a car in every home), a competitive arena for the firm (that describes the primary interests of the firm in certain industries and the exclusion of other industries), some corporate values (that include some explicit or implicit set of principles all employees try to respect), and the contribution the firm wants to make to society.

The second element is the development of a specific perception about what customer's needs may be in the future, how the industry may evolve, and which resources and capabilities the firm may need. This outlook must take into account not only what the company might want to do, but also the gaps existing between customers' expectations and the actual service offered by other companies. Very often, when managers look at the gaps between the expectations of customers and the value finally perceived by them, they may detect some opportunities for improvement, both for existing companies and for new companies wishing to enter the industry. So, the business concept should not only have a clear perspective about the customers that a firm has, but should integrate this view with a specific way of serving customers' needs through an efficient value chain. The main advantage new companies have is that they are starting from scratch and can examine ways of doing business and serving customers with a new, fresh look and a more innovative value chain. This is something that existing companies can do only with difficulty, because of the inertia and the resistance to change that an organization usually has to face.

The third element is an understanding of the evolution of competition in the industry, the potential emergence of new substitutes, the changing role of suppliers, and the evolution of the industry's value chain (Porter 1985). Obviously, this understanding will have an effect on the strategic vision and the perception of customers' needs. They all have to contribute to a new perspective of how value will be created along the different steps of the industry's value chain.

- Strategic vision

- A perception of customers' future needs

- A perspective about the industry's value chain

- The organization of the firm's value chain as an integrated, interrelated system, linked up with the strategic vision

- The choice among alternative options

Fig. 6.1. Business concept: Main elements

The fourth element of a business concept is the organization of the company's activities as an integrated, interrelated value chain. These activities should all be geared not to the individual efficiency of each one but to creating the maximum possible value in the entire interaction with the customer. This approach looks at the value chain not only as a sequence of activities but also as a network—rather than a sequence—of interrelated activities that tend to be mutually supportive (Porter 1996). Moreover, we argue that the business concept should consist of activities that right from the start form an interrelated system designed to provide a specific value to customers. This perspective has significant consequences for the management of people, the role of individuals and groups, the design of the organization itself, and, particularly, the compensation and control systems. An innovative business concept requires that each one of these elements of the organizational design not only adapts passively but also contributes actively to consolidating it.

The fifth element of the business concept is the choice among some alternative options that have an impact on the value chain. Basically, strategy consists of choosing among options to achieve certain goals. In the same way, choosing a business concept requires an election among several options. The business concept of a company that seeks the mass market is not the same as that of a company that specializes in certain customers. The business concept of a firm that operates in a particular geographical area cannot be the same as that of an organization that is present in different geographical areas with different demands and needs.

These critical options can basically be summarized as shown in Fig. 6.2. First, customer segmentation has to be considered. What type of customer does the company wish to serve? Does the firm intend to reach the mass market? Or, on the contrary, does it seek to specialize in a particular type of customer?

Secondly, there is the value provided. What type of distinctive value does the company intend to offer its customers? Does the company wish to offer value based on low prices? Does the company wish to offer a service with a clearly superior quality? Does the company seek to break the cost–service proposition currently offered by other companies?

- Customer segmentation

- Value provided

- Key activities in the value chain

- Investment priorities and capability development

- Outsourcing decisions

- Geographical scope

Fig. 6.2. Business concept: Some alternative options

Thirdly, what will be the key activities in this value chain. Does the company have the resources and capabilities to carry out these activities more efficiently than its competitors? Will the company be able to combine these key activities in an innovative way? Will the company's other activities support or strengthen these key activities?

Fourthly, in the light of the key capabilities and activities, what should be the company's investment priorities? Which capabilities require a substantial improvement and a differential investment and which do not?

Fifthly, having defined the way in which the company will offer the customer a superior value and having established the investment priorities in activities and capabilities, which of these activities must necessarily be developed within the company and which can be outsourced? What may be the medium-term consequences of permanently outsourcing certain activities? In addition to the possible bargaining power that the supplier may gain over the company, what impact will outsourced activities have on the value offered to the customer? What effects may it have on the organization's learning? What effects may it have on the capacity for improvement and innovation?

Sixthly, there is the matter of geographical scope. Which geographical areas should the company be present in? Does the presence in certain geographical areas have any effect on the company's costs or revenues? Does entering a particular market sooner or later make any difference?

In the rest of this chapter we will explore how firms develop new business concepts and speed up growth. In Chapter 9 we will introduce the notion of the business concept again to discuss its effects on the limits to corporate growth.

4. DEVELOPING A NEW BUSINESS CONCEPT

We can view the development of a new business concept from four different practical perspectives. Each one is the result of identifying growth gaps, which are real opportunities through which a firm can innovate its business concept and grow (see Fig. 6.3.). We will distinguish four gaps; first, the gap between

- Gap between customers' current and future needs

- Gap between customers' current needs and the products or services currently offered

- Expectations gap in current products or services

- Efficiency gap in the operational processes

Fig. 6.3. Growth gaps: Opportunities for developing new business concepts

customers' current and future needs; secondly, the gap between customers' current needs and the products or services currently offered; thirdly the expectations gap in current products or services; fourthly, the efficiency gap in the production, distribution, and service operations. We will discuss these concepts in the following sections.

4.1. Developing the products and services of the future

The first gap an innovator can identify is that which exists between the customers' current needs and their future needs. In other words, the innovator must reflect on the ways in which customers' future needs can be satisfied better with a new product or service concept. Innovations such as the VCR, the scanner, the personal computer, the mobile telephone, or the mountain bike come under this heading. We can see that these are not always revolutionary innovations but, sometimes, more or less simple products that already exist—for example, a bicycle or a mobile telephone—that are now produced or offered in a different way, with a more attractive price-value ratio.

This type of gap is not always observed by current customers, who may be perfectly satisfied with their products or services and not envision better services in the future. Nevertheless, this gap or opportunity may be perceived by innovators. As we will see, it is a different type of gap from those we will examine later on. Managers face this gap with a very high chance of failure, because of the difficulty of identifying customers' real needs, or the probability of doing so with a low efficiency. In other words, in this type of innovation, companies are not moved by their customers, rather it is the companies that move their customers, not with a more or less attractive advertising campaign but with an unquestionably superior product or service. Clark and Wheelwright (1993) offer a highly original presentation of the process leading to the development of new products and the correct management of this process.

To illustrate this situation more clearly, we will briefly describe the evolution of a very innovative company that has managed to create the future in a relatively traditional, fragmented, and unattractive industry. Multiasistencia, a Spanish company created in 1983, has revolutionized the home and company market for repair, maintenance, and emergencies services (see further Huete 1993).

In 1997 Multiasistencia had about one and a half million insurance policies, received more than a million calls a year requesting its services, and gathered together more than 4,000 professionals (plumbers, electricians, carpenters, etc.) who provided the services required by Multiasistencia's customers.

In the eyes of its founder, Nicolás Luca de Tena, Multiasistencia's business concept was founded on two principles. The first principle was to offer clearly differentiated services to its customers. These services consisted of a fast service, quality work, and an extremely clear pricing system that contained no hidden surprises. Secondly, there would be an operations and logistics base where the service's quality and cost would be difficult to imitate or replicate. A high level of customer attention and service quality had become the mainstay of the organization's culture. The company's founder firmly believed in these values and had sought to inculcate them time and time again in his employees. He sought to give precedence to innovation, enthusiasm, the ability to share, and teamwork, and reinforced these messages through the company's personnel recruitment, remuneration, and promotion processes.

The way in which Multiasistencia's operations were organized contained many original ideas. The company ran both its own and franchised offices, which shared the same working methodology, the same operating procedures, and even the same interior design. When a customer rang Multiasistencia, the operator immediately contacted a professional who was to solve the problem. This professional, as soon as he arrived at the customer's home, had to call the company. The work performed by the professionals affiliated to Multiasistencia was subject to a series of quality controls to ensure that the standard of service was consistent with the company's goals. From the customers' viewpoint, these professionals were the personification of the company's service. For this reason, the company devoted a lot of time and effort to recruitment and training. Multiasistencia did not employ professionals as employees but contracted their services as and when required. The company sought to use self-employed professionals who would render their services to Multiasistencia's network of customers. The professionals recruited by Multiasistencia noted a very marked improvement in their professional and financial standing.

Initially, the company offered its services to individuals and companies operating in the catering industry (hotels, restaurants, etc.). In 1986 Multiasistencia won a major contract with American Express. This was the first of the many contracts that Multiasistencia subsequently concluded with other corporate customers who offered Multiasistencia's services together with their own products or services.

Multiasistencia's customers could be divided into three main groups. First, there were corporate customers. These were insurance companies, banks, or professional associations that included Multiasistencia's services among those provided to their customers. The second group comprised private individuals who had signed a contract with Multiasistencia. By paying an annual fee, these customers were entitled to a round-the-clock service 365 days a year from the company. Finally, there was a third group who, without having signed any prior agreement with Multiasistencia, requested its services when necessary. The assistance provided by the company in these cases was charged at a higher price and was limited to the customers who had signed a contract.

Multiasistencia's experience can help us synthesize a few ideas about the creation of future products and their implications for business concepts (see Fig. 6.4.). The first is that Multiasistencia's growth has been spectacular from its creation, not just in terms of figures, but because of the business concept developed. The company has created a new way of understanding an industry that, in the past, suffered from a high degree of fragmentation and poor service quality. It has managed to create a different industry and a type of company that, until then, did not exist, by envisioning and making real a service that was needed but which, until then, nobody had offered.

Secondly, Multiasistencia has been able to fill in a gap between current and future needs in the home repairs and services industry, just as other companies—for example, Reuters or SAP—have been able to do in other industries. However, it is also interesting to note that to create the future, one does not need to be very big or have a lot of resources or operate in a high-growth industry. Multiasistencia was not born big nor did it have a lot of resources. Its founder and his associates created a business concept that sought to offer an impeccable service and they have succeeded in turning this concept into a reality through a highly efficient organization.

Thirdly, the company's founder had a clear philosophy about the company's purpose and the quality of service that had to be offered, and was able to transmit this to all his associates, in an industry in which, 'a priori', it is considered objectively complex to guarantee a minimum quality level.

Finally, Multiasistencia has achieved an enviable level of operating efficiency. This enables the company to offer a very high-quality service at very reasonable prices. The investment in building an IT infrastructure, in-house training of all personnel, and a service-driven culture are other factors that account for the company's success.

- A unique business concept

- A service to fill the gap between the present and the future

- Clear corporate philosophy

- High level of operational efficiency

Fig. 6.4. The development of the products and services of the future

4.2. Developing new products or services to meet customers' current needs

The second gap that may be perceived by entrepreneurs is that between customers' current needs and the products or services currently offered. The difference between the first gap and this one is that this second gap refers to the needs that customers already have. When there is a large gap between customers' needs and what companies actually offer, the potential for innovation is high, either by new companies or by existing companies that decide to develop new products or services. Ultimately, these companies decide to break with their traditional business concept, discard some of their basic assumptions, and serve their customers' needs better. Stalk, Pecant, and Burnett (1996) propose the concept of 'breaking compromises' to define this strategy.

The US airlines industry offers a highly interesting case for studying the development of a new type of service: Southwest Airlines (see Hallowell and Heskett 1995). This industry underwent a sweeping change after 1978, with the deregulation process initiated by the Civil Aeronautic Board (CAB). Until then, the industry had been highly regulated: air fares were set by the CAB and airlines had no freedom in deciding which routes they wished to fly outside the company's home state. Within that state, there was complete freedom to fly. However, the wave of deregulation that started in 1978 had important consequences for this industry. On the one hand, large companies (a total of eleven, controlling 80 per cent of the market in 1978) initiated a rapid expansion within the country, establishing the so-called hub-and-spoke system, which consisted of organizing centres in certain airports that were used as connections for flights to any other destination in the country. Thus, to provide a service between two cities, an airline chose a reference centre; the flight departed from the city of origin and headed to the centre, from where, a second flight connected with the destination.

The hub-and-spoke model was considered to be the industry's major innovation in the 1980s and seemed to be a forerunner of the system that large companies would use to defend themselves against small companies that sought to enter the industry, taking advantage of the opportunities offered by deregulation. This was the second trend in the industry after 1978: the entry of small companies that started to offer frequent services between certain cities, with prices and costs that were much lower than the large, established companies.

One of the companies that drew a lot of attention in this new market was People's Express. This company's business concept was very different from that of the large companies. Not only did it base its strategy on very low fares, attempting to appeal to potential flyers for whom the large companies' fares were too high; its approach to the business was also different. This approach consisted of seeking low operating costs, with low salaries, multifunctional personnel (performing both check-in functions on ground and service functions during the flight), low in-flight service, and a relatively high number of routes. This combination had a very clear consequence: a People's Express flight between Newark and Washington DC could cost a third of a flight with one of the large companies. With such attractive prices, People's Express's growth mushroomed. In less than three years after starting operations, it was billing $1 billion.

However, People's Express's model had an important flaw: the hypothesis that in this industry there are no scale economies. In actual fact, there are economies of scale in activities such as the booking system, the maintenance system, or the management and operation of the hubs. However, as soon as the company started to increase the number of routes served, without seeking a minimum size, the low cost position ceased to be sustainable. Furthermore, large companies such as Delta, American Airlines, or United Airlines started to react to People's Express' fares by offering lower fares. Thus, the unique position held by People's Express in the market for a few years ceased to be unique when some large companies started to imitate its strategy.

This weak cost position was exacerbated by the fact that the company decided to buy Boeing planes, instead of leasing them as in the past. This purchase, in the midst of a major price war in the market, left the company with a stifling financial burden. People's Express's business concept was not viable and, eventually, the company merged with Texas Air and disappeared. However, that business concept did show that low fares could significantly increase the demand for air travel. It also showed that fares would become a very important competitive weapon in the industry in forthcoming years. Finally, the concept indicated that the hub-and-spoke model might not be the most suitable for serving certain routes.

Southwest Airlines followed a business concept that was similar in some aspects (and different in others) to that of People's Express. This company started operations in 1971 in Texas. Although there were initially many doubts about its viability—among other reasons, because there were already two airlines that offered services in that state—Southwest sought a different positioning. Low fares were a central element of the company's strategy, but not the only one. The first advertising campaign contained a message conveying the idea that flying with an airline that looked after its customers could be a fun experience.

Its strategy included regional flights, frequent departures, punctual arrivals, and a variety of special offers at such low prices that the plane became a competitive replacement for the car for short distances. In fact, the average duration of the company's flights was sixty minutes and, in the company's eyes, its immediate competitors were the train and the car.

However, the deregulation of the industry that began in 1978 challenged some of the hypotheses on which some firms based its business. As we have already mentioned, the prevailing idea in the industry was to look for growth in new markets using the hub-and-spoke system, with a sophisticated booking system and a high level of service during the flight. This was the path that some of the industry's large companies started to follow.

The business concept adopted by Southwest had other features (see Fig. 6.5.) that led to the development of a new service. The first was a conception of travelling as a fun experience: this idea permeated all aspects of the company's relationship with its customers, from the first contact to the end of the flight. The aim was to show that flying need not be boring. To achieve this goal, a carefully designed personnel selection and training policy was implemented. Employees were treated as part of a family and great care was taken in the recruitment processes to find those candidates that best fitted the company's profile.

The second feature was the design of the point-to-point routes system, without any destinations in between, thus breaking with the hub-and-spoke system. The company carefully avoided expanding into routes that would make it necessary to stop off and connect with another flight, with the requirement this would involve of creating a service and maintenance centre.

The third feature was the careful selection of new routes for the company's growth. Southwest expanded, but it left aside the emerging opportunities that did not offer a clear growth path. In fact, the company focused more on expanding the market in which it was already operating—that is, increasing the number of passengers on an existing route—rather than starting a completely new route.

The business concept adopted by Southwest was not only innovative and clearly different from the rest of the industry, but its results confirmed its viability. Indeed, by 1997, this company was the seventh largest airline in the USA, with a return on shareholders' equity of about 17 per cent—versus the industry average of 6 per cent—and an even greater growth potential. It seemed that the business model favoured by Southwest was valid and viable, which no doubt has contributed to the existence of a significant degree of consistency between the business concept and its different components.

In fact, a comparison between Southwest and any of the major competitors such as American Airlines, for example, shows a marked contrast between their business concepts. Thus, while Southwest clearly staked its strategy on direct routes between cities, American chose a hub-and-spoke model. While American developed a strategy based on services that generated high costs and were not always appreciated by customers, Southwest adopted a low-cost

- Different positioning

- Focus on something additional to low prices

- Different business concept

Fig. 6.5. Developing new products or services to meet current needs

policy. American opted for nationwide market share, while Southwest opted for market share in each individual route. Finally, American based its strategy on achieving economies of scale based on the company's total size, while Southwest sought economies of scale in each individual activity.

4.3. Repositioning current products and services

Creating a new business concept often implies being able to offer new products or services. However, on other occasions, creating a new business concept may simply mean repositioning existing products or services better on the market, to match customers' current expectations, eliminating those dimensions that hamper their use and adding others that are necessary to improve their acceptance. Kim and Mauborgne (1997) describe some companies that have used product repositioning as a means to speed up growth. The main difference between this and the previous two gaps is that in this third gap, the product or service already exists, but needs to be repositioned. The firm has to discover this gap in the expectations that customers have and close it with a new approach.

Those companies that are able to identify this gap and provide a suitable answer have enormous growth opportunities. The Spanish financial services industry provides an interesting example: Banco Santander (see further Canals 1993b). This bank experienced dramatic growth between 1987 and 1998, increasing its assets ten times. Although the group's profits grew at a slower rate, the figures are no less extraordinary, from 26,000 million pesetas (156.3 million euros) in 1987 to 130,000 million pesetas (781.3 million euros) in 1998. In January 1999 Banco Santander announced its merger with Banco Central Hispano, another Spanish bank. The new bank created is Banco Santander Central Hispano (BSCH).

The starting point for this spectacular growth was September 1989, when Banco Santander launched the superaccount, a high-income checking account that revolutionized the industry. Until then, Spanish banks did not compete on price (interest rates). The main factor in attracting and retaining customers was the location and density of the branch network and, to a lesser extent, certain promotional events.

Taking advantage of the liberalization of interest rates approved by the Bank of Spain a few years before and with the process of the single financial market in Europe about to begin, Banco Santander started a revolution in the industry, offering a traditional product, the checking account, with a higher interest rate. The superaccount was an immediate success. Banco Santander's volume of deposits grew by 40 per cent in just one year. The main reason for this success was not only a very well managed and executed marketing plan but, above all, the satisfaction of a need that was latent and that no other financial institution had seriously addressed: remuneration of the traditional checking accounts at market rates.

In a context of growing financial awareness and the emergence of new competitors to the traditional bank industry, such as investment funds, Banco Santander's managers perceived the need to respond to this gap in the market with a product that had been shown to be important, particularly in the US and Britain. Banco Santander had also seen that, faced with the imminent squeeze on financial margins in the traditional banking industry, banks had to find other ways to make up the corresponding fall in revenues. The path chosen by Banco Santander was to offset a smaller financial margin with higher volume.

The experience of this launch also shows the importance of being the first in the market and not waiting for others to fill in the holes in the market (see the framework developed by Lieberman and Montgomery 1988 on first-mover advantages). Indeed, Santander's speed contrasts with other banks, which were slow to act. By the time they started to react to Santander's offensive, this bank had already gained many new customers. Consequently, the success of Banco Santander's initiative was due to a combination of factors from which certain lessons can be drawn (see Fig. 6.6.): an innovative view of customer's needs, the launch of a new product that filled a need that was not satisfied by the financial products existing at that time; the search for higher growth and a higher market share, to offset shrunken margins; and, finally, speed in design and execution to be the first to act and then to capitalize on the advantages of being the first. However, the consequences of this action by Banco Santander have been even more far-reaching. The superaccounts have revolutionized the bank's marketing strategy and its internal procedures. Since 1989 Banco Santander has launched several innovative products, such as mutual funds or personal mortgages, penetrated significantly new market segments such as capital markets and corporate banking, and expanded on a significant scale abroad, both in the US and in Latin America.

To summarize, the launch of the superaccount was the manifestation of a wish to fill a major gap in the field of financial services that no other bank had wished to fill in the past. In part, this was due to the traditional conception prevailing in the Spanish banking industry, according to which a bank's profits were derived from high margins sustained by prices regulated by the financial authorities in a market that was protected from competition. Banco Santander broke away from this way of thinking by showing that good performance could

- An innovative view of customers' needs

- The launch of a new product that filled a need

- The search for higher growth and a higher market share

- Speed in design and execution

Fig. 6.6. Repositioning current products or services

be achieved through a new margin–volume combination. This, in turn, consisted of identifying needs that were insufficiently covered by current services.

4.4. Operational efficiency: A necessary condition for creating the future

Creating a new business concept may have another important dimension: organizing the company's activities according to different patterns from those followed by other companies. This way of organizing may enable it to develop a superior capability in the execution of the company's projects and a higher operational efficiency.

Consequently, this dimension for creating the future consists not only of envisioning new products but, above all, of executing processes more efficiently than competitors in order to serve customers. This approach sometimes involves questioning currently prevailing hypotheses on a product's price and cost, and proposing a new relationship between cost, price, and value offered. As Brown and Eisenhardt (1998) point out, before a company undertakes a radical change, it could first try to make current operations as efficient as possible.

Komatsu, a Japanese manufacturer of earth-moving equipment, offers an interesting illustration of this (see Bartlett and Rangan 1985). Until the 1970s this industry was traditionally dominated by US companies such as Caterpillar, J. I. Chase, and Deere. Komatsu started business on a very modest basis in 1921. Its growth did not really start to get off the ground until the 1960s, when the Japanese government ceased to consider this industry one of its priorities and allowed Caterpillar to enter Japan through an alliance with Mitsubishi. The entry of Caterpillar in Japan and the increased rivalry in the domestic market revitalized Komatsu. Instead of losing heart and looking for a small niche in the market, Komatsu's president, Yasinari Kawai, started a series of activities aimed at consolidating the company. In 1970 Komatsu had less than 10 per cent of the world market share and even this share was mainly thanks to its dominant position in the Japanese market. In 1985 this share had doubled. In 1997 its global market share was about one-third.

What are the factors that have driven Komatsu's impressive growth? The combination of forces is very varied. First, it adopted a product concept and product lines that were different from Caterpillar's. Until the 1970s, this company had been known for offering high-quality products, high performance, and high prices. However, there was a growing market for high-performance, small and medium-sized machines at lower prices.

Secondly, it developed a different distribution concept. Caterpillar had depended on exclusive distributors who contributed to adding value to the end product but at a high cost for customers. The emergence of new customers in high-growth countries enabled Komatsu to grow without requiring an expensive dealer network, by making direct contact with the governments that were contracting public works projects or the construction companies themselves.

So far, these two factors seem to fit in with the way the companies we have observed in some of the previous sections went about creating the industry's future. However, what really sets Komatsu apart is the management's ability not only to rethink the industry's future but also to put it into effect by continual improvement of its operating efficiency.

The stages followed by Komatsu in the 1970s to drive its growth by improving its efficiency show a clear sequence. First, Komatsu set about improving its products' quality. With the increased rivalry on the Japanese domestic market, quality became a vital issue for Komatsu. During the first half of the 1970s the company's managers implemented a series of quality improvement plans for the different products, with very clear indicators for determining the degree of fulfilment of its programmes. The second step consisted of reducing costs by means of systematic projects to replace complex components with simple components that were more functional and interchangeable. Komatsu then expanded the product range. Until then, Komatsu had been a low-end producer. With the commencement of international operations, it became vital to have a broader range of products to cover different customers' needs. Thus, between 1975 and 1981, the range was almost doubled, from forty-six to seventy-seven products.

The next step was the EPOCHS programme. This programme pursued several goals. First, the project aimed to improve the efficiency of the production processes by modularization. Secondly, it set out to achieve more effective coordination between the marketing and production departments, so that customers' needs were immediately communicated to the design and production engineers. Thirdly, it implemented new quality plans in the production process. Finally, this project led to a further increase in Komatsu's product range, particularly at the top end. Operational efficiency was driven by a corporate philosophy rooted in continuous improvement and customer service and certain growth goals in the international markets. In fact, during the first half of the 1980s, Komatsu started to gain a major presence in the US and this presence has continued since then.

One of the most important lessons we can draw from Komatsu's story is that its business concept shows a unique combination between the corporate vision, a very clear strategy, and an extraordinary capacity for operational implementation. This capacity for setting long-term goals, transferring them to immediate goals, and then implementing action programmes, shows that the companies that invent the future are those that not only create new products or services, but are also able to maintain and improve them over time thanks to an exceptional management capacity. Thus, creating a new business concept has to do with imagination, creativity, and sensitivity to new, emerging needs, but at the same time it is influenced decisively by an ability to visualize the company's activities from an innovative viewpoint and achieve a greater efficiency in its operations (see Fig. 6.7.).

- Strategic vision

- Strong improvement-driven internal culture

- Investment of resources in key projects and divestment from secondary projects

- Relationship between corporate purpose, culture, strategy, and operational efficiency

Fig. 6.7. Operational efficiency and growth

5. DEVELOPING NEW BUSINESS CONCEPTS: UNLEASHING PEOPLE'S INITIATIVE AND CREATIVITY

In this chapter we have presented different dimensions of the capability that a company and its people have to create a different, better business concept. This is a risky, complex process in which many people interact. Ideas are generated and exchanged at different levels and some aspects of the way the company operates, previously considered fundamental, should now be challenged with the purpose of improving them constantly.

As we have seen in this chapter, the development of a business concept requires reconsidering certain basic issues about the company: what vision the firm has; who the company's customers are or should be; which future products or services should be developed; which markets should be considered a priority; what price–value combinations should be offered to customers; and finally, how the company's activities should be restructured to respond to these challenges.

Confronting these complex questions requires something more than clear concepts. It is a process in which managers' creativity and rationality must interact at a very deep level. Managers and their associates hold the creation of the future in their hands. This future does not come about by chance or by applying certain strategic planning techniques that point the company in the direction it should follow. Rather, there is always someone, whether it is one person or several, behind each business idea, and behind any definition of the future of the firm.

Management's responsibility is to be able adequately to stimulate and coach people through this process, so that the current status quo does not block the renewal of the company and the definition of new business concepts. At the same time, managers must maintain that delicate balance between freezing some projects because they are supposedly incompatible with current ways of operating and pushing the company towards new areas. In this process of defining business concepts, senior managers have an essential role to play. It is not a process that should be driven only by a company's top executive— although, without doubt, this function is indispensable—but rather it is a process developed, shared, and implemented by the top management and undertaken by the entire organization.

It is an accepted fact that renewal processes may be easier when a company is in a state of deep crisis and people accept the need for a change. On the other hand, when a company is doing well and there does not seem to be any need to change, that is precisely the time when the definition of a new business concept is more complex.

The case of Indo may help us understand this discussion better (see Canals 1993c). Indo is a Spanish company that manufactures spectacle lenses and frames and that had been one of the leaders in the European market. In the early 1990s the company was still profitable. However, the stagnation of the domestic market because of slower growth in consumption and the appearance of two special types of threats in frames—low-cost products from South-East Asia and the concept of the frame as a fashion product associated with well-known international brands—seriously challenged the growth model followed by Indo.

The combination of these phenomena put Indo in a very difficult situation. Slackening sales and dwindling profits led the company to restructure and subsequently reinvent its business. This consisted of outsourcing production processes, investing abroad to push down production costs, and relaunching the marketing function—until then based on superior R&D and subsequently more focused on marketing promotions and advertising. None of these actions, which went directly against the philosophy prevailing in Indo until then, was easy to carry out. However, the situation of crisis enabled Indo's management to introduce a change project and to share it with all the company's personnel, who were convinced that it was necessary to save the company. However, if it had not been for the fact that the company was in serious difficulties, the change process would have been much more costly and difficult to implement.

On the other hand, when companies are growing steadily and their profitability is improving continuously, the process of changing or reinventing the company becomes much more complex. In such cases, a culture is needed that facilitates and fosters the need for continuous change, with a top management team that accepts renewal as a constant rule. This is the case of companies such as SAP, Hewlett-Packard, or Intel, where renewing and cannibalizing star products are part and parcel of their culture. If we look closely at this approach, we can say that it is very demanding and that it shatters many people's expectations, starting with the sales teams responsible for the really successful products. However, if one looks at it from the viewpoint of continually renewing and reinventing the company, it is a requirement that without doubt helps people reassess the process on an ongoing basis.

The definition of a new business concept is a complex process that is originated, guided, and driven by people with a strong concern to improve continually the company and to carry out better professional work providing a better service to customers and employees. This process may require imagination on the part of managers to discover future pathways among present events and to propose new concepts. However, alongside these capabilities—which are always useful—one should not overlook the importance of a set of values and attitudes shared by the company's managers and, in general, by all of the company's employees that enormously facilitate the recreation process. We would like to highlight the following.

The first consists of the capability to accept and view current success as merely temporary. Business success is not a consequence of a series of planned actions: it is a combination of many factors, which may indeed include these actions. However, it is also the outcome of other factors, such as the reaction of customers and rivals, or the creation of public opinion in favour of certain products, services, or companies. Companies that view business success as permanent, as a deserved result of the effort made, are doomed to enjoy it for very little time. On the contrary, managers who cultivate a realistic, humble attitude, who acknowledge that success today does not guarantee success tomorrow are more inclined to try again and succeed. Hence the importance of this basic attitude.

The second attitude is an acute sense of entrepreneurship at all levels of the organization (Stopford and Baden-Fuller 1994). This dimension is not developed overnight. It is the result of at least two elements. The first is a type of mentality among the company's managers that leads them not to be completely satisfied with what has already been achieved but to strive for new achievements, driven by an enormous will to excel, and to work increasingly to broaden and deepen the company's social justification. The second element is related to the company's formal systems—that is, the degree of centralization or decentralization in decision-making, the compensation and control systems that have been articulated, and the way new business ventures are organized within the organization. There is a long, rich experience that shows that certain formal systems favour entrepreneurship while others discourage it.

The third attitude is for senior managers to be not just executives but people who are committed to the development of the people who work with them, and for whom they have a deep respect. Coaching or mentoring are processes by which managers perform a role that is more akin to an adviser or coach than to an executive who is accustomed to thinking and designing action plans to be executed by others. This management philosophy has many repercussions within the company, not just in terms of fostering this individual initiative but also of unleashing the development of the potential that all individuals have and that is not always expressed because the context has not allowed them to develop harmoniously.

Furthermore, when one views this activity in terms of a coaching process, the sense of professional success or failure takes on a very special meaning. The so-called successes are always starting points for new goals, never winning posts that foster self-complacency. Likewise, failures are never irreversible phenomena but rather specific experiences from which one tries to build a better future. This perception of success and failure undoubtedly helps create an atmosphere in which it is worthwhile trying, with prudence, different ways of doing things, developing new products or considering new ways of serving customers. As a result, the possibilities for creating or recreating the company's business concept with a chance of success are increased.

Meanwhile, the mentoring process itself helps eradicate any self-compla-cency that might exist in the company and imposes a kind of inner demand and healthy ambition to do things a little better each day. Indeed, in companies with a good mentoring process, these goals are viewed not just as organiza-tional goals but as goals that form a vital symbiosis with the managers' own improvement processes. Thus, managers come to view the organization as a great context for personal development. In this sense, the ambition for profes-sional success is replaced by the ambition for personal improvement, to develop all of the potential lying within each individual to give the best of oneself in one's work and to enable others to benefit from this.

In addition, this is a two-way path. That is, it is a process in which not only those who are mentored improve but also those who act as mentors—the former because they receive the experience and wisdom of other senior managers who encourage them and help them develop in new areas, the latter because they have the opportunity to broaden part of their professional chal-lenge not only by acting themselves, but also by making others act and develop thanks to their experience.

Undoubtedly, mentoring requires a very high level of trust in the organiza-tion and this is never a spontaneous process. Trust demands personal integrity, clear ethical standards, total transparency, shared values, an unquestionable sense of equity and fairness, and generosity of senior managers towards the other employees. In this sense, generosity in time, resources used, and projects backed is usually the best means of obtaining a high level of commitment to the organization from the rest of the employees. On the other hand, a lack of generosity or a perception that senior managers are only pursuing a personal agenda usually lies at the root of a lack of commitment and, ultimately, makes a subtle noose that strangles the company's possibilities of expansion. Indeed, an organization without the commitment of its employees is doomed to an ephemeral or mediocre life.

By way of conclusion, we would like to stress that creating new business concepts is not an automatic process that can be made through formal plan-ning systems, using more or less sophisticated techniques. It is, above all, a creative process performed by people. Moreover, there are a series of top-management attributes or characteristics that are conveyed to the entire organ-ization and that can accelerate or slow down the process. These attitudes are never determining factors on their own. However, their absence may endanger an organization's capability to reinvent itself or to be able to create the business concept of the future.

6. SOME FINAL IDEAS

In this chapter we have discussed the notion of the business concept and its main elements. The continuous creation of new business concepts is an indispensable prerequisite for corporate growth and long-term survival. Without it, growth will quickly run out of steam. Nevertheless, the creation of business concepts requires more than a simple reflection. It has to include a credible strategic vision, a perception of customers' future needs, a better way to serve them, and the efficient organization of the firm's activities to deliver superior value.

We have also introduced the concept of growth gaps, a set of dimensions along which the business concept creation process can be viewed. The first gap entails the perception of new, emerging needs that could become consolidated if the company is able to offer the right products or services. The second growth gap encourages the design of new products or services to cover current needs omitted or neglected by the companies operating in an industry. This neglect may be the result of indifference or complacency on the part of the industry's leaders, which prevents them from changing and taking a new look at what else they could do.

The third growth gap is the potential repositioning of existing products or services to meet customers' expectations and improve the satisfaction of customers' needs. This repositioning could be in price or some of the product's dimensions, adding or removing features depending on the real customers' needs. Finally, developing new business concepts is directly related to the ability to operate more efficiently, or to put into practice certain ideas that would shape the company's vision of its industry. This represents the fourth growth gap.

The development of a new business concept cannot be limited to a planning process. It is dependent on both the creativity and the rationality of the people who work in an organization. Senior managers' responsibility in this sense is to guide and coach people and foster the company's continuous renewal process.

Resources and Capabilities: Enabling Growth

1. THE ROLE OF RESOURCES AND CAPABILITIES

Resources and capabilities have become essential factors in business strategy. The evidence presented in Chapter 3 seems to point to the fact that they are also decisive in corporate growth.

What is the role played by the firm's resources and capabilities in its growth process and, ultimately, in its sustainability? The answer is complex and has been approached in different ways. To start to unravel it, we will discuss the growth process followed by two companies: Walt Disney Company and Saatchi & Saatchi. In Section 2 we will discuss more formally the role of resources and capabilities in corporate growth. In Section 3 we will analyse what determines the value of resources and capabilities for growth. The deployment of resources and capabilities in new activities will be explored in Section 4.

1.1. Walt Disney: The growth empire

Walt Disney has been one of the most exceptional companies of the last twenty years of the twentieth century. Until the early 1980s, this legendary company had been steadily declining: its performance had been mediocre and its share prices had fallen to the point of being considered a clear target for a hostile takeover bid in Wall Street (see Collis 1988).

Walt Disney's origins date back to 1923, when Walt Elias Disney and his brother Roy started a studio in Hollywood under the name 'The Disney Brothers'. In 1928 they released the first cartoon film, *Steamboat Willie*, featuring Mickey Mouse. One year later stories started to be published with Mickey as their main character, while the film that had made him so popular started to be distributed in Europe and Latin America.

After several box-office hits in the 1930s and 1940s (including *Fantasia*,

Dumbo and *Song of the South*) and Disney's first television programme for the USA, called *An Hour in Wonder World*, Disney started a new business that would have a decisive influence on the company's future direction: theme parks. In 1955 Disneyland, in Anaheim (California), opened its doors to the public. Ten years later, Walt Disney purchased a large piece of land (11,000 hectares) in Orlando, Florida, where it opened Disney's second large theme park, Disneyworld, in 1971. In 1976 Disney reached an agreement with Oriental Land Company to develop a theme park near Tokyo. This was the first major venture in theme parks abroad and Disney approached it differently: it transferred ownership of the park to the Japanese partner and concentrated on designing and planning the park. Meanwhile, Disney's creative genius consolidated itself during the 1960s, with new box-office and television hits that strengthened the company and helped create what came to be known as 'Disney's magic'.

However, in the late 1970s and early 1980s, Disney's magic seemed to be faltering. The company was unable to generate new products that could boost growth. Furthermore, other Hollywood studios were starting to compete with Disney with products that appealed to young people's imagination, such as George Lucas's trilogy, with *Star Wars* at the top. Thus, Disney entered a period of stagnation in projects and performance and the stock market started to penalize the company. However, it was obvious to everyone that Disney had an enormous potential in its creators, its products, and the intrinsic value of the Disney brand.

In 1984, after several attempted changes of ownership, Disney's board appointed Michael Eisner as Walt Disney's CEO. A few months after starting his mandate in the company, the new chief executive announced what would be his goals. Particularly important was his intention to consolidate Disney as a world leader in the entertainment industry, to maintain and enhance the integrity of the Disney brand, to preserve the company's creative and entrepreneurial spirit, and to achieve an annual growth rate and return on shareholders' equity of 20 per cent. In order to achieve these goals, Eisner embarked upon a mammoth task: mobilize all of Disney's resources that were underused and could contribute to relaunching the company. The new management team was convinced that Disney's problem was not the shortage of resources to produce new successful films but the inadequate management of existing resources.

The first area of action in revitalizing resources was to make a better use of its film library. Until then, the company's policy had been periodically to reshow classic films. Now, this division sought to introduce the sale of these films on video to the public and to license movie packages to major television channels in the USA and throughout the world. In short, the goal was to improve the marketability of the enormous pool of existing films and eradicate a routine that had become disastrous for the company.

The second area of action was to regenerate Disney's film studios. In previous years Disney had not managed to emulate its competitors' success. The new management's goal was to restore Disney's position as a leader in entertainment for children and adults, with the emphasis on family entertainment. This meant increasing the capacity of the existing studios in Disney's Touchstone division. In less than two years Disney had doubled the number of movies in production and contracted scripts, directors, and actors on a massive scale. A few years later, in 1988, Disney had become world leader in revenues from film releases. As was logical, the company took advantage of the increased production of commercial successes to boost its video sales to the public and hike up its royalty charges to the television channels.

The third area of action was to optimize the use of the 28,000-acre theme park in Orlando. First, the range of attractions in the park itself was improved to increase the number of visitors. Thus, the so-called Disney-MGM Studio Tour was added to the park, becoming a movie theme park within a larger park. A second move was to initiate a real-estate development plan to build hotels and convention centres in the immediate vicinity of the Orlando theme park with the aim of turning the area into a vacation and leisure centre.

With these actions, Disney's revitalization has become a firm reality. The company has not only succeeded in expanding at the planned rates, but its return on capital invested is in line with the goal set by Eisner back in 1984. Disney's growth process cannot be understood solely in business or financial terms. The new management team's effort was founded on the conviction of the unique value of Disney's resources and capabilities, which, in the mid-1980s, were not being used in the best possible way. Behind Disney's relaunch—and its new projects—there was a management team able to generate innovative ideas around a basic theme: how to get the best performance from available resources. Disney has accelerated growth not only by preserving these resources but by exploiting them adequately with a more creative management and taking them to new businesses, where the company's capabilities and the value of its brand have made them sparkle as if touched by a magic wand.

1.2. The rise and fall of Saatchi & Saatchi plc

In the 1980s, Saatchi & Saatchi became the world's most ingenious and popular advertising agency, billing £2 billion in 1986, with more than 10,000 employees and a presence in almost eighty countries (see Collis 1987). This growth had taken place over a period of fifteen years, after the brothers Charles and Maurice Saatchi formed their first agency in 1970. More than just an agency, this company was a conglomerate of advertising agencies and marketing firms. Its business concept in the advertising and marketing world had created a completely different view of how these companies would be in the future.

In the 1970s the advertising industry was highly fragmented, with a very large number of small agencies. The Saatchi brothers saw a business opportunity in this fragmentation. If they could create a large agency, their ability to win major accounts would increase. At the same time, the size would enable them to attract talented professionals, form a solid human team with a large critical mass, be known by more potential clients, and gain a higher market share.

This was the first of the principles on which the Saatchi brothers' philosophy was based: growth to achieve a bigger scale. As it was not possible to accelerate this process by fast internal growth, they chose a different path: the acquisition of competing companies. This mechanism had a high financial cost—the price of the companies acquired—but a major advantage: the number of competitors in the industry would decrease. To accelerate the process, the Saatchi brothers devised an ingenious scheme for buying companies: companies with a low price/earning ratio (PER) were acquired. Twenty per cent of the price was paid when the transaction was closed; the rest of the price would be paid over a period of five years. An important part of the deal was that the managers of the acquired agency would keep their jobs and the deferred price would be tied to achieving the performance goals set in the purchase agreement.

By this means, two birds were killed with the same stone. First, the need for financial resources was reduced, thereby enabling the process of buying other companies to be accelerated. Eventually, the financial resources would be taken from the earnings generated by the companies after they had been acquired by Saatchi & Saatchi. The second objective was to give the acquired company's management a strong incentive to achieve the goals that had been set, as this was the necessary condition for receiving payment of the deferred purchase price. As a result of both aspects, Saatchi & Saatchi's financial situation started to improve, not only in terms of size but also in profitability. Furthermore, the acquisitions did not seem to overburden its financial structure, as borrowing did not increase substantially, thanks to the methodology followed in organizing the acquisitions.

The second principle of Saatchi & Saatchi's philosophy was globalization. The future, according to Maurice and Charles's vision, would be global products with global brands. This vision received academic backing from Harvard Professor Ted Levitt in the early 1980s. In a famous article published in 1983, 'The globalization of markets', Levitt enthusiastically advocated the end of market fragmentation. The world, he concluded, belonged to global brands.

Saatchi & Saatchi viewed globalization not only as a target against which to position itself and develop an advantage over other advertising agencies, but also as an enormous opportunity for achieving economies of scale in the creation, marketing, and distribution of advertising. A global agency's costs would be much lower than those of a local agency. One of the most successful cases of global advertising was that for British Airways, produced by Saatchi & Saatchi and known as 'Manhattan landing'. This TV advertisement cost about a million dollars and was used in forty-five different countries with the same design and format, simply dubbing in the language used in each country.

The third principle of the company's philosophy was the integration of professional business services. This principle, conceived in the wake of the financial successes in the early 1980s, led the company to diversify towards other marketing and business research companies. The Saatchi brothers' dream was to build a business services supermarket that would include the financial capacity of an investment bank, the reputation of a strategic consulting firm, and the expertise of auditing services, combined with Saatchi & Saatchi's experience in advertising. The perception of the synergies to be gained by integrating services was supported by a hypothesis: managers would have increasingly less time and, instead of engaging professionals for each function, would prefer to contract the services to a single company that could take care of all the details.

This dream took the company to the edge of the abyss. For integration to be possible, first companies that could help achieve the goal of integrating services had to be acquired. Consequently, the company continued with its acquisition policy. There were two purchases that proved to be particularly costly, both from the financial viewpoint and because of the impression it created among stock-market analysts about Saatchi& Saatchi's future.

The first was the purchase in 1986 of Ted Bates, the third largest advertising agency in the world, whose performance was considerably above the industry average. With a book value of $390 per share, the purchase price was $893.5 per share, giving a total price of $450 million. Because of the opposition of the selling shareholders, Saatchi & Saatchi had to pay 90 per cent of the purchase price at the time the transaction was closed. The stock market reacted negatively to this agreement, which seriously weakened the company's financial position.

The second acquisition attempt—which never actually materialized—was Midland Bank, the third largest UK commercial bank. This operation sought to serve a twofold purpose: add a large bank to the group and take to the banking industry the concentration and consolidation strategy that had been implemented in the advertising agencies industry. However, the stock market said 'enough was enough' and Saatchi & Saatchi's shares started to fall, thus limiting the possibilities for obtaining further capital to finance future purchases. Since then, the company has been fraught with serious strategic, human, and financial problems. In 1995 the Saatchi brothers were forced to leave the company by new shareholders who had little confidence in their management talents.

Saatchi & Saatchi brought fresh insights to the advertising industry. However, their business concept proved to be flawed on several dimensions. It is sometimes pointed out that certain companies owe their success to different, superior views of serving and creating value for customers. Without doubt, Saatchi and Saatchi introduced a different conception of the agencies' role, the importance of integrating their service with other business services, and the globalization of products and brands. In this sense, ideas were not lacking. And, for a few years, these ideas generated growth, although it was not sustainable.

The vision developed by the firm—founded on globalization and the integration of professional services—never achieved the full approval of the business community. However, the company's most serious problems were not only the lack of proportion between the goals it set out to achieve and the resources and capabilities required to achieve them, but also the failure of its business concept.

Creating and consolidating a global company requires, first of all, a team of professionals who share the same business concept—in this case, the creation of advertisements and a specific approach to customer service. However, the principle of complete decentralization in each of the local agencies effectively prevented Saatchi & Saatchi from structuring a shared, consistent vision of the business. This concept also presupposes the possibility of sharing a brand image globally. This idea seemed to contradict the role of local firms, since they are the ones that have a presence on the national markets rather than the parent company. A global-services firm requires a global brand supported by some design and implementation criteria that are applied consistently in all countries. Saatchi & Saatchi did not invest enough in a global brand or in developing professionals and building an organization able truly to offer the kind of service they were claiming.

In this sense, Saatchi & Saatchi is the opposite case of Walt Disney, in that it tried to accelerate growth by stretching existing resources, and deploying them according to a dubious business concept. Its experience shows that an abundance of resources is not enough to achieve sustainable growth. Resources should have a unique value and be deployed according to a business concept, as we shall see later.

2. THE ROLE OF RESOURCES AND CAPABILITIES IN CORPORATE GROWTH

The cases of Walt Disney and Saatchi & Saatchi show, among other aspects, the importance not only of having resources and capabilities, but also of matching the design and implementation of a growth strategy with the available resources and capabilities. Although the resources available are not a definitive limit to a company's growth, they do provide an important reference for reflecting on whether the strategy has some basic ingredients for its success.

A new view of corporate strategy has been developed in the academic world, articulated around the concept of the resource-based view of the firm (Wernerfelt 1984; Dierickx and Cool 1989; Prahalad and Hamel 1990; Amit and Schoemaker 1993; Peteraf 1993; Barney 1995; Collis and Montgomery 1995). This approach points out that the development of sustainable competitive advantages is directly related to a company's resources and capabilities and not only to a good positioning in the industry, as Porter (1980) argued.

Initially, these ideas may look like a rehashing of old concepts. However, the rehashing has had a beneficial effect, as it has enabled subtleties to be detected that, until then, had passed unnoticed. These ideas can be viewed as old hat because the concept of distinctive competence was put forward as early as 1957 by Philip Selznick. Several years later, Ken Andrews took the concept and made it one of the central themes of his classic book *The Concept of Corporate Strategy* (1971). For these authors, a distinctive competence is that which makes a company unique, different from its competitors. When this uniqueness ceases to exist, the competence no longer distinguishes the company that possessed it and it becomes the common property of many competitors, thereby losing part of its value.

C. K. Prahalad and G. Hamel (1990) lent further support to this concept. Indeed, these authors point out that the development of core competencies is the one factor that accounts for a company's growth and profitability on two parallel dimensions. The first consists of using, renovating, and leveraging resources, as we have discussed in the case of Disney. The second dimension consists of making adequate use of resources in directions that are consistent with their value, precisely the opposite of Saatchi & Saatchi's venture. This dimension is the key in corporate diversification.

For these authors, a core competence is that which makes a very particular and valuable contribution to customer value. Through its brand image and the quality attributes associated with it, the Disney brand—and its capacity to regenerate itself and be included in numerous products and services—has become one of the company's distinctive competencies. Having a superior technology or engineers able to create innovative products is not, by definition, a distinctive competence. This competence will be truly a core or distinctive competence when it enables the firm to offer a clearly superior service, to the extent that it becomes a source of sustainable competitive advantages. Of course, core competencies (for example, in the development of new products or marketing new brands) are directly related to the resources and capabilities that lie at the heart of any organization.

A second feature of a distinctive competence is that it must be unique, something that cannot be readily imitated by competitors. When a competence is readily acquired or developed by competitors, its value for the company tends to decline and the competence ceases to be distinctive.

The concepts of resources, capabilities, and distinctive competencies share many attributes and their distinction is very subtle (Barney 1995). While resources can be readily identified (both tangible resources—for example, capital—and intangible ones—for example, reputation), this is not always the case with capabilities (Amit and Schoemaker 1993; Collis and Montgomery 1995). We will discuss these concepts in the next two sections.

2.1. The role of resources

In a first approach, it is advisable to distinguish between tangible and intangible resources. Let us start with the former. Tangible resources are readily identified: they are assets reflected on a company's balance sheet—assets such as production, technological, and financial resources. Although these resources have a book value that is recorded in the financial statements and a market value that varies depending on these assets' supply and demand, their specific value for a company may be different from those two values.

Thus, a particular asset—for example, a process technology—may have a certain market value. However, its value for a company may be greater when that technology is combined with other resources or capabilities also held by the company—for example, production capacity—or when these resources are managed or coordinated by the company's managers. Tripsas (1997) provides an empirical confirmation for this hypothesis when studying the impact of certain complementary assets on the value of certain resources and capabilities for the company.

One example can illustrate this point. In the automobile-components industry, a small local company, with virtually no competitive advantages, may have assets whose market value is less than the value they may have for a multinational corporation that could use those assets—and the company's location—to cover a particular market or to expand its production capacity quickly. In this case, these assets' value when held by one company may be different from their value for another possible buyer. This is the main reason why some multinational corporations investing in fast-growth countries are prepared to pay large sums for companies whose book or market value is less than the price offered by the acquiring company. The reason is that the same resources, managed another way and within a different organization, may offer a higher profitability.

From the point of view of their value and contribution to a company's growth and strategy, we can ask three main questions about the value of these tangible resources. First, is their current use efficient? Secondly, will their use in the company's future projects be as or more efficient than that of rivals? Thirdly, if the company were to be starting business today, would it choose these resources to carry out its operations? The case of Walt Disney just described offers useful answers to those questions. Each of these questions can be addressed in different ways. In principle, none of them gives a final answer on the resources' true value. The crucial issue that these questions seek to put under the spotlight is that having acceptable resources is not sufficient by itself to implement a certain growth strategy. The question is whether these assets are those that the company really needs for that strategy to be successful.

The second category of resources comprises the intangible ones. The value of these resources does not appear in the companies' financial statements. Some important intangible resources are the company's brand image, corporate culture, or reputation. These resources are highly interrelated. A company may have a low-profile brand image because it offers an industrial product. However, its reputation among its customers may be extraordinary. Generally speaking, the brand's value depends, among other factors, on the company's reputation. Any improvement in this variable has a decisive influence on the brand's value. In turn, the company's reputation may grow if the organization's culture contributes to inducing all of its employees to improve the customers' perception of the quality of the products or services offered by the company (see Barney 1986 and Kotter and Heskett 192 on the role of culture as a valuable resource).

The main problem raised by these intangible resources is that it is difficult to identify and define them on a practical level and give them a value. On the other hand, a firm's reputation can be developed and strengthened by the unique capabilities it has. In other words, resources and capabilities are inter-related, which makes their distinction more difficult. We will come back to this point in the next section. However, it is also true that, as the industrial society becomes a services society, where knowledge and information are the main-stays of business growth, the importance of intangible resources will come increasingly to the forefront.

Let us take two of the intangible resources that we have mentioned above: the brand name and the company's reputation. A company that decides to contract a certain business service will use some criteria to choose a supplier: price, the supplier's previous experience, another company's experience with the supplier, the supplier's brand image, its reputation, etc. Some of these factors are obviously tangible, such as price. Others are clearly intangible. However, even in the tangible dimensions such as price, both the buyer and the seller play with intangible items, such as the brand image or the company's reputation.

The consulting industry provides a very good example of this. A certain type of project may seem similar for all firms, but some firms will charge much higher fees than others for this service. What lies behind this difference in fees? This service's value, like other business services, is based on experience: its true value for the buyer is not clear until it has been rendered. In such cases, a renowned brand or a certain reputation offers, in the buyer's eyes, a guarantee as regards the final result to be achieved.

An indirect way of valuing a company's intangible resources is to use the market-value/book-value ratio. Sometimes, this ratio may conceal an appreci-ation of tangible assets. At other times, it may conceal the value of intangible assets and the ability of an organization's managers to generate value from the resources they manage. Many strategic decisions or growth strategies are grounded on the use and leverage of intangible resources, such as the brand image, or the possible transfer of certain resources—such as the corporate culture—to other businesses where these resources may have a certain value. (See Prahalad and Hamel 1990 and Collis and Montgomery 1997, for whom this issue is a keystone of their conception of corporate strategy.)

Just as with tangible resources, it is important to assess carefully the poten-tial of the company's intangible resources for contributing to the successful articulation and implementation of a growth strategy. Sometimes, the percep-tion or belief that a new business can share the same brand image as another existing business in the company may lead one to think that the new business will be just as successful as the previous one, simply because it has the same brand. This is one of the many growth pitfalls associated with a simplistic inter-pretation of a company's success factors. Normally, a company is successful not just for one reason but for many reasons—which, in turn, will be interrelated—and some of these can be controlled by the company and others cannot.

A real-life case will help us understand better the consequences of excessive optimism about the transfer of intangible resources. Johnson & Johnson, the world leader in care products for babies, decided in the early 1970s to invest in the—at that time—growing industry for disposable nappies. In fact, disposable diapers were the fastest growing consumer product in the USA. At that time, the industry leaders were Procter & Gamble, with a 70 per cent market share, and Kimberly Clark, with a 20 per cent market share. These two companies had developed a very efficient production technology for a product that was very complex to manufacture.

Johnson & Johnson thought that its extraordinary brand image, and access to distribution channels, would enable it to enter the business and reach the same homes where it was already present with other baby products. However, it came up against an unexpected obstacle: the difficulty of manufacturing nappies at a low cost, so as to be able to price the product competitively. Although some market tests indicated that the product's quality was superior to that of its direct competitors, the production difficulties were enormous and the company was unable to produce at a reasonable cost. Furthermore, the market did not accept prices higher than those of its rivals. As a result, Johnson & Johnson's entry into this industry was a total flop and after a few years it finally withdrew. The value associated with the company's reputation and brand image was unable to make up for a deficient production capability.

2.2. The role of capabilities

We have defined organizational capabilities as the capacities that an organization's professionals have developed over time in combining resources and designing organizational processes, either individually or collectively. A company like Procter & Gamble, world famous for its extraordinary competence in marketing consumer products, has accumulated a series of capabilities that enable it to design and launch new products with success rates exceeding those of most of its rivals.

The process by which these capabilities are developed—which end up becoming true distinctive competencies and growth drivers—is complex. Basically, their development is related with the way in which knowledge and learning are acquired in organizations, and with the way people learn from their experiences and those of other people. Consequently, these capabilities may become a series of activities that—to put it simply—a company can execute very well. These capabilities include most business functions: development of managers and people in an organization, production, logistics and operational excellence, the capacity for product innovation, marketing, and service provided to customers. These capabilities have normally been developed by people in a tacit way. What turns these capabilities into growth drivers is their special value and uniqueness that other rivals cannot easily imitate. We will illustrate this aspect with two well-known companies, Banco Santander and Canon.

Banco Santander

Banco Santander has been one of the highest growth European banks in the 1990s, as we discussed in Chapter 6 (see Canals 1993b). Behind this spectacular growth one can identify some critical strategic decisions, of which we will highlight three: the launch of the superaccounts (high interest-bearing checking accounts) in 1989, the acquisition of Banesto in 1994, and the bank's internationalization with the acquisition of financial institutions in Europe, the USA, and Latin America. Any of these risky growth decisions could have ended as a complete business failure. One of the reasons why this has not been so is the existence of a series of enormously valuable capabilities that this bank group's management has been able to develop and mobilize.

Of great importance are the work and dedication of a group of highly competent managers and the enormous resources that the bank invests each year in their ongoing education and development. These professionals have accumulated some capabilities that are absolutely crucial in the banking industry, such as the capability to market new commercial and investment banking products. This includes the quick development of new financial products and their massive distribution through a variety of channels, with powerful advertising campaigns supporting the launch.

An example is the superaccounts, a financial product that enabled Santander to become the leader in deposits in the Spanish banking industry. Later on came the supermortgages, investment funds, and consumer loans.

A second capability developed by this bank is its global risk management. By means of a control and monitoring system supported by exceptional information technology, Banco Santander has achieved highly sophisticated risk management, by products, customers, currencies, and geographical areas, at a level held by few banks in the world. Logically, the information provided by this system enables the bank to make quick investment or divestment decisions in certain products or currencies; this is crucially important in the banking of the late twentieth century.

A third capability, related to the previous one, is that of generating and managing information about customers and markets with speed, quality, breadth, and precision. Each of these characteristics is fundamental to a good information system and all of them seem to be present in this bank. It is acknowledged by its competitors that Banco Santander possesses an enormous capability in the development of information systems that enable, swift, responsive decision-making.

The capabilities described have been developed by Banco Santander over many years, and they have become mainstays of its growth strategy, as we discussed in Chapter 6.

Canon

The case of Canon—its capability development process and its impact on growth—is also very illustrative (see Ackenhusen and Ghoshal 1992). In 1998 Canon was one of the world's leading photocopier manufacturers. The growth path followed by this company had been truly spectacular. Canon started manufacturing plain paper copiers in 1962, many years after Xerox, the unquestioned world leader until the 1980s, had established itself in the market with some very advanced products.

Canon did not manage to develop and manufacture an advanced product until 1968, with the so-called NP (new process) system, which offered a real alternative to the classic xerography. However, important though the innovation was, the situation in the industry in the late 1960s was not easy. Xerox had managed to dominate the industry, both in the USA and Europe and—to a lesser extent—in Japan. It had achieved this not only through its technological dominance but also because it made a series of strategic decisions that created high entry barriers for possible rivals. These barriers included a complex system of patents that prevented imitation of Xerox's technology and products; a very extensive and efficient distribution network; a delivery concept based on machine rental rather than sale, which required continuous interaction with the customer; and, finally, the reputation it had acquired.

Canon realized that it could not compete with the same weapons as Xerox and had to choose a different path. It also knew of IBM and Eastman Kodak's attempts to enter the industry during the 1970s, both of which had failed. Consequently, Canon made several important decisions, in particular, the choice of a different market segment from Xerox's. Xerox targeted companies that handled a large volume of photocopies, while Canon opted for machines that could operate satisfactorily with lower volumes.

On the customer side, Canon also progressively developed a network of distributors, agents, and in-house sales personnel with a view to attaining an effective but flexible presence in the most important markets. For its part, Xerox had only exclusive agents. More important than that was the product concept developed by Canon, giving high quality and reliability at an increasingly lower cost. By this means, Canon not only achieved a better value-for-money ratio than Xerox over the years, but it also neutralized one of Xerox's key advantages: its distribution system also provided technical assistance. If the photocopier was reliable, then no extensive technical service network was needed, which effectively eliminated one of Xerox's major advantages, its powerful distribution network.

Canon's story provides confirmation that the dilemma between low cost and differentiation is not absolute but relative. Since the 1970s, Canon has been able to offer increasingly better photocopiers at prices that are not necessarily higher than those of technologically inferior products. The fact is that the dynamics of international rivalry demands continuous improvement in quality and cost. Competing on only one of these variables while neglecting the other could be suicidal.

It could be thought that Canon's success was due solely to the development of a good international expansion. This was a key factor. However, its best decision was to develop a product that was much more reliable and had a higher growth potential than its rival, thereby invalidating some of the advantages acquired by Xerox.

The process by which Canon developed these high-quality machines was also unique. Canon did not take major risks. It rather preferred an incremental but inexorable process of continuous improvement, until it came up with a product that was really going to be preferred by users. This process lasted from the early 1960s to the mid-1970s, and during this period a new Canon photocopier model appeared virtually every year.

Together with this basic product-development capability (which, in this case, would be equivalent to a 'core competence'), Canon showed a series of characteristics or ways of doing things that complemented its capabilities, so that a company that, in the early 1960s, had been tiny was able to become a world leader in a technologically complex industry.

The additional characteristics that define Canon's capabilities are as follows. First, it had a conception of technological innovation that was based not on huge leaps forward—which are always tremendously risky—but on an incremental, adaptive process that consisted of four stages: borrow technology from other companies, learn its operation and dynamics, adapt it to one's own needs, and improve it. Secondly, it had an obsession for quality, so that the product would give its user the best service possible. Thirdly, it maintained a consistent international strategy, seeking the advantages of concentrating activities in certain critical areas, such as R&D and production, and of decentralizing in others, such as marketing and distribution. Finally, as regards marketing activities, Canon developed a reputation for an extraordinary flexibility to adapt to local markets, combining direct sale with exclusive distributors and other non-exclusive agents, instead of sticking to just one distribution formula.

Capabilities and growth: Some reflections

We can draw a few conclusions upon the capabilities of Banco Santander and Canon. First, these capabilities have become major mainstays of the firms' growth strategies. Secondly, none of these capabilities is simple or easily acquired. It is not a question of buying assets available on the market, like a sophisticated computer network. We are talking about the interaction of people who, with certain resources, have been able to develop a set of capabilities that enables them to serve their customers better, creating value for everyone. Thirdly, these capabilities are not sustainable competitive advantages by themselves (see further Dierickx and Cool 1989; Barney 1995; Collis and Montgomery 1995, 1998). Some of these capabilities can be readily imitated; others are more difficult to imitate. However, all of them can be substituted or replaced by other, more efficient ways of doing things that contribute to giving superior value to the customer.

Finally, if capabilities are to be truly valuable, they must be directly related with some of the company's businesses. Thus, it would make no sense for a company that confines itself to buying and selling raw materials to develop or possess an excellent manufacturing capacity. It would be a capability without any value for that company. For this reason, when assessing a company's capabilities, it is important to place them in the context of the activities that the company must perform to offer value to its customers, either now or in the future. Those capabilities that do not contribute to this purpose have no value for the company, nor can contribute to its sustainable growth.

3. WHAT IS THE VALUE OF A COMPANY'S RESOURCES AND CAPABILITIES?

In Section 2, we discussed the nature of a company's capabilities and resources. We observed that their value depends on each company's specific context. Certain resources and capabilities may have a greater value within one firm than in other firms; in other words, a particular organization may make a better use of some resources in certain markets or businesses, or in certain stages of the company's growth process. In particular, the value of resources and capabilities is very closely related with what the company wants to do or actually does, and with its present strategy and growth plans.

It is important not to lose sight of the connection between these resources and capabilities and the company's growth strategy. In the final analysis, they will be valuable for the company if they serve not only to maintain the company's competitive position today but to guarantee value creation and growth in the future. From the point of view of corporate growth, a company must reflect upon the value of its resources and capabilities (see Fig. 7.1). First, what resources and capabilities does it need to develop a particular growth strategy? Secondly, what is the availability of these resources and capabilities within the company? Thirdly, what is the impact of the set of resources and capabilities the company has on the growth decision? Fourthly, what is the action plan to acquire or develop the resources and capabilities that the company needs but still lacks?

The question that follows naturally is more specific: can we consider that certain resources and capabilities are truly valuable for a company's growth strategy? Hamel and Prahalad (1994) argue that core competencies are those that contribute disproportionately to a product or service's final value for a particular customer. Let us try to be more specific in this respect.

Resources and capabilities that are essential for corporate growth have to possess some of the following qualities: they must be unique, valuable for customers, and difficult to imitate (for an alternative viewpoint, see Ghemawat

Fig. 7.1. Growth strategy, resources, and capabilities

1991 and Grant 1995). The more marked these qualities are, the higher their value will be for the company.

A first characteristic of the resources and capabilities that have an impact on the company's value is their uniqueness. It is not sufficient for a company to have a production capability that is competitive *vis-à-vis* other companies. In that case, it will be on a par with others, but that capability will not be a unique source of competitive advantage for the company. This will happen only when it is better, alone or in combination with other capabilities.

A second characteristic is that these resources and capabilities must have a value on the market. An industrial company may have a technology that is far superior to that of other companies. However, if it is not commercially viable, it will be useless. This is what happened with the computing technology developed by IBM and other companies in the 1950s. The commercial non-viability of the products deriving from it neutralized any value that it could have had.

This consideration leads us to another point regarding the value of resources and capabilities. In order to be a source of competitive advantage, resources and capabilities must have a value on the market. However, to be unique and difficult to imitate, they must not be traded on the market. If this were to happen, the value of these resources for the company possessing them would fall dramatically. Those resources and capabilities would cease to be unique and would no longer be a truly distinctive advantage *vis-à-vis* the company's competitors.

It may also happen that the resources and capabilities do have a value but this value does not last as the resources are easy to substitute. If they are to have a distinctive value, resources and capabilities must be difficult to substitute. Technology or manufacturing substitution processes render obsolete those resources and capabilities on which a company's competitive advantage formerly depended. As a general rule, technological progress tends to substitute resources and capabilities that were considered valuable for a reasonably long period of time. Hence, competitive advantages that are sustainable for ever simply do not exist. In fact, companies such as Intel or L'Oréal, who have been leaders in their industries for decades, have achieved this goal because of a continual rediscovery and regeneration of their competitive advantages.

Fifthly, the resources and capabilities should not be easy to imitate. The time taken to substitute products by others may be longer or shorter, but complete or partial imitation of a product or service by its competitors is very fast, and will be increasingly so because of the explosion of the information available and the speed with which it can be disseminated. Obviously, a resource that a competitor can imitate immediately is not a valuable resource for building a sustainable advantage. It is difficult to predict whether a resource or a capability will be easy to imitate or not. However, in certain industries, some resources are available on the market or can be acquired with relative ease. For example in the personal-care industry, many companies can produce quality shampoos similar to those of Johnson & Johnson, using similar production techniques and the same distribution channels. However, the unique resource that Johnson & Johnson has is not just manufacturing but its brand image and the capability to use it in marketing campaigns to support the products that make up its portfolio.

To summarize the previous discussion, we could say that resources and capabilities may become a source of sustainable competitive advantage and a solid platform for corporate growth in so far as they have a lasting value. In turn, the value will depend on their uniqueness and how difficult it is to imitate or substitute them. We could add that it will tend to be greater when that resource or capability is combined with other resources or capabilities, within the same organization, so that the whole is no longer a resource or capability of lasting value but a veritable cluster of resources or capabilities. Fig. 7.2 shows the critical questions we must ask to ascertain the value of resources and capabilities for the growth strategy or for any other strategic decision of a company that is going to use that resource.

4. THE ROLE OF RESOURCES AND CAPABILITIES IN THE COMPANY'S GROWTH: HOW CAN THEY BE USED AND LEVERAGED?

In the previous sections we have stressed the importance of resources and capabilities in evaluating a company's growth strategy. Both the presence and the absence of certain resources or capabilities may be decisive for that strategy's success. Even in the case of absence, a company may undertake projects aimed at acquiring or developing the resources and capabilities it currently lacks and that are needed for a particular growth strategy.

Hamel and Prahalad (1993) have proposed the concept of resource leverage,

- They should be unique
- They must have a value for customers
- They cannot be acquired on the market
- They are difficult to substitute
- They are difficult to imitate

Fig. 7.2. The value of a company's resources and capabilities

both intensively in current projects and extensively in future projects—that is, projects in which the company may not have a strong presence yet. In this context, they refer to strategy as 'stretch and leverage'. This view is useful in thinking about corporate growth. They set the classic concept of 'fit' in strategy (that is, the fit between a strategy's internal resources and the outside opportunities) against the concept of 'stretch'. They define this concept as that situation in which there exists a gap between the resources available to a company and the level of aspiration it has as an organization and to which its managers must contribute.

The 'stretch-and-leverage' approach consists of several distinct steps. The first is to concentrate resources to achieve a goal pursued by the organization. A classic example of the concentration of resources has been developed by Komatsu, as we discussed in Chapter 6. For years, its primary objective was to catch up with Caterpillar, a US company that was world leader in the industry. All of Komatsu's projects were aimed at improving its performance compared with Caterpillar's. The company's objective was very clear: to catch up with the leader.

The second step is to develop new resources and capabilities from within the organization. Resources generated in-house usually come from ideas proposed by employees. Consequently, creating environments that encourage innovation and entrepreneurship, and that do not excessively penalize mistakes, seems to be essential for accumulating new resources.

The third step is to acquire resources and capabilities outside the company that complement or enhance internal resources and capabilities. External resources may be acquired in one of two ways. The first is to recruit professionals from other organizations who bring with them a different outlook. The second is to establish alliances that enable the company to learn other companies' capabilities. Alliances have been, and still are, used not only by companies that wish to catch up with the leader but also by leading companies who are aware that they cannot be in the front line of competitive battles in all industries. The alliances formed by IBM or Motorola in the personal-computer industry, or by Sony and Toshiba in consumer electronics, clearly show the importance of this way of accumulating resources and capabilities.

Finally, a fourth step is to look for complementary properties between resources and capabilities with a view to their subsequent combination. In a previous section we showed that resources and capabilities may increase in value if they are unique and also when they are combined with other resources and capabilities that are also unique. Thus, the capacity of the successive operating systems developed by Microsoft, combined with the computing power of Intel's microprocessors, provided computer manufacturers such as Compaq (which has become the world leader in personal computers) with an enormous advantage over theoretically stronger rivals such as Apple or IBM.

Compaq's competitive advantage is to be found not so much in a particular resource but in the combination of internal resources and capabilities combined with external ones, each of which on their own would have less value for Compaq than the whole.

5. SOME FINAL IDEAS

This chapter started with a reflection on a business success story, Walt Disney, and one of a business project that ended in failure, Saatchi & Saatchi. After reviewing these experiences, we have learnt that both stories contain a factor that is important for corporate growth: the role of resources and capabilities.

An emerging view of corporate strategy stresses the importance of identifying and developing resources and capabilities as core elements of any growth strategy or any other strategic choice that a company faces. Indeed, we have seen that an inadequately corrected imbalance between the resources and capabilities required for a growth strategy and those available may doom a strategy to failure. On the other hand, the existence of limited resources is always a starting point in examining a decision, never a final situation. Resources and capabilities can be developed inside a company or acquired from outside a company—never on an open market as, in this case, those resources would cease to be unique and valuable—by means of alliances with other companies.

Resources and capabilities, therefore, must fit a company's strategy. A growth strategy that relies on unsuitable resources and capabilities is a strategy that is born with a handicap, and as such is likely to be destined for failure. Suitable resources and capabilities are essential for the development of a strategy.

Resources and capabilities must have several characteristics to make a contribution to the firm's growth: they must have a value for the company and that value must be sustainable. Resources become valueless when they are not unique.

Strategic Investment Decisions: Creating New Growth Pathways

1. INTRODUCTION

In Chapter 6 we discussed the effects of a unique business concept on corporate growth. Companies that have experienced sustainable growth in recent years, such as SAP, British Airways, L'Oréal, Glaxo Wellcome, and Nokia, have created business concepts based upon new approaches to serve customers. One of the essential factors shown by these companies to turn a business concept into a reality has been their ability to evaluate and implement certain strategic decisions and, in particular, make certain investment decisions that have defined the pathway for their future growth. Certainly, growth can sometimes be the outcome of a set of small steps. Nevertheless, as the case of the companies analysed shows, there is no doubt that some key strategic decisions have a great impact on corporate growth.

The study of strategic decisions in the firm's evolution and its growth process has a very long history in the field of management (March and Simon 1958; Child 1972; Eisenhardt and Zbaracki 1992). Many of these strategic decisions (expansion of the product scope, entry into new markets, the adoption of a new technology, or the acquisition of a competitor, for example) entail investment decisions. These strategic decisions have been studied from different viewpoints (Hitt and Tyler 1991; Eisenhardt and Zbaracki 1992; Hart 1992). Bower (1970) analyses the resource allocation process among various alternative investment projects. Burgelman (1983) tries to formulate a model that explains the process of launching new business units within existing companies.

The experience of the companies we have studied shows the enormous importance that certain strategic investment decisions have had on their subsequent growth. We are, therefore, dealing with a factor that may be essential in explaining the growth process. The unique importance of investment decisions in business strategy has been analysed in detail by Ghemawat (1991). In a pathbreaking study, he shows that business strategy should focus on the analysis of some irreversible investment decisions ('commitment') that will determine in many ways the firm's future. In the companies we have studied, the role of certain investment decisions on corporate growth is unquestionable. As a consequence, those strategic decisions play a key role in our model.

The development of a unique business concept is fundamental. Brilliant ideas about the future are very useful and necessary. What is more, a brilliant business concept provides the starting point for a company, but not the end point. However, a business concept, more often than not, requires a more or less significant commitment of resources. Strategic decisions are alternatives that, by definition, exclude others. Thus, the investment in the development of a certain product that leaves out other products, or in a certain technology that leaves out other alternative technologies, or in a certain type of production or distribution process that excludes other alternative processes, is a decision that not only entails a major commitment of resources but also defines a certain strategy.

Strategic investment decisions are often related to the development of the company's capabilities. In accordance with the resource-based view of the firm, achieving a certain market position is not only to be attributed to a lower cost structure or a better differentiation. Behind these and other qualities, there are some resources and capabilities that, when adequately combined, enable the company to achieve that competitive position. Consequently, the creation of a business concept implies a definition of what capabilities will be crucial for the company in the future and a programme for developing or acquiring such capabilities (Hamel and Prahalad 1994). In turn, this programme requires a strategic decision, and an investment of resources in a certain direction, which excludes other alternative directions.

The plan in this chapter is as follows. In Section 2 we will discuss three real cases of strategic investment decisions that speeded up growth: an investment in services, an investment in new products, and an investment in new manufacturing capacity. The nature and characteristics of those decisions will be analysed in Section 3. We will present a description of the decision-making process in growth decisions in Section 4. A methodology to evaluate strategic growth decisions is given in Section 5.

2. INVESTMENT DECISIONS, STRATEGY, AND CORPORATE GROWTH

The unique nature of certain strategic investment decisions is that, in one way or another, they commit the company's future and define its growth possibilities. These decisions provide new business opportunities or give new life to existing businesses. These investments tend to be irreversible. Thus, if the project is not successful, the resources invested tend to lose value. Therefore, it would be just as bad to invest in projects without a hope of success as not to invest and let opportunities pass by. Managers must be able to tread the tightrope between the financial risk that a certain investment may not deliver the expected return and the strategic risk that the decision not to invest may weaken the company's competitive position.

In order to understand better the importance of these decisions for a company's growth, we will analyse three cases in this section. The first is an investment decision in services. The second is the development and launch of a revolutionary new product. The third is an investment decision in manufacturing capacity.

2.1. Investment decisions in services: Euro Disney and Port Aventura

The internationalization of theme parks began in 1976, when Disney opened its first park outside the USA. Japan was the country chosen. However, the park that, without doubt, has caused the most stir—and also the most worries—for Disney has been Euro Disney, on the outskirts of Paris, which opened in 1992. Six years after that park opened its doors, the results were still disappointing. However, in 1995, another theme park, Port Aventura, started to operate on a rather more modest level near Tarragona, Spain. The results, three years after it had first opened, had been more successful and contrast sharply with those obtained by Euro Disney, in spite of the value of the Disney brand (see Huete and Segarra 1996).

Any explanation of the two parks' results cannot be confined to stressing the so-called weather factor. The fact that Port Aventura is close to the Mediterranean Sea is a basic factor in its success, but not to explore other arguments would be to give a very superficial view to the situation. Investment decisions have played a singular role in these two cases.

Let us start with Euro Disney. The park opened with thirty-five different rides, several dozen restaurants and shops, a golf course, six hotels with a total of 5,200 rooms, and a residential complex with 400 apartments. The results in the first year of operations were disappointing. The park attracted almost 11 million visitors—a success in terms of customers—but the losses were enormous. The following years showed the same trend, until the park broke even in 1996.

What are the factors that account for these results at Euro Disney? Among others, the conception or vision of the company's future, and the investment decisions that were implemented accordingly, were of paramount importance. In fact, Euro Disney's business concept was an almost exact replica of the model used in the USA: a leisure location where families expect to spend their vacation. Thus, in line with this vision, the park must have hotels and apartments, as well as all manner of shops and entertainment activities for a relatively long stay. However, the reality that Disney's managers had to face was that, in Europe, theme parks do not seem to play this role in their visitors' minds. As experience has subsequently shown, European visitors consider theme parks for shorter stays. Consequently, in Europe, a theme park can be smaller—in terms of hotel facilities—than in the USA. The capital required would then be less and the financial burden to be borne by the company would be substantially lower.

In part, the problem was exacerbated by the fact that the essential factor in the business concept used by the parent company, Disney, was the real-estate development adjoining the park, which included the residential and hotel complex. As a result, the park's capital requirements were much higher than those strictly necessary to develop its entertainment content. Thus, certain investment decisions founded on a particular business concept brought Euro Disney to the verge of failure, which it only partially succeeded in avoiding by renegotiating its debt and bringing new investors into the project.

Port Aventura tells a very different story. This company had the financial backing of its main shareholders, La Caixa and Anheuser Busch; the latter also provided the guiding principles on which the park would be organized. Busch used as its reference its theme park in Williamsburg (Virginia), which had been successful.

Port Aventura's philosophy was to offer families the opportunity to go on an attractive journey for a few hours. Following this approach, Port Aventura started with five thematic areas and thirty-two rides. As an integral part of the service, Port Aventura had forty-five catering points within the park, with a capacity for serving 4,500 meals per hour during four different shifts. However, Port Aventura did not seek to build a hotel complex or turn the park into a long-stay vacation environment but rather targeted it as a very short-stay destination. Obviously, with this approach, Port Aventura's capital requirements were minimized.

Port Aventura was an immediate success, even in the first year, both in visitors and in profits. Indeed, in 1995 the park was visited by a total of 2.7 million people, 200,000 more than the initial target. The park also managed to cover expenses, when, in the initial plan, losses of about 65 million euros had been budgeted for the first year. In 1996 and 1997 the results were even more encouraging.

Nevertheless, at the end of 1998, Port Aventura faced a new problem. Competition from other theme parks in southern Europe was fierce, the number of visitors was flat, and the average spending by visitor was not growing. Its managers realized that the business concept based on one-day visits to the park could not be sustained. They decided that they needed to change that model and offer visitors the possibility of staying overnight in the park. That meant an additional investment in hotels and also in new attractions. The investment strategy had to be changed.

Euro Disney was too ambitious with its investment plans, Port Aventura too modest. Both had to think again about their investment strategy: Euro Disney to cut it down and Port Aventura to expand it. And both stories reflect extraordinarily well the sheer importance of investment decisions for growth. One more lesson can be drawn from those cases. The minimalist option in investment followed by Port Aventura helped it escape from the financial crisis that beset Euro Disney. Nevertheless, Port Aventura's main challenge at the end of 1998 was how to rethink its investment strategy so that it would not miss growth in the future.

Investment decisions play an essential part in accounting for the growth process and in the continued pursuit of a certain strategy throughout a company's life. These decisions also help explain some of the difficulties faced by a company when it attempts to implement an organizational change process. Fixed assets that have been (or may be) the key to a firm's success may become, at some point, formidable obstacles to change, as the Euro Disney case shows.

2.2. Investment decisions in new products: the case of Gillette

To study the investment in new products, we will discuss the case of Sensor, a revolutionary razor developed by Gillette over a period of almost ten years and launched on the US market in January 1990 (see Esty and Ghemawat 1993).[1]

In the early 1980s, Gillette enjoyed a dominant position in the world razor market. In the USA, its market share was in excess of 60 per cent and, worldwide, it was estimated that its market share was similar. However, this share was slowing down. The main reason for this drop was the increased penetration of disposable razors, driven by its main competitor Bic. Disposable razors were a continuous threat to Gillette for several reasons. First, in this segment, it was difficult to develop and sustain product differentiation. As a result, competition between companies ended up focusing on price, which was the decisive variable. Price wars were continuous and Gillette had to counteract them with products of a clearly superior quality without breaking with the existing price standards. There were no major moves in product innovation, given the enormous investment required and the small chances of recouping the investment later because of the price wars and lower profitability.

By the end of the 1970s, Gillette's senior managers, concerned by the course being followed by these events, initiated a project, called Flag, whose purpose was to create and launch in the next few years a truly revolutionary razor, with tilting head and independently mounted blades that could adapt to the face's profile. Even though it was a consumer product, the design and production complexity involved in this project was enormous. Thus, for example, the razor assembly operation involved more than a hundred welds per second by laser, a technique that, until then, had only been used to make high-precision electronic devices. The challenge for Gillette was to manufacture this razor on a high scale. By the time it was launched in 1990, the accrued investment in the

---

[1] The purpose of this section is not to discuss in depth all of the dimensions of new product development, but only their effect on the company's growth. For an excellent analysis of new product development, see Clark and Wheelwright (1993) and Thomas (1993).

Flag project amounted to $75 million in R&D and $100 million in manufacturing equipment. In addition, it was estimated that the cost of the launch plan could amount to a further $100 million, making it the most expensive new product launch ever.

Once the product was developed, Gillette's senior managers had to decide whether it should be disposable or with replaceable cartridges. Both options offered very clear advantages. It seemed that launching the razor with replaceable cartridges could halt the growing trend towards the competitors' disposable products. Also, that segment was the one that offered the highest margin and, therefore, was initially the most attractive. For their part, the advocates of the disposable option defended the idea that disposable razors were the future and that Gillette had to contribute to this future by launching a product whose quality would be unsurpassable. Also, launching the razor with cartridges would mean cannibalizing the Atra Plus razor with tilting head, which had been launched only a few years before and had a strong market position, which was limited only by the slower growth of that segment. If the new razor was to be launched as reloadable, it would undoubtedly have an immediate impact on Atra Plus, and this was used as an argument in favour of marketing the new product as a disposable razor.

At the heart of this dilemma was the need to define the most desirable market position for Gillette in the future. However, the alternative finally chosen could have very clear consequences on the project's final outcome and on the company itself. Finally, in 1989, Gillette decided to launch the new product as a reloadable razor, with the aim of halting the growth of disposable razors, even though this meant cannibalizing part of the sales of Atra Plus.

Sensor, as the new razor was finally called, was successfully launched in January 1990, first in the USA and, a few months later, in Europe. With this launch, Gillette consolidated its leadership in the industry, it accelerated corporate growth to an annual rate of 15–20 per cent on a sustained basis until 1998, and succeeded in halting the advance of the disposable razors.

Many lessons can be drawn from the Sensor case for corporate growth. First, with this project, Gillette revitalized its business. Going beyond a more or less satisfactory level of current performance, Gillette's managers decided to break with the past and make a commitment to innovation and investment as a means for ensuring future growth. Secondly, Gillette's future required investment decisions that not only committed very large sums but also risked cannibalizing some of the company's existing and relatively innovative products. Therefore, the dilemma facing the company was whether it should continue pursuing short-term efficiency by exploiting existing products to the end or whether, on the contrary, the company should break with the past and some of the products that had predominated until then. (Ghemawat and Ricart 1993 and Levinthal and March 1993 provide an interesting formalization of the issues related to static and dynamic organizational efficiency.) It is obvious that, whichever alternative was chosen, it would have an enormous impact on Gillette's subsequent development and, in particular, on its growth possibilities.

Therefore, the launch of Sensor highlights the effects that these investment decisions had not only on Gillette's growth as such but also on the process and direction followed by that growth. This type of investment decision defined a certain technology, a manufacturing capability, and a distribution system—among other possibilities—that would become powerful growth engines and that would guide the company in a certain direction for a long period of time.

2.3. Investment decisions in manufacturing capacity: the Volkswagen Group

As opposed to new product launches, the case of Seat, the Volkswagen group's Spanish subsidiary, shows the impact on growth and performance of investments aimed at improving manufacturing capacity and introducing new production processes.

Seat was a Spanish automobile manufacturer that was acquired by the Volkswagen Group in 1985. In the early 1980s, the company hit serious problems caused by the growing globalization of the automobile industry, increasing competition, inadequate product quality, and a weak financial structure. After several years of licensing agreements with Fiat to manufacture the Italian company's models, the two companies separated in 1980. Seat needed a partner who could bring capital, technology, and products and this was what Volkswagen agreed to do.

In 1986 Seat had a large production plant in Barcelona (see Canals and Dávila 1995). This plant had an annual production capacity of about 500,000 vehicles. However, its productivity was only about sixteen cars per employee per year, almost three times less than the plant that GM Opel had opened near Zaragoza, Spain, a few years earlier.

Initially, Volkswagen decided to modernize Seat's Barcelona plant. However, with the growth in demand for automobiles in western Europe during the late 1980s and the prospects of an emerging market in the central and eastern European countries, Volkswagen's managers decided to build a new production and assembly plant—and the technologically most advanced plant in Europe—in Martorell, near Barcelona. The cost of building the new plant was budgeted at about 1,500 million euros. It would have a production capacity of about 300,000 cars per year and expected productivity would run at about fifty cars per year per employee, one of the highest in Europe.

Volkswagen's strategy with Seat was to transform it into a company manufacturing vehicles targeting the low and middle ranges of the market, with low prices, Latin image, and German technology, which would supply the south European, Latin American, and, when the time came, central and eastern European markets. For Seat, this new plant meant not only an impressive modernization initiative but also an enormous increase in total capacity (almost 60 per cent). The sharp downturn of the European market in the 1990s and the slow takeoff in eastern Europe generated excess capacity and plunged the company into a deep crisis.

To come out of the crisis, it was necessary to consolidate Seat's original capacity in Barcelona—after Volkswagen had invested almost 1,500 million euros in it over the last few years—increase production capacity at the new plant, reduce the company's headcount, launch new models, and integrate Seat almost totally in the Volkswagen group. In 1999, six years after the crisis had broken out, the company's situation had improved dramatically. Seat has the second most modern plant in Europe and its productivity runs at fifty cars per employee per year.

In spite of the vicissitudes that the company had suffered during these years, the risky investment in a new plant was crucial for guaranteeing the company's future. This new plant had improved the firm's productivity and achieved quality levels that are similar or, in some cases, superior to those of the Volkswagen group, with production costs below those of other European manufacturers. These factors, combined with German technology and an innovative automobile design, have enabled Seat to position itself as a viable company with a future within the European automobile industry.

As in the case of Euro Disney, if the previous approach had been continued, Seat would have become unviable both commercially and financially. The new investment in Martorell and the appropriate changes in the relationship between Seat and the parent company enabled this automobile company to be turned around.

The case of Volkswagen and Seat also shows another dimension of strategic investment decisions. The degree to which investments in new products influence the company's future depends on their importance in the company's activities and the degree of specificity of the manufacturing capabilities. In the case of investments in manufacturing, the final impact also depends on a company's uniqueness—that is, the differences between its attributes and those of its competitors' manufacturing facilities.

3. SOME ATTRIBUTES OF STRATEGIC INVESTMENT DECISIONS

As we have just discussed, the choice of basic capabilities and their development through investment decisions are decisive for a company's future and influence a company's capacity for further growth.

The reason why investment decisions are so important is because they may create new growth platforms. They are decisions that influence a company's strategy over a long period of time. As Ghemawat (1991) describes, investment decisions have certain features that help explain the persistence of business strategies and performance levels. Furthermore, Ghemawat points out that strategic investment decisions contribute to a better understanding of the source of differences in performance among companies within the same industry. In other words, the differences in corporate performance within the same industry are due in part to investment decisions in certain resources.

What attributes do these decisions have that generate such an enormous impact? Ghemawat points out a number of reasons for the far-reaching effects of strategic investment decisions on the company's strategy, to which we have added other attributes that we have observed (see Fig. 8.1.).

The first reason is that strategic decisions induce the company to move along a certain path for a certain period of time. Thus, when a retailer like El Corte Inglés in Spain decided to expand its business scope and enter the field of hypermarkets by creating Hipercor, it committed some valuable resources to the new business for a certain period of time. In such cases, it is not possible to divest instantly. Consequently, when a company enters a new business, launches a new product, or invests in a new technology, it is effectively enclosing its future direction and growth for the next few years within a certain framework from which it will be difficult to exit. This difficulty in exiting is not only a result of the financial resources committed. The experience observed in several companies in different countries shows that the decisions to withdraw from an industry, or to abandon a major business project, are enormously costly in both financial and personal terms.

Strategic investment decisions limit the company's further development to a certain path because the investment's specific outcome (a technology, a new product, or a new business) is usually a set of resources with a certain degree of specialization and complementary with other resources. These factors make the investment decision highly irreversible. For the same reason, it is not easy to sell them on the market and recoup the investment. This helps explain why a company persists in a certain strategic direction for a long period of time.

The second reason for the impact of those decisions is that, by choosing one path, the company waives the option to choose alternative paths. In other words, a strategy is not only associated with a requirement of resources depending on the goals to be achieved, but also entails an opportunity cost by not pursuing other goals that could be equally feasible. Toyota's decision to invest in the UK in the 1980s to manufacture and sell cars from there to the entire European market was a decision that committed that company's future

- A path for future development determined
- Alternative paths ignored or rejected
- Lag in the execution of projects and lag between perception of needs and execution
- Organizational inertia

Fig. 8.1. Strategic investment decisions: Some features

growth in Europe. The decision to site its plant in Britain gave Toyota access to a very large market with a well-educated population in a country with good infrastructures. However, the investment in England closed the door—at least for a time—to gaining a greater presence in Germany and other European countries. It is still a fact that a country's domestic market is the main source of customers for many automobile companies that operate in Europe.

Another reason is the lag between the decision, its execution, and the arrival of the expected results. The reason for this lag is complex and is due to the appearance of unexpected factors (such as changes in consumers' preferences) or expected factors that are difficult to quantify, such as the learning process in the use of a new technology. This lag not only prolongs the time taken to achieve the expected results but also prolongs the persistence of the strategy chosen or a certain growth path while waiting for the results.

Another factor that accounts for these decisions' importance on corporate growth is inertia (Rumelt 1995 suggests an interesting typology on the reasons for this phenomenon). This factor describes the difficulty in changing from one way of operating to another, not only because of the financial cost this entails but also because of the subjective cost of having to do things differently from how they have been done until now. Any strategy involves particular production, marketing, or distribution policies, which try to satisfy customers' needs in a certain way. Changing any of these variables requires making changes to the company's strategy, which may be costly, from a subjective viewpoint, for many managers. Consequently, it is not just a question of the financial cost involved. The personal, subjective cost of this change for the decision-makers may also be enormous and may unleash a negative reaction to any change that the company may wish to implement.

4. THE GROWTH DECISION-MAKING PROCESS

Bower (1970) and Burgelman (1983) have documented extensively the decision-making process regarding investment decisions and the corporate resource allocation process. Bower suggests a sequential process consisting of two phases: definition and impetus. Both phases, in turn, are conditioned by a structural context (configured by the company's formal organization and control systems) and a situational context (determined by certain specific circumstances affecting the company). The project definition phase is usually led by a front-line or middle manager, who suggests, defines, and proposes the project. The impetus phase is led by a more senior manager, who gives his or her backing to the project and pushes it up to the company's executive committee.

In some of the firms we have analysed in this study, the decision-making process shares some of the features observed by Bower, but with a number of aspects that are slightly different, including a different sequence. Furthermore, the process does not always start from the lower levels of the company's organization and move upwards towards its top management. The process can be more complex and diverse. Thus, the structure of the corporate growth decision-making process, as can be observed in some companies, consists of six stages: the discovery of opportunities inside or outside the company, the generation or definition of a business idea, the translation of that idea into a certain project, the study and deliberation of that project at the different levels in the organization, the decision taken by the executive committee, and, finally, the implementation of the decision and execution of the project (Fig. 8.2.).[2]

We will discuss the elements in this process in the rest of this section. Nevertheless, we want to highlight a few key points. The first is that in this sequence of stages, as in Bower and Burgelman's models, the internal context plays a key role in the decision-making and the resource-allocation processes among different investment projects, as we have already pointed out in Chapter 4.

A major difference with respect to Bower's model is the importance of the industry's external context in this type of decision. We have observed that the external context provides a reference that is continually present during all stages of the process, both when the idea is generated or emerges—sometimes,

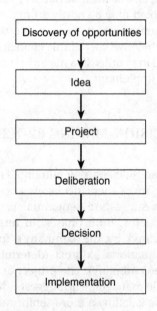

Fig. 8.2. Corporate growth: The decision-making process

---

[2] Some authors (e.g. Garnsey 1998) describe different phases in the growth process. In this section the centre of our attention is the decision-making process, not the firm's evolution through the growth process.

as a result of detecting opportunities within the industry—and in the successive stages of screening information and approving the project. References to competitors, customers, suppliers, substitutes, or evolution of the demand are constant in this process.

Another factor (and a difference with respect to both Bower and Burgelman's models) is the importance of the decision implementation process. In this case, we wish to highlight not only the importance of implementing the strategy as a prerequisite for success, but also the interplay between the external and internal contexts when defining the specific way in which the investment decision will be implemented. We will come back to this point later.

Finally, another aspect of the process that we have observed is that it is not always a bottom-up process (as Bower observed), in which a front-line or middle manager proposes a project to a senior manager. This may be a common case, but it is not the only one. In fact, some organizations combine this possibility with others, under which certain opportunities or ideas are defined or proposed by senior managers and are subsequently explored in detail by other members of the organization. This is the most frequent case in diversification decisions or in mergers or acquisitions. Thus, the direction followed by the project as it progresses through the various stages is not only bottom-up nor only top-down. Both possibilities are feasible and, in fact, even within the same decision, both end up becoming intermingled. In the following pages we will discuss in more detail each of the stages summarized in Fig. 8.2.

4.1. Discovery of opportunities

The first stage of the process we have observed is the identification and discovery of opportunities, both in the external context and inside the company. Normally, before defining a specific project, certain growth opportunities—whether inside or outside the company—have been perceived by its managers.

The opportunities perceived within the company usually arise from a better use of the resources and capabilities currently available: a higher efficiency in manufacturing capacity, a better distribution system, or a new product developed in the company's own laboratories. In all cases, we are talking about opportunities available within the company.[3] On the other hand, the opportunities perceived outside the company have a somewhat different nature. While in the former case, the availability of these resources is a basic given in the decision-making process, in this case the company may or may not have the necessary resources and capabilities to take the opportunities.

BBV's spectacular growth process since 1994 shows the difference between

---

[3] This dimension coincides with what Ghoshal *et al.* (1997) define as entrepreneurial judgement. Kirzner (1973) defines the similar notions of alertness to information and awareness of opportunities.

the two dimensions and how it found opportunities both inside and outside the firm (see Chapters 1 and 3 for a description of this process). Among the specific growth decisions that were made, BBV's management took a more active approach to market new products, using the bank's existing resources, like its distribution network or its brand name. This is a clear case of making better use of resources—only partly used until then—to encourage growth.

A second important decision made by BBV was the rapid market penetration in Latin America, acquiring controlling holdings in those countries' banks. In this case, the decisions were made after a search process of the opportunities that existed in the countries concerned. After studying the situation, senior managers asked for a commitment of the necessary resources to undertake this expansion.

Both inside and outside, opportunity discovery processes are important and decisive, but their impact varies depending on each firm and its industry. In the case of Glaxo Wellcome, for example, a new product launch could initially be motivated by external considerations, such as the existence of a type of disease without a suitable drug for treating it. However, in the process of discovering the active compound for that drug, new possibilities could appear to develop compounds for other treatments that were not initially planned by the research team. These are, therefore, two complementary processes that set the direction for growth decisions.

4.2. The idea

The second stage of the process we have observed is the definition of the idea once the opportunity has been perceived. An idea is nothing more than a preliminary conceptualization of how the company can make use of an opportunity that has been detected. In the case of SAP, the decision to launch S/3 was based on an intuition about a potential customer need—that of integrating different systems—and the exploration of the company's capabilities to find solutions for that need.

This intuition led to a series of reflections that gave rise to the specific idea about how the German company could meet that challenge. Consequently, the idea is not the project. The difference lies not only in the level of preparation but also in the fact that, in the project stage, the possible decision has already gone beyond the stage of defining the business idea that managers may have. However, the idea is still a concept in a primitive state of development, which has been examined by a few people, who are not necessarily the ones who will eventually define the project. Sometimes, it may be a sales representative who perceives the need to improve the product's functionality. In other cases, it may be a functional manager. Finally, in other cases, it may be the CEO.

The importance associated with the generation and configuration of growth and business ideas within the company is based on the conviction that these ideas will evolve into specific projects that will be studied and assessed. These projects' quality will depend, in part, on the variety and richness of the ideas generated. Thus, during BBV's growth process within the 1,000 Days Programme, the suggestions made by different members of the organization were incorporated in the project's design and its implementation plan. Therefore, the configuration of the idea is an essential ingredient of the growth process.

4.3. The project

The third stage is the preparation of the project. On the basis of what we have been able to observe in the companies, the project can be distinguished from the idea on three basic dimensions. The first is the degree of preparation and examination of the different variables comprising the project, which seek to evaluate the desirability of a particular growth option for the organization.

The project's second distinctive variable is that it is usually studied by the people responsible for executing it or by the people who may have a certain responsibility in its execution in the future, if the project is approved. This is not the general rule but, in the cases studied, it is fairly frequent.

The project's third distinctive variable is the involvement (or advisable involvement, if this is not yet the case) of a multifunctional group of people in its preparation. Thus, in the case of Nokia, involvement in the process is not confined to the laboratory scientists or to the sales executives. Instead, both areas are involved, together with financial and manufacturing managers. In fact, it is essential for the project to be studied by a multidisciplinary team not only to ensure a higher quality in the assessment, but also to obtain both the project's final approval and, more importantly, involve the critical personnel responsible for implementing the project right from the early stages of the project's definition.

4.4. Deliberation

The fourth stage that can be observed is that of deliberation. This is an irregular stage, characterized by the fact that the idea, now in the project phase, is moving vertically and horizontally within the organization. It is a stage that faces an enormous amount of uncertainty about the project's final result. However, in the companies studied it is an essential stage to detect possible shortcomings, enrich the idea's main factors, and identify all possible obstacles that may arise from its implementation.

In this stage, the aim is to enrich the project's quality as much as possible and reflect upon any obstacle that might emerge during the implementation. This stage is fruitful so long as the organization and its people are willing to consider projects that are not strictly within their field of responsibility and to share information—in the case of the project's leaders—and new projects with other members of the organization. It is at this stage that it becomes clear that, ultimately, the project's success depends on the degree of trust existing within the organization. In companies such as BBV or SAP, where employees feel encouraged continually to propose challenges, this subprocess is extremely dynamic.

4.5. Decision

The next stage is the decision on the project that must be made by the executive committee. A large number of factors are involved in this final decision. The project's quality, its internal consistency, its fit with the industry's context, the company's resources and capabilities, the internal political process through which the project has reached the company's executive committee, the background of the executive committee's members, the current situation on the capital markets, and the company's current share price are some of the factors that we have seen to play an important role (depending on each case) in the final decision on the strategic choice that the company will follow.

Subjective considerations—which are inherently difficult to quantify—have a greater weight than would be expected in certain decisions. Thus, in some of Telefonica's international expansion decisions, the criterion to be the first mover in a market in the full swing of deregulation seemed to predominate over profitability criteria, at least in the short term.

A similar phenomenon takes place in the mergers and acquisitions we have observed. The acquisition of Wellcome by Glaxo showed that quantitative, financial, or business reasons are not always the most important factors. Indeed, the very process by which financial issues are studied shows that the preferences and perceptions of those responsible for preparing the information have an enormous influence on the project's final outcome. Ultimately, the decision to acquire another company also contains certain subjective components that are based more on a perception about how the operation can work.

In fact, it should come as no surprise that this is so, as in such decisions, in addition to the uncertainty inherent in any commitment of resources, the decision-makers must also face the specific uncertainty of what the company they are acquiring is like; what the nature and quality of its relationships with customers and suppliers is; and, finally, how the people and organizational integration process between the two companies should take place. Given this situation, it is not surprising that qualitative and, sometimes, subjective factors play such an essential role in such decisions.

Nevertheless, apart from the surprise that these observations may cause, it is more important to note that, in the complex decisions regarding the company's growth, decision models based on absolutely rational assumptions, or even on processes having a limited rationality, have very little validity. However, it would be a mistake to go to the other extreme of thinking that decisions in such cases are the outcome of a political negotiation process among the various agents involved.

In most of the decisions we have examined, managers perform a serious and coherent analysis of the decision involved and its potential consequences. What happens is that, even in these cases, managers involved in the process cannot foresee the ultimate consequences of their analyses. However, the effort to present an analysis that has an internal consistency, rich in information and describing a number of different scenarios, is of enormous help in obtaining a prudential synthesis for evaluating the corresponding investment decision. Hence, the importance of being accurate and comprehensive in this task.

4.6. Implementation

The final stage observed in the growth decision process is the execution of the decision and the implementation of the strategy approved. This stage takes place after the company's decision-making committees have given their verdict and it is essential and absolutely critical for the project's success. Correct decisions that have been adequately studied and formulated may become stuck because of a rudimentary execution or implementation. On the other hand, a decision made in a context of enormous uncertainty may be successful if it is implemented appropriately.

In the implementation process, we have observed three features that seem to be essential if the project is to have a positive final impact. The first is the involvement in the decision (in its prior study and in all the different deliberation stages) of all those who, within the organization, are or may be related with the decision to be made and all those who may be involved in its implementation. The intention here is to include aspects of the project's implementation right from the beginning of the decision's deliberation process. This is an important step, which may avoid important errors or omissions in the deliberation phase.

The second feature is the preparation of several contingent scenarios, with their corresponding action plans. There are many factors that may cause a growth project to fail. However, there are some whose potential importance may become enormous. These factors need to be studied in greater depth, establishing different possible scenarios. Having done so, we must then ask the question: if this scenario happens, what should be done? It is vital to evaluate these possible contingencies in advance; the decision's risks can be weighed better and one has time to reflect on the best courses of action if these eventualities should occur.

The third feature is the flexibility of the management team, particularly of those people who are most involved in seeing the project through. In some cases, we have seen that personal or subjective considerations—'we must save this project, because it is crucial for that person'—have predominated over prudent considerations that advised halting the project or refocusing it if significant unexpected events should occur during execution. In this case, the collegiate implementation process, the integration of different viewpoints, and the flexibility of the people involved in implementing the project or its overall design are critical for ensuring adequate implementation.

One final remark about the decision-making process. In this process, other variables of the growth model we have introduced earlier have a considerable influence: the external and internal context or the resources and capabilities. It is obvious that these factors are not just stages or landmarks in the growth process but variables to be taken into account in the final decision. Indeed, in this final stage of the process, the managers' role is to synthesize the available information and formulate a prudent judgement regarding the best option to follow.

To illustrate the structure of this process, Figs. 8.3 and 8.4 show the basic elements of the growth decision-making process that we have just described in two specific cases: BBV's penetration in Latin America and the launch of Zantac, the most successful drug in Glaxo's history. In both cases, we highlight

Process stage	Critical dimensions in BBV
1. Discovery of opportunities	• Market potential • Market deregulation • Possibilities of offering financial services adjusted to the local needs • Deployment of available resources and capabilities
2. Idea	• Stronger presence in the region after deregulation • Quality and innovation leadership in the region in commercial banking
3. Project	• Analysis of the best way of penetrating each market • Possible decisions to acquire local banks
4. Deliberation	• Vertical movement (top-down) throughout the organization • Horizontal movement • Constant support by the Management Committee
5. Decision	• Establishment of investment priorities • Collegiate approach by the Management Committee • Reasonable acquisition prices
6. Implementation	• Integration of the banks acquired • Appointment of a management team • Transfer of commercial and technological know-how • Transfer of new products

Fig. 8.3. The growth decision-making process: BBV's penetration in Latin America.

Process stage	Critical dimensions in Glaxo
1. Discovery of opportunities	• Need for anti-ulcer therapy • Weaknesses of rival therapies • Available resources and capabilities
2. Idea	• Experimentation with new compounds • Sales potential
3. Project	• Development of the specific therapy • New marketing concept for the drug launch • New pricing policy
4. Deliberation	• Vertical movement (top-down) throughout the organization • Horizontal movement • CEO's vision of the industry's future
5. Decision	• Constant support from the CEO • Importance of qualitative criteria, alongside quantitative criteria
6. Implementation	• Highly motivated research and marketing teams • Development of new marketing skills

Fig. 8.4. The growth decision-making process: Glaxo and the launch of Zantac

the essential dimensions of each of the decision's different stages, showing how it was born, evolved, approved, and, finally, implemented. We can see that, in both cases, the perception of the internal and external opportunities and the creation of an idea to exploit these opportunities were essential, although, of course, the concrete form given to these dimensions is specific to each division and each company.

5. THE EVALUATION OF GROWTH DECISIONS

In previous chapters we have presented an explanatory model of corporate growth. In this chapter we have introduced the final building block, the strategic investment decisions—that is, decisions that determine the company's future evolution and its growth. It is sometimes said that such decisions (such as the development of a new product or entry into a new market) provide the explanation for a company's growth, which is true, but only in part. Indeed, such decisions are also determined and influenced by the other factors of the model.

In this section we wish to use this model to present a methodology for assessing growth decisions, based precisely on the model's own rationale. The reasons for proposing a methodology to assess such decisions should be obvious from the study of their importance in previous chapters. In the field of corporate strategy, some authors have suggested criteria for assessing a company's strategy or certain strategic decisions (see e.g. Andrews 1971; Porter 1980; Rumelt 1984; Ghemawat 1991). Of all these, it is Ghemawat (1991) who proposes a strategy assessment model that can be transposed most readily to the evaluation of growth decisions.

In this section we present a model for evaluating growth decisions that is consistent with the corporate growth model that we have developed in the previous chapters and on which it is based. This model consists of six elements: the assessment of the company's internal context, the assessment of the external context, the definition of the business concept, the analysis of resources and capabilities, the financial evaluation of the decision, and scenario design (see Fig. 8.5.). In the rest of Section 5 we present a brief synthesis of these factors, some of which have already been introduced in the course of this book for other purposes.

5.1. The internal context

In Chapter 4 we analysed the importance of a company's internal context for its growth. Among other factors, this context is defined by the following elements: the structure and formal systems, which include the organization design and the control and compensation systems; the company's purpose; the corporate

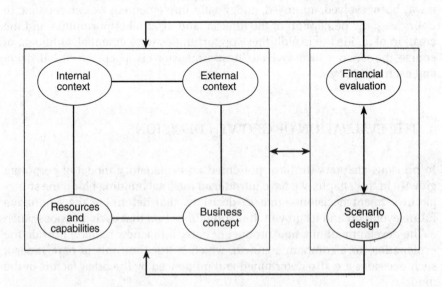

Fig. 8.5. Growth decisions: An evaluation model

culture and values; and the role of the top management team. Finally, there is also the company's recent history, which influences—either by fostering or by blocking them—new growth projects and initiatives that its managers may consider.[4]

When assessing the internal context of growth decisions, it is vital to consider the following issues:

- Is the growth decision consistent with the internal context?
- Does the internal context support the growth decision?
- Are the formal structure and management systems suitable for the new direction that the company will follow?
- Does the company have the right managers and employees to undertake the growth decision?
- To what extent does the growth decision strengthen the corporate purpose?
- To what extent does the growth decision enhance the corporate culture and values?
- What is the role of senior managers in the decision?
- What is the decision's impact on individual and organizational learning?
- What effect will the decision have on the company as a group of people?

Particularly important in this aspect is the role of the senior managers' preferences in the decisions that are assessed. These preferences must be considered both to give them the weight they really have and to prevent the preferences from unconsciously distorting the analysis of the problem and, therefore, its solution. As we have discussed in this chapter, how the project's process is managed is critically important. Sometimes a poorly managed process leads to disastrous decisions.

Within these preferences, there are two issues that may be used to focus the discussion. The first is what a company's top management team wants or intends with its growth decisions. Sometimes, the goal may be fairly personal, such as growing, having a presence in the industry, or imitating what competitors do. Obviously, this type of goal may become incompatible with the company's development. However, as part of the investment decision process, it is a good idea to specify such goals, so that each aspect of the decision is put in its right place.

The second important question in this context is what the company should do with respect to this decision. In this case, 'should do' does not have a technical content—for example, whether or not it should be in this market—but an ethical content. It, therefore, includes a consideration of the company's responsibilities regarding its employees, shareholders, customers, suppliers, and the community in which it operates. In many growth projects, these responsibilities are clear and do not pose many problems. In others, on the contrary, the decision's effects are enormous. Think, for example, of an investment decision that

---

[4] Each of these factors has been described conceptually and their practical importance has been shown with real cases in Chapter 4. We will not repeat the analysis here.

is vital for the company's future, to such an extent that, if it is not implemented, the company will end up closing. Or of a growth decision that may entail a significant staff cut. Unfortunately, in such cases, the decision criteria are not unequivocal: we cannot generalize about what should be done in each case. The only message we would stress is that it is necessary to take these dimensions of the problem into account, because, otherwise, the solution will be incomplete and, therefore, incorrect, even though its effects may not be felt in the short term.

It is also important to consider the effects that growth decisions will have on the company's employees, as these are enormous. We have grouped these effects under two categories. First, there is the learning that employees and managers gain during the project, in the course of exploring new processes or technologies or undertaking new projects. Secondly, there is the personal learning in the decision-making process itself and the motivations of the decision-makers. One indicator of this learning is the level of trust within the company, which may increase or decrease during the implementation of the project.

5.2. The external context

The growth opportunities made available to a company by the external context in general may be decisive in accounting for the growth process, as we discussed in Chapter 5. When studying the external context in assessing growth decisions, one should take into account the conceptual model presented in Chapter 5: the industry's value chain (see also Porter's (1980) model). Consequently, the factors that must be included in the analysis of the external context include the degree and nature of rivalry, the threat of substitution, buyer power, supplier power, the threat of new entry, and finally, the configuration of the industry's value chain, how it is organized, and who controls the chain.

When assessing a growth decision in the light of the external context, the following questions should be considered:

- What is the industry's value chain today?
- What will the value chain be like in a few years' time, after the decision that is currently being assessed?
- What will be the decision's impact on customers?
- How will this decision change the basic value proposition offered by the company to current or prospective customers?
- What is the industry's attractiveness today?
- What possibilities does the industry offer for developing a new product, entering a new market, or increasing production capacity—to mention only a few of the possible growth decisions?
- How will the nature and intensity of rivalry change in the industry?

- How will rival companies react to this decision?
- Will the decision lead to the entry of new companies?
- What will be the new relationship between the company's products and services with other complementary services or products?

It can be inferred from the nature of these questions that the analysis of the external context cannot be confined to a static consideration—how the context influences the company and the possible strategic decision today—but rather how it will affect the company in future years. One must also ask how the investment decision will affect customers and the industry's structure, on the one hand, and the industry's value chain, on the other. Truly innovative strategic investment decisions are those that bring about a dramatic change in the industry's value chain, shifting the leading role from certain agents to others.

5.3. Defining the business concept

By analysing the internal and external contexts and reviewing the resources and capabilities required, it becomes much easier to define and evaluate the business concept upon which corporate growth will be based.

Among other things, the evaluation and definition of the business concept includes the following questions:

- What is the strategic vision that drives growth?
- What may be the future of the industry and the future of the company within the industry in, for example, five years' time?
- How does the company expect to serve the future needs of its customers?
- What is the gap between its current or prospective customers' current and future needs?
- What is the company's current positioning and what should its future positioning be?
- What is the gap between customers' present needs and the value offered by the current products or services?
- What resources and capabilities does the company need to address these needs?
- What is the efficiency gap presently incurred by the company?
- How must the company's business concept change if it is to preserve its leadership in the industry?

These questions should find an answer in the light of the previous considerations on the internal and external contexts and the evaluation of resources and capabilities. However, this is an iterative process, since the definition of the business concept will influence some of the answers given to the earlier questions.

In addition, the reflections on the business concept play a very important role in shaping the decision that the company must make. Questions about the business concept open the door to an explicit consideration of the appropriate decisions and help define their content and specific elements.

One important consideration of the company's business concept is that it must reflect an outlook of the future of the industry and the company and must be focused on the market and the customers. It is a question of reflecting not how managers perceive the company but how the company is perceived by its customers. The idea is, therefore, to view the company from the viewpoint of the market and its customers. The customers' perception encompasses at least three dimensions: the price they must pay, the value they obtain with the product or service they buy, and the cost of using the product or service, including looking for information about the product. These dimensions are directly related in the customer's mind.

Customers also compare these dimensions with other firms' offers. Consequently, a company's positioning always has, by definition, a comparative dimension, that is, a relative position in the market with respect to the position held by other competing companies. It is not just a question of doing things well but of doing things better than the rest, at least on some dimension (price, quality, service, aftersale service, etc.). This comparative dimension with competing companies is fundamental for defining and assessing strategic decisions.

For this reason, positioning is not only a marketing issue. In other words, it is not just a matter of thinking about the products and services offered by the company, although this is an integral and important part of the positioning; it is also essential to consider how the company's cost structure directly affects the choice made by a customer. For a time, an attractive array of products or services may hide an inadequate cost structure. However, this situation is not sustainable and may cause a deterioration of the company's financial position and its ability to grow in the future.

5.4. Resources and capabilities

The importance of resources and capabilities in the company's growth process is enormous. Excess resources may be the driving force for undertaking a growth process. However, in the light of the analysis carried out on this issue in Chapter 7, it is clear that the study should not be restricted to the existence of idle resources and capabilities that could be used for growth. Indeed, when assessing strategic growth decisions, the vital question to ask is whether the company has the necessary resources or capabilities to turn the growth project into a palpable reality, at least as regards what is under the direct control of the company. In other words, it is essential to ask whether the company has the appropriate resources and capabilities to guarantee the growth process. These resources and capabilities include, as we have seen in Chapter 7, financial resources, fixed assets, technology, production and distribution capacity, and information systems, among others—in short, all the resources and capabilities associated with the company's value chain. The importance of each one varies depending on the specific decision being assessed.

When resources and capabilities are not available, or they do not exist in sufficient quantity or quality, it is vital to design a plan that helps the company obtain them, whether through internal growth, from third parties, or form alliances with other companies that already have them.

A particularly necessary capability in growth decisions is management. Growth may require greater attention by managers on certain tasks or projects that, until then, were not on their agenda. If this effort is not offset by a reduction in other previous tasks, the effectiveness and quality of attention to key problems and challenges may decrease substantially and what was intended to be a project to boost the company's growth may end up being a project that drains strength from the company's development.

As a general rule, there is a certain tendency to overestimate the resources and capabilities available and underestimate those that are actually required. In this stage of the assessment of the project, the aim is to ascertain those resources and capabilities that the company needs and those that it actually has, so that it can draw up a plan for developing or acquiring them in order to ensure the project's success. This evaluation should be clearly reflected in the financial evaluation of the growth decision. Thus, for example, in the case of a new production or distribution technology in which the company has no prior experience, it would not be prudent to assume that the company will become immediately efficient in its use. Therefore, when estimating the costs associated with the production process, one should take into account the absence of that basic capability.

5.5. Financial evaluation

The emphasis on financial considerations in the business world is the cause of important omissions. The assessment of strategic decisions has sometimes suffered from this shortcoming, when certain financial criteria imposed subjectively have forced decisions to be studied from a purely financial viewpoint.

Such an analysis is vital for assessing growth decisions. However, it must be carried out within a much broader context, in which the internal and external contexts, the resources and capabilities, and the business concept find an appropriate and necessary place. Indeed, the financial analysis should incorporate the findings obtained from the reflection on all of the above factors and not from others established from outside. Thus, financial analysis should use as its starting point not artificial estimates of prices and costs but a careful analysis of the elements comprising the model presented in this book: the internal context, the external context, resources and capabilities, and the business concept.

Financial analysis seeks to offer a preliminary picture of the financial viability of growth decisions by using criteria such as the investment's net present value, rate of return, or pay-back period. The purpose of this section is not to give a detailed discussion of these criteria, which would be more fitting in a financial text (e.g. Brealey and Myers 1996), but to highlight certain aspects of their use to assess growth decisions.

These classic financial criteria for assessing investment decisions are extremely useful. However, their limitations, from a strictly financial viewpoint, are also well known: the treatment of the risk and uncertainty of the flows associated with the growth decision; the time period to consider; the consistency of the results, depending on whether the investment's net present value or rate of return is used; and, finally, the choice of the discount rate to be used. Some of these problems have been tackled by using the theory of financial options to evaluate investment decisions. We do not intend to discuss these issues here, which would take us away from our main purpose, but simply state the existence of these problems associated with the financial criteria used to assess investment decisions.

Moreover, there are intrinsic problems related to the use of financial criteria in assessing investment decisions related with growth decisions. One of them is the consistency between all the components of an investment decision. A well-designed financial plan must reflect, first of all, the positioning that the company seeks to attain or already has in the market and should adequately combine the various policies required by a certain growth decision. Thus, it is important to ensure consistency between the different policies. Hence it is vital that people from different departments within the company evaluate such questions from an interfunctional, integrative outlook.

If the project is studied only by the financial department, the outcome will have a limited value. Indeed, although this department may be responsible for coordinating the project, all the departments affected by the project must give their opinion on the different policies that will structure the project: sales, purchasing, production, logistics, R&D, distribution, and marketing. In principle, it would not make much sense if the finance department were to suggest hypotheses for the marketing plan, the distribution costs, or the behaviour of the experience curve. For these reasons, it is important to consider the financial analysis not as a series of more or less precise cash flows but as a business project in which the different functions or departments must articulate coordinated and consistent policies if the project is to get off the drawing board. Unfortunately, when these figures are prepared exclusively by the finance department, without working closely with the departments that have to put these plans into practice, the criteria applied may have little practical use.

To summarize, the use of financial criteria for assessing strategic decisions is valid and useful but insufficient and must be complemented with the other criteria that we are considering in this section.

A note on the use of options theory

Some strategic decisions may enable the company to undertake new growth options in the future. However, the assessment of these growth options is not always reflected adequately in the classic financial criteria. To analyse these decisions, financial theory has developed a number of models that can be applied under certain conditions. The problem is that these models, even though they claim to be simple, are still complex.

The application of options theory to the assessment of growth projects is the result of some fundamental observations. First, there are investment projects whose uncertainty about their future is similar to that of the prices of certain financial options. The second observation is that, in those projects, the use of the net-present-value criterion tends to underestimate the results because it does not take into account the options that the project may make available to the company in the future, if the company undertakes it. For example, the value of IBM's investment to enter the personal-computer market, if one used the net-present-value criterion, could have given negative results in quite a few of the scenarios considered. However, if IBM had not entered this business in the early 1980s, today it could be a marginal player in the computer industry.

The technical discussion of the financial valuation of options is fairly complex and we will not go into it here. (For a general review of the main methods used to value options, see Bowman and Hurry 1993, Dixit and Pindyck 1995, Luehrman 1988, and McGrath 1997, who explain how to apply financial options to investment projects.) However, a qualitative explanation of these ideas will help us understand them better. A growth project A—for example, entering the personal-computer business—includes an option when investment A may enable a growth project B in the future—for example, developing new software. The financial valuation of the growth decision must therefore include the current value of investment A, plus the value of the option in investment B, including a weighting factor that adjusts for whether or not investment B is made in accordance with the progress of investment A.

An option's value basically depends on certain factors in addition to the cash flows it generates. First, the wait period until the investment is made. In principle, the longer this period is, the greater will be the possibilities of obtaining more accurate forecasts. Obviously, this value will decrease if a competitor takes the lead and makes the investment before the company. A second factor is the growth decision's risk. Generally speaking, by deferring the investment decision, it is possible to reduce the risk or at least gauge it better. The third factor is the nature of the option: there are options that are unique to the company while other options are shared among competing companies. This is the typical case of a new technology developed by several companies although none of them has started to market it yet to avoid cannibalizing present sales.

To summarize: certain investment decisions can be viewed and analysed as if they were financial options. Modern options theory does not always offer a single, definitive solution to the question of how to evaluate a growth strategy, but it does contribute certain elements that undoubtedly enrich traditional financial analysis.

5.6. Scenario design

The financial evaluation discussed in the previous section has a static dimension. It provides the baseline scenario, the best possible estimate at a given time about the evolution and execution of a growth decision.

However, in order to gain a better understanding of the company's evolution over time, it is vital to reflect on alternative scenarios. Scenarios do not reduce the uncertainty surrounding the firm's evolution. However, they do help reveal certain aspects, problems, or potential conflicts that could otherwise remain undetected. In other words, scenarios help us consider issues that are crucially relevant to the success of growth processes. We therefore think that it may be particularly useful to include them in the assessment of strategic growth decisions.

Scenario construction as a methodology has undergone significant progress in recent years (see e.g. Wack 1985 and Van der Heijden 1996; De Geus 1997 discusses the effects of the development of scenarios on the firm's survival). In this section our purpose will be not so much to discuss the techniques as to consider the reflections that a scenario definition process should include. These reflections will be quantitative and qualitative. The former must then be included in the financial assessment process, defined in the previous stage, with the intention of enriching the scenario construction.

We will group these reflections in three main categories. Each one poses the question: 'What if?'. The first encompasses the external-related factors such as the evolution of the demand and the foreseeable changes in its behaviour, the emergence of new substitutes or new business concepts that make the current concepts obsolete, the evolution in rivals' strategy, imitation processes, the evolution of the industry's installed capacity, and the impact of new technologies. Each of these factors is difficult to predict. However, focusing our attention on them and considering the possible effects they may have on the growth decision may help bring to light certain unexpected dimensions. Furthermore, in many cases, these reflections may give rise to subjective estimates about certain variables (for example, the speed with which a new product will be imitated or the emergence of a new form of distribution) that have an impact and can be included in the corresponding quantitative estimates.

The second category of factors is related to the company's internal factors. One of these is the company's resources and capabilities and its true value in the future of the firm. Another essential aspect is the organization's adaptation to cope with the growth process. Sometimes, a certain type of organization, for example, a divisional one, may be very useful for certain stages of the company's life but less practical in other stages. Thus, an international expansion decision may advise in favour of changing the organization structure. If it is not changed, the decision's effectiveness may be significantly impaired, as the organization will not be optimally positioned to adapt.

A third factor is the ability of people and the organization as a whole to cope with the change inevitably involved in any growth process. This variable is particularly important when the growth decision implies not an increase in the sales of traditional products but entry into new businesses or countries. The contexts will be different and an ability to adapt to new realities is essential.

The construction of scenarios helps visualize possible contingencies—which do not necessarily have to happen in the end—and to think about possible action plans, both to prevent them and to solve them if they actually end up happening.

5.7. The evaluation of growth decisions

The methodology we have presented in these pages to evaluate growth-oriented strategic investment decisions is summarized in Fig. 8.5. As we pointed out at the beginning of this section, this methodology is based on the explanatory model of business growth that we have discussed in previous chapters.

Three closing remarks should be made about its use. This methodology does not pretend in any way to replace critical, creative thought on strategy or corporate growth. In fact, the questions that have been raised in the course of these pages have sought to foster and revitalize this creative process, never to shut the door on it. Therefore, it is a model that remains open to management creativity and the uniqueness of each growth decision. The second remark is related to the first. The methodology described does not guarantee the success of the decisions it is used to assess, nor does it eliminate uncertainty. It only allows us to consider some key factors in an integrative manner, seeking to avoid the exclusion of certain aspects, as so often occurs in real-life decision-making processes. Finally, this model seeks to give greater pre-eminence to prudence, a virtue that managers need in any decision-making process, and never to replace it.

6. SOME FINAL COMMENTS

In this chapter we have discussed an essential factor in explaining corporate growth: the strategic decisions and, in particular, the investment decisions that commit the company's future course to a particular direction for a long period of time.

Reinventing the company's future normally hinges on the need to develop certain capabilities (commercial, technological, operational, etc.) that can enable the future chosen by the company to become a reality. These capabilities require investment in projects such as launching new products, building new production plants that, in one way or another, condition the company's future and growth potential, or entering a new country.

We have discussed some strategic decisions undertaken by Euro Disney, Port Aventura, Gillette, Volkswagen, BBV, Glaxo, and Telefonica. We can deduce from this analysis that these investment decisions drive and enable growth, tend to be irreversible, enable managers to learn and assimilate certain capabilities, account for the persistence of the strategy and business performance over the years, bar the company's access to other alternative options, and prevent any change in the strategy for a relatively long period.

Finally, we have presented—with reference to the cases of BBV and Glaxo, among others—a model for the company's growth decision-making process consisting of six stages. It provides an explanation for the particular way some firms explore these decisions. The cases studied enable us to define a number of attributes in this type of strategic decision-making process.

Therefore, it is reasonable to conclude that a critical factor in managing corporate growth is the rigour with which the company chooses and appraises certain strategic decisions—particularly, investment decisions—that may have a decisive impact on its future and performance.

The Limits to Corporate Growth

1. THE CONCEPT OF STRATEGIC HARMONY

In previous chapters we have presented a model that tries to offer a comprehensive view of corporate growth. It has the following building blocks: the internal context, the external context, the business concept, resources and capabilities, and strategic investment decisions.

In this chapter we want to explore the limits and constraints to corporate growth, or, in other words, what factors may halt a company's growth process. Penrose states that 'in order to find a limit to growth, or a restriction on the rate of growth, the productive opportunity of a firm must be shown to be limited in any period. It is clear that this opportunity will be restricted to the extent to which a firm does not see opportunities for expansion, is unwilling to act upon them or is unable to respond to them' (1959: p. 31–2). We want to understand better why firms seem to be unable to discover new opportunities or why they are not able to tackle them. For this purpose, we will introduce the concept of strategic harmony, which we define as the concordance of all of the firm's activities with each other and with the firm's strategy, organization, and external context. This notion is essential to understand the limits to corporate growth.

The traditional strategy approach has stressed that the company's evolution over time depends on the fit or consistency between the firm's strategy, its organization, and the industry (Andrews 1971; Porter 1980). Indeed, many successful companies such as Ikea or Nokia show a good fit among these factors. There is also another dimension to the notion of fit that stems from the business concept that we defined in Chapter 6: the coherence and interrelation among the various activities carried out by the company. (Milgrom and Roberts 1995 offer a more formal discussion of this notion and introduce the parallel concept of complementarities.) This combination of activities may enable a firm to attain a unique positioning in the market (Porter 1996), different from its competitors and, consequently, may put it on the track of sustained growth.

The concept of strategic harmony encompasses the traditional fit or consistency notion and the consistency among the firm's activities. It encapsulates a paradox. The greater the internal strategic harmony among a certain set of the company's activities, the stronger its short and medium-term competitive advantage can be. However, if the company is unable to consider other options and change when necessary, strategic harmony may become a formidable obstacle to change when a competitor appears with a new business concept. Consequently, a company's strategic harmony cannot obviate the need to change and adapt to guarantee its long-term survival. On the other hand, without strategic harmony in the short term, long-term survival would be more difficult.

The concept of strategic harmony is essential in a discussion of the limits to corporate growth. Sometimes, the lack of growth is attributed to a slackening demand or an intense rivalry. Those factors are important, indeed. Nevertheless, these and other factors fall into the broader concept of strategic harmony—or lack of strategic harmony, in the case of low growth—in the three dimensions presented: strategic harmony between a firm's strategy and its context, between a firm's strategy and organization, and between the firm's activities and its strategy. When strategic harmony among these factors fades away, corporate growth is seriously threatened.

In this chapter we want to explore the reasons behind the lack of strategic harmony—or the disharmony—among these factors and link them up with the limits to corporate growth. But before starting that analysis, in the next section we want to present a case of disharmony, to shed light upon its nature and effects on corporate growth.

2. THE NOTION OF STRATEGIC HARMONY IN PRACTICE

In Chapter 6 we introduced the notion of the business concept. The business concept is founded on the vision that managers are able to develop about their customers, suppliers, and rivals, and the unique positioning of the firm in the industry. According to that view, managers decide about the configuration of the company's different activities, its value chain, and the strategic choices associated with it.

This concept of strategic harmony highlights the importance of harmony among these factors, reinforces the business concept, and pinpoints the fact that the company as a whole is more important than each of its individual parts, no matter how decisive they are. In fact, for some companies, their main source of competitive advantage is not so much a certain product or low production costs, but a combination of activities that facilitates the continuous development and marketing of new products (as Nokia or Intel do), or the combination of some factors that enable a company to have lower total costs than its competitors, such as Compaq in the personal-computer industry.

In order to explore this concept more deeply, we will discuss the business concept of Wal-Mart, one of the fastest-growing companies in the USA since

1980, and will examine the strategic harmony between its activities, its business strategy, and its external context. This discount retailer was founded in Arkansas by Sam Walton in 1969, since when the company's market value has grown continuously. By the end of 1997 it ran about 1,500 stores in the USA, Latin America, and Asia (see Ghemawat 1987; also Ghemawat 1986 on the sustainability of performance). This company's spectacular growth must be contrasted with the experience of some of its competitors in the USA, with many years of experience in retailing and with such familiar brand names for consumers as Sears or Kmart. Thus, while these and other companies have failed or experienced a mediocre growth, Wal-Mart has grown strongly year after year.

What has been the basis for Wal-Mart's growth? It is easier to understand a company's success factors with hindsight than to predict them; even so, the task is dauntingly complex, as many factors are involved and, although they can be identified, it is difficult to estimate each one's exact contribution to the company's evolution. Some factors that may have been critical for a number of years subsequently lose importance and their place is taken by a new combination of factors. At the risk of overlooking some of them, we can identify some of Wal-Mart's main distinctive factors. They are combined in a coherent way and have helped its growth. The relationships among those factors can be observed in Fig. 9.1.

The first factor is its corporate philosophy. Wal-Mart has synthesized this philosophy in two famous mottos. For its employees, 'We care about people'; for its customers, 'We sell for less'—two concise but incisive sentences that have guided Wal-Mart's actions. Of course, any manager could argue that a company cannot be run merely on a lofty, inspiring declaration of principles, and this is true for Wal-Mart as well. However, principles and a corporate

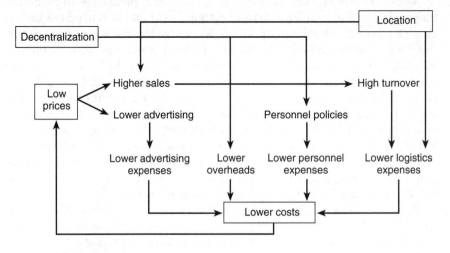

Fig. 9.1. Wal-Mart's strategy

mission perform a similar function for the company as the soul does for the body: they are a driving force that inspire, give life, and are constantly there to guide its actions. Hence the importance of a simple, clear philosophy that is consistently followed by the company.

The following link, which connects these principles to Wal-Mart's business strategy, also has two sides to it: employees and customers. For its employees, the company has recruitment, compensation, and training policies. Wal-Mart is a company that has adopted an innovative approach to the management of people. Some of the actions that characterize it are the profit-sharing scheme linked to the improvement of each store's management, a participative culture that encourages its employees to implement continuous improvements, and a high level of decentralization in decisions concerning the product categories to be kept or replaced, inventory management, or purchasing.

For its customers, the essence of Wal-Mart's strategy has consisted of two principles. First, there is the 'We sell for less' policy. Wal-Mart consistently offers products with the lowest prices available in a particular geographical area. The second has consisted of a wide product mix, much more varied than that of any other discount retailer in the USA. Against an average of about 30,000 items stocked by the discount stores, a typical Wal-Mart store may hold more than twice as much.

So far, we have defined a corporate philosophy and certain specific policies that seem to have contributed to Wal-Mart's success. However, do these policies translate into a higher profitability? And, if so, can they be readily imitated by other companies operating in the industry? A low price policy can only be sustained by two means: first, an extraordinarily high operational efficiency that helps operate with low costs; secondly, high volume so that lower margins are offset by a higher turnover. Both mechanisms are critical in the case of Wal-Mart.

Wal-Mart's efficient cost structure rests on several pillars. We will mention three. First, an extraordinary logistics system based on holding inventories in large warehouses, and not in the stores. Stores are for selling, not for inventories. This improves space management, where it is most expensive. A communication system between stores, warehouses, and suppliers enables the company's inventories to be kept to a minimum, while also facilitating identification of the best-selling products. Secondly, Wal-Mart stores are located in areas where the land and rentals are cheaper than in the main urban conglomerations on the USA's east or west coast. Wal-Mart's main shopping centres are located in the Midwest. Thirdly, Wal-Mart's marketing costs are lower than those of its rivals. The reason for this is also very simple. The 'We sell for less' policy saves running advertising campaigns or special promotions, items that usually rank fairly high in the budgets of other retailers.

These and other tightly coordinated policies implemented by Wal-Mart enable it to benefit from a lower cost structure than the industry average. Furthermore, Wal-Mart's low prices and wider product range mean that the flow of shoppers to its stores is greater than in other companies. The combination of marketing policies within a very well-thought-out business strategy generates an enormous flow of public. In addition, Wal-Mart's initial location in small and medium-sized towns has translated, in practice, into the consolidation of local quasi-monopolies, as some of these towns' populations are so small that there is not space for another discount retailer.

We have discussed the case of Wal-Mart and the business concept its founder, Sam Walton, had and how it was converted into a tremendously efficient firm. The elements of this business concept show a strong internal coherence. It is interesting to compare Wal-Mart's concept with the business concept held until a few years ago by the country's largest discount chain, Kmart. In 1996 this company was approximately twice as large as Wal-Mart. However, Kmart's and its market value was only about half that of Wal-Mart. Whatever reference parameter was chosen, the comparison invariably tipped the balance in favour of Wal-Mart.

These results are the outcome of two different approaches to the discount business, which are summarized in Fig. 9.2. This shows that Wal-Mart's business concept is very different from Kmart's. Indeed, Wal-Mart's vigorous growth can be accounted for only if one starts from the idea that its business concept, its way of doing things, has not consisted of imitating Kmart but of offering something completely different. By devising a business concept that has attracted its customers' attention and won the unswerving support of its staff, it has succeeded in overtaking the industry's historic leader. Furthermore, the business concept itself helps us understand why Kmart has taken so long to react to Wal-Mart. Kmart's different policies, which are shown in Fig. 9.2., were in concord and worked as a closely, coordinated system, also consistent with the external context. When this system was made obsolete by Wal-Mart's strategy, the change was difficult: for Kmart, it was not just a matter of changing a part of the system but of changing the entire system.

Wal-Mart's business concept and its strategic harmony have persisted for many years. With the appearance of new, specialized competitors (the so-called category killers) or the restructuring and relaunching of traditional companies such as Sears, the question now is whether Wal-Mart will be able to

Factor	Wal-Mart	Kmart
Location	Small towns	Large cities
Pricing policy	Always low prices	Regular promotions
Real estate	Cheap	Expensive
Logistics	Decentralization	Centralization
Purchasing	Decentralization	Centralization
Advertising	Irrelevant	Critical
Stores	Space control	Rental

Fig. 9.2. Business concepts in the US discount industry

continue repeating the recent years' growth rates. A key factor in its ability to keep growing will depend on how well Wal-Mart can adapt its business concept and strategic harmony and create new business concepts. Otherwise, its concept, that was essential to its past success, may hamper its future evolution.

3. STRATEGIC HARMONY AND THE LIMITS TO CORPORATE GROWTH

The notion of strategic harmony is essential for explaining a firm's sustainable growth, even more than the availability of resources or the external opportunities. On the other hand, the absence of strategic harmony may lead to the company's stagnation or decline. (Burgelman and Grove 1996 offer a very interesting and complementary view, by introducing the concept of strategic dissonance.)

The factors that may lead to growth stagnation or decline can be grouped, in turn, under two main categories. On the one hand, there are the company's internal factors, in particular the disharmony among themselves or with the firm's strategy or the external context. Under this category, we would highlight internal resistance to change and the lack of adaptation of people, organizational structures, and policies to the new realities of the industry in which the company competes. It is common to see organizational decline for internal reasons. An organization form like the functional structure may be appropriate when the company has not yet reached a large scale and competes with a few products on more or less similar markets. Nevertheless, the functional structure is not very appropriate when the company has different products, competes on different markets, and is highly internationalized.

External factors and the disharmony between them and the firm's strategy and activities are the second reason that may hamper corporate growth and impede the company's adaptation to the new realities of its current or prospective customers. We include under this category both product imitation by competitors and substitution of products by new ones, which may emerge from within the industry in question or from outside.

IBM had serious doubts in the early 1980s about launching its PC (see Mills and Friesen 1996 for an interesting discussion of IBM's evolution and crisis in the late 1980s). If it had not invested in this emerging market, today IBM would probably be a marginal player in the industry. Its rapid reaction enabled it successfully to counteract the first major attack. However, a decade later, IBM was losing world market share in this industry to Compaq and other firms, which operated with lower costs. Compaq realized that the growth of personal computers would explode on the corporate and consumer markets if two conditions were met: first, the computer should be user-friendly; secondly, prices should be lower. The first condition seemed to be fairly guaranteed in the early 1990s. The second was still not certain in 1992. That year, Compaq undertook two decisive actions. First, it made a drastic price cut on several PC models, which would enable it to overtake IBM in market share later on. Secondly, it made a strategic investment in a new production plant, with markedly lower production costs, so that the price cut would be backed up by lower costs and higher operational efficiency.

In the next sections we will discuss three major obstacles that limit corporate growth that go beyond the lack of opportunities: the disharmony between the firm's strategy and its external context, between the firm's strategy and the resources and capabilities needed, and between the firm's strategy and its implementation. The first is related to the category of external factors. The other two have to do with internal factors that limit corporate growth.

4. THE DISHARMONY BETWEEN THE FIRM'S STRATEGY AND ITS EXTERNAL CONTEXT

According to the notion of strategic harmony defined above, a tightly integrated and successful business concept makes it more difficult for other companies to imitate it or replace it with a new business concept.

Looked at from this viewpoint, it is obvious that a business concept like Wal-Mart's, that shows strategic harmony along the dimensions discussed, is more sustainable. In this sense, one can say that the business system as a whole is more valuable than each of the activities considered individually. And the more integrated the system is, the more difficult it will be to replicate it. The main risk associated with a very coherent set of activities is that managers may be unable to foresee (and act in accordance with) the next change that takes place in the industry. Past successes may prevent them from seeing coming changes and reinvent the business concept. When an organization is unable to anticipate, lead, or respond to changes in its industry, a rift appears between the firm, its context and the changes that are taking place in the industry.

IBM is an example of this disharmony. During the 1980s IBM tried to convince its customers that the future of information technology was in large mainframes, not in the personal computer. Even though the company invested in its PC division, it was not considered to be the company's division of the future. This attitude influenced the way the company approached the promotion of certain products, the development of new models, or the solutions offered for networks of small, integrated computers. An outlook on the future that is fundamentally different from the industry's reality or from customers' needs is, at the very least, a very risky outlook. It is true that companies that do not innovate and that confine themselves to following their customers' dictates will never be acknowledged leaders of their respective industries. However, to consider a view about the future that has no basis in reality has a very high chance of failing. By the end of the 1980s, faced with the unrelenting growth of the PC market, it was obvious that IBM's resistance to the PC revolution was no longer tenable. A significant part of the restructuring undertaken by the company since 1993 has consisted of rehabilitating and strengthening the role of the personal computer.

The disharmony between strategy and external context may have different causes depending on the industry and the company. However, there are some factors that contribute to this disharmony and that we will discuss in the next section.

4.1. The erosion of capabilities

The first case of disharmony we would like to examine is the loss of value of the company's capabilities. As a general rule, a company's capabilities do not disappear physically, unless they are associated with people or assets whose services can be sold on the market. Nevertheless, capabilities may lose value for the company and its customers, for a variety of reasons.

First, capabilities may lose value as a result of the substitution of the current products by new products with superior attributes. The appearance of personal computers has meant that mainframes have lost value for some companies. This is why the demand for large mainframes has not grown at the same rate. Mainframes have been partially substituted by PCs. The advent of new products not only makes the old products obsolete but it also has the same effect on the capabilities of the companies that offer them. Therefore, the substitution effect of certain products by others rapidly cuts into the bottom line of established companies.

Secondly, imitation may take place when other companies with similar capabilities compete on the same basis, causing the company to lose part of its special appeal for customers. Thus, when Apple introduced its first personal computer based on a superior software, its distinctive features were very clear for many users. However, when IBM and other compatible models started to manufacture computers with Microsoft software that offered some of the advantages of Apple's Macintosh, Apple started to have problems.

The third reason for the loss of value of a company's capabilities is a change in demand. This factor may seem a special case of substitution. The differential factor is that in the previous case we referred to substitution as a process in which new products come into play. This third case is slightly different. Customers may expect other capabilities from the company (for example, a more efficient service), but the company is unable to listen to the customers' new needs or adjust quickly to serve them.

These cases share an attribute in common—namely, that certain key factors cease to be valuable and give rise to disharmony between the firm and its external context. This may happen when the industry changes, because of the entry of new competitors that imitate existing products, a radical change in the patterns of demand, or, finally, the advent of substitutes that oust the old products and make obsolete the distinctive capabilities associated with them. Ghemawat (1991) offers the conceptual foundations for the distinction between substitution and imitation effects. We will discuss these concepts below, together with the third factor.

Substitution

Substitution is a process by which prospective customers are attracted towards a new product or service concept that is different from those traditionally offered in the industry. This process is the outcome of innovation and techno- logical change: a product starts to decline and eventually disappears because another emerges with better functionality and a lower cost for the customer. Substitution does not increase the product's supply, as may be the case of imitation. Substitution uses a different mechanism: it acts on the demand side, shifting it from the products or services currently offered to others that have a higher value for customers.

One of the innovators' most valuable advantages is their ability to detect customer's possible needs and offer them a new product or service concept that solves those needs better. In the US retail industry Sears offered consumers the integral department store concept, where they could find virtu- ally all the products needed. Later, discount retailers such as Kmart introduced the concept of low prices for a certain type of product, with a smaller range than that offered by Sears. The result was a new concept of customer service. More recently, Wal-Mart has reinvented the concept of discount stores, offering consumers the possibility of improving the value offered until then by com- panies such as Kmart.

Consequently, one of the innovators' unique talents is the ability not only to develop new products or services, but to understand the prospective customers' future needs, breaking with an existing model of product (some- times, including the cannibalization of its own products) or service, and offer- ing an alternative model with greater value for the customer. This innovation process constitutes one of the key features of substitution.

Imitation

Imitation is related to the replication of a scarce resource or product by a competitor (Ghemawat 1991). The rhythm of the imitation process depends on the effectiveness of the mechanisms—such as the interrelation among activi- ties—that prevent a firm from imitating what others do. Product imitation has one immediate effect: its supply increases and, consequently, it loses value on the market. Thus, although imitation may be necessary for a company that has been left behind in the rivalry dynamics, it may also give rise to effects that are not always positive, as it invariably implies competing head-on with the incumbent. Direct confrontations, such as price wars or launching similar products, are not always beneficial.

As a general rule, the imitation process can take one of several paths: pricing, product development, advertising, investment in similar production plants or distribution networks, or an increase in production capacity. The imitation process is simpler in the case of pricing, product promotion, and advertising in industries such as consumer goods, airlines, and telecommunications. On the other hand, in capital goods, high-tech, or automobiles, imitation usually requires investment in production plants, R&D, or available production capacity and, consequently, is slower and more complex.

Changes in demand and consumers' patterns

A special case of substitution that can bring a company's growth to an end is the change in demand caused not by the substitution of a product or service by another superior product, but simply by a change in the demand as a result of changes in tastes or preferences, a change in the prices of substitutes or complementary products, or a variation in families' available income. Changes in demand are unrelated with the industry the company is in and are not always associated with the rivalry dynamics, as is the case with imitation or substitution. Nevertheless, this mechanism is very close to the effects of substitution.

A good example of this is the crisis experienced by US automobile manufacturers in the 1970s as a result of higher prices for a complementary product, oil. This increase brought about a drop in automobile sales. The preference of customers for large models had blocked the development of smaller cars with lower fuel consumption. This limitation in the product range enabled Japanese and European manufacturers to start making serious inroads into the US market.

Sometimes, the starting point of the US automobile manufacturers' problems is pinpointed to the 1980s, with the appreciation of the dollar and the strong penetration of Japanese manufacturers in the US market. However, the problem's roots go back further, although the context of the 1980s helped precipitate the crisis of the industry's three largest manufacturers. At the origin of this crisis was the increase in the oil price. We do not know whether the industry's history would have been written differently if there had been no oil shock in the 1970s. However, there is no denying that the shock had a significant influence on the subsequent unfolding of events.

As a result, changes in demand can bring corporate growth to a halt, unless firms develop new products or services according to the new patterns of consumer behaviour.

4.2. Anchored in the past: The wrong type of innovation

The design of policies that are anchored in the past is another factor that heightens the disharmony between strategy and the firm's external context and may stop corporate growth. It can be explained by various reasons. The first is sheer conformism: managers do not look for new business opportunities. The

European banking industry in the 1980s is a paradigmatic example. In several European countries like Spain, banks did not compete in price or in product differentiation but simply in geographical presence. In practice, this led to a situation of high prices for the consumer, lack of product variety, and limited growth.

The banks that broke away from this situation of zero growth in revenues and profits were Banco Bilbao, with its merger with Banco Vizcaya in 1988, and Banco Santander, with the launch of the superaccounts in 1989. These two options put an end to a situation of stagnation. Other banks such as Banesto, Central, or Hispanoamericano were not in a position to answer the challenge to them at that time. In fact, a view about the future that was essentially obsolete prevented them from responding satisfactorily to the new challenges made by BBV or Banco Santander. Since then, those banks have had to make enormous efforts to reverse their decline. Part of their problem was their assumption that the world was going to be basically the same as in the recent past. Their outlook had not changed and this immobility prevented them from looking for new opportunities for the future.

A second reason is a focus on products instead of customers. There are innovative companies, with very innovative views about the future, that ignore customers' actual or future needs. A particularly significant case in this context is that of certain multinational companies that insist on launching pan-European brands (particularly in consumer products) for markets that are basically different. History is fraught with failures in this context and even highly successful companies have been caught unprepared. The observation of these phenomena leads us to suggest the following hypothesis: when a product is associated with deeply rooted traditions—such as cleaning products or coffee—any change in the end consumer's habits has a very high cost.

On the contrary, in those products where demand patterns are less strong or less deeply rooted, or when the new product's advantages are very clear, the possibilities for globalization are greater. In such categories, we could place products such as cars—which are becoming increasingly standardized, at least in Europe—consumer electronics, or certain types of fashion goods, where tastes tend to be shared beyond geographical boundaries. The failures related with launches of pan-European brands share a common reality—companies' obsession in putting products above customers. Again, we are faced with a crucial dilemma here: the need, on the one hand, to preserve current advantages and, on the other hand, to break away and innovate. In the case of globalization, many companies have wished to be innovative and ground-breaking but perhaps they have not succeeded in convincing their customers of the advantages they offer.

The third reason is the inability to see beyond current customers. Christensen and Bower (1996) show that the truly innovative companies, those that have led each cycle of technological change, have not been the leaders in the previous cycle. They propose an explanation for this phenomenon. Companies that are leaders in a certain stage of the industry's evolution seek to satisfy the current needs of current customers. Very often, these customers do not consider a radical product change because they are satisfied with the product they already have or they perceive that this change would involve some additional costs that they are not prepared to accept. Furthermore, the large volumes required by revolutionary new products cannot be attained with smaller or less important customers. Consequently, a leader's current customers usually tie the company to a certain product line, where changes are incremental, not revolutionary. On the other hand, smaller, innovative companies or new entrants have only one option if they are to penetrate and win a presence on the market: break with the current model existing in the industry and offer a different product or service. This explains why, in some industries, the leaders of each new technological cycle have been new companies that did not exist in the previous cycle. Growth is led by these new entrants, not by incumbents.

4.3. The tyranny of past leadership

A third factor that gives rise to the disharmony between the firm's strategy and its industry is the tyranny of past leadership. Market leaders are afflicted with that disease. This tyranny may appear under different guises. One is that leadership prevents firms from considering other scenarios. Caterpillar's declining leadership in the world earth-moving equipment industry is an example. Until the mid-1980s, this US company had enjoyed virtually absolute control of both the US market—the largest regional market—and the world market, as we discussed in Chapter 6. However, the emergence of Komatsu was an enormous challenge for Caterpillar because it questioned some of the fundamental elements of its business concept. Indeed, Komatsu had succeeded in manufacturing smaller, simpler, and cheaper earth-moving equipment than Caterpillar. However, Komatsu had also devised an alternative to one of Caterpillar's major strengths: the exclusive dealers network, which enabled the US company to control certain national markets and, also, offer a high-quality maintenance service. However, by focusing on simpler machines, Komatsu eliminated the need for maintenance of vehicles. Furthermore, instead of selling machines to construction companies in industrial countries—a relatively mature market—Komatsu decided to sell directly to governments in fast-growth countries, which were the leading civil-works contractors. Obviously, governments did not demand a dealers network but simply a good product, a good price, and a good service. This story has many lessons to offer. However, one of them is that its market leadership prevented Caterpillar from offering new products earlier, because they could have disrupted its traditional business concept, or exploring new distribution alternatives and thus reaching new customers or new markets, as this action could have destroyed one of the company's strengths, its network of exclusive distributors.

A second dimension of the tyranny of market leadership is the fear of internal cannibalization—that is, the substitution of certain products by better ones. This problem is an alternative form of the previously mentioned dilemma between preservation and renewal. Cannibalization is an extreme version of this problem. If the current products work well, sell well, and are appreciated by their customers, why change them? The answer is not easy, but the history of the rivalry between Caterpillar and Komatsu seems to point to one thing at least: if the innovation effort is made by a competitor and it succeeds, customers may change their perception of the products and the company may go from being a leader to being a follower. Thus, cannibalization may sometimes be indispensable. Companies such as Hewlett-Packard, Nokia, and Intel break time and time again with the current product range and regularly launch new products. Thus, for example, Hewlett-Packard seeks to obtain 80 per cent of its revenues from products whose average lifetime is less than five years. Such cases clearly indicate the importance of considering product cannibalization and breaking away from past leadership to sustain corporate growth.

5. THE DISHARMONY BETWEEN THE FIRM'S STRATEGY AND ITS RESOURCES AND CAPABILITIES

The disharmony between the firm's strategy and the appropriate resources and capabilities to develop the firm's activities may also prevent corporate growth. We are referring not just to financial resources, but to all the resources and capabilities that are needed (commercial, production, technology, etc.) to implement the company's strategy. Those resources and capabilities constitute the basic platform upon which the firm carries out its different activities, and allow it to seek some tight interrelations among them. The case of Wal-Mart discussed earlier in this chapter provides a good reference to an understanding of the importance of these relationships among activities. Now, we want to refer to the lack of strategic harmony from a deeper perspective: the disharmony between the firm's current stock of resources and capabilities and its overall strategy.

The case of the medical electronics unit of EMI, the British firm that developed the first scanner for medical diagnosis, is a clear example of this situation. EMI made several decisions with respect to the launch of this revolutionary product in 1972 that had an effect on its ability to expand in the future. The first was to outsource production of certain essential components of the scanner to specialized workshops that would manufacture to order. EMI would complete assembly in its own plant. The second was to launch the scanner in the USA and, at the same time, to build a maintenance service and sales base in that country from scratch. In short, in 1972 EMI did not have the necessary production capacity nor any presence in the USA.

The scanner's launch in 1972 was a resounding commercial success. However, the initial success was like a kind of narcotic that made the company's managers forget that they did not have the required production and marketing resources and capabilities to implement the strategy. This problem was compounded by the fact that not only did they not have them at the time of launch but neither did they succeed in developing them during the first years after the launch.

As the company and the market grew, it became increasingly evident that it was vital to have an effective control over manufacturing and to improve coordination between manufacturing and sales, on the one hand, and R&D and sales, on the other hand. The geographical distance between the manufacturing and R&D centres in Britain and sales and service units in the USA only served to worsen the problem. In the late 1970s the company went into a state of crisis, owing to a combination of internal problems (mismatch between strategy and required resources and mismatch between strategy and organization), a downturn in the market, and a growing presence in this market of large manufacturers of medical equipment such as General Electric and Siemens.

Resources and capabilities enable a company to respond to the challenges it encounters. However, when faced with a relatively rapid pace of external change, some firms may not be able to react quickly, either because they lack the resources or capabilities that are needed to respond to that challenge or, quite simply, because they do not know how to use them in the new environment. Thus, firms allow growth opportunities to pass them by. In this case, the cause of the lack of growth is to be found not in external factors but in internal ones.

When General Motors delayed an immediate response to the growth of the compact-car segment in the USA in the late 1970s, it lost a major growth opportunity. Part of the problem in the slowness of General Motors' reaction was its managers' perception of the importance that a possible compact-cars division would have on the company. The popular saying at that time was: 'Small cars, small profits'. However, a complementary explanation for General Motors' lack of reaction would be that the company's resources and capabilities for the design, manufacturing, and sale of automobiles were not up to the new paradigm that Japanese manufacturers were imposing on this segment and that would later spread to the entire market.

When the compact-car segment started to grow, in the mid-1980s, and the Japanese manufacturers became industry leaders, General Motors acknowledged that it could not react fast enough to the new competitive situation. In an attempt to lighten the problem, it reached an agreement with Toyota to manufacture in a General Motors plant in California a small car that had already been designed and marketed by Toyota. The purpose of this initiative was to learn how to make these cars and how to manage procurement, assembly, and distribution from the industry's leading Japanese company. At the same time, General Motors created a separate division whose purpose would be to design, produce, and market by the early 1990s a compact car that could be recognized as market leader. This division launched Saturn, the new car, in 1992. Although this division has been a success, its integration in General

Motors has been relatively low and it has not made a great contribution yet to its renewal.

This case shows that a company may have abundant resources and capabilities. However, if these are not what the company needs at that time, they may be useless. Consequently, the limit to growth, from this viewpoint, is not that resources or capabilities are unavailable but that the available resources or capabilities do not adapt to the company's needs and the challenges of the industry to enable growth to continue. Otherwise, these resources may be useless.

In addition, these resources may not only be useless for the company's future expansion but may also constitute an obstacle to change. Ghemawat and Ricart (1993) point out that the company's static efficiency (in other words, the short-term improvement in operations) tends to generate capabilities that may be different from those required for the company's dynamic efficiency (in other words, the company's ability to change).

Leonard-Barton (1992) also suggests that certain core capabilities may become core rigidities that prevent firms from changing and improving their competitive position in the future. In both cases, these available capabilities or resources may limit the company's future growth.

After all, it is not just the lack of resources or capabilities that may bring corporate growth to an end, but the lack of the right ones to face the current and future needs of customers. This disharmony, when it is not addressed by the firm, can have a dreadful effect on the firm's growth potential.

6. THE DISHARMONY BETWEEN THE FIRM'S GROWTH STRATEGY AND ITS IMPLEMENTATION

The discordance between a firm's growth strategy and its implementation also raises serious obstacles to growth. In a nutshell, this disharmony encapsulates the impossibility of executing or implementing the strategy or the actions required to drive the growth that the company needs because of the managers' inability to change.

It may happen that, in some cases, the company does not have the resources and capabilities that are needed to undertake the change. However, even if the necessary resources and capabilities are abundant, the main obstacle to change may be the managerial action itself. At the very heart of managerial action is an ability to perceive and understand the real world, a description of a set of problems, a generation of alternative actions, the choice of a particular option to follow, and the implementation of that decision (Barnard 1936; Simon 1993). These components of managerial action may be absent in certain decisions. We must not forget that companies are communities of individuals who manage certain financial, technological, or production resources. Therefore, the ability to change will ultimately depend on these people.

On the basis of the companies we have studied, we can distinguish the following factors that seem to limit the effectiveness of managerial action in the implementation of a growth strategy: the incorrect definition of the problem, the lack of valid alternatives, the inadequate organizational design, organizational processes and routines that hamper change, and inconsistency in the decision-making process (see Fig. 9.3.). Rumelt (1995) provides another classification of factors that constitute obstacles or frictions to organizational transformation: distorted perception, dulled motivation, failed creative response, political deadlocks and action disconnection.

6.1. Incorrect definition of the problem

The inadequate definition of the problem is a first obstacle to managerial action. The reason may be lack of information, the incorrect interpretation of what is happening, or confusion in the information available owing to the problem's complexity.

Lack of information is a problem related to the company's information systems, which, in some processes, may be ineffective in grasping reality and transmitting it adequately. This refers not only to a lack of information in a strict sense, but also to the regular absence of the specific information that would be gathered, for example, if certain management control systems were used. This absence tends to conceal a significant part of reality.

Incorrect interpretation of what is happening may be an immediate consequence of the lack of an adequate information system. However, it may also occur when managers are unable to assimilate and view under a new light what is happening in the industry, what customers want, or what the company's own internal problems are. The organizational processes or concepts described earlier may play an important role in this phenomenon by preventing managers from taking an accurate snapshot of reality and interpreting it correctly. Hypotheses about the business such as 'Small cars, small profits' (as occurred in the US automobile industry) create rigidities in the way reality is understood that prevent it from being addressed with the freshness required by the new challenges facing the company.

The case of EMI discussed earlier also sheds some light on this. One of the problems it faced was the physical separation and lack of communication

- Incorrect definition of the problem
- Lack of valid alternatives
- Inadequate organizational design
- Organizational processes that hamper change
- Inconsistency in the decision-making process

Fig. 9.3. Limits to growth related to strategy implementation and managerial action

between its sales network (mainly located in the USA) and its production and R&D departments in Britain. Each department's individual interests generated a climate of mistrust between the department managers that precluded an unbiased evaluation of the data on the company's critical situation. This preclusion was a decisive factor in delaying a more accurate diagnosis of the situation and a suitable action plan to redress it.

Finally, one should not underestimate the difficulty in integrating information on multiple aspects of reality. Reality is complex, with subtle facets that the information is unable adequately to portray, or with implicit or hidden interrelations that managers are not always able to perceive. This difficulty makes defining the problem accurately an even more complex task.

6.2. Lack of valid alternatives

An essential element in problem solving is to assess the merits of the various alternatives proposed. However, this exercise is valid only when the alternatives are relevant. Otherwise, it is a superfluous exercise that biases the final decision and may lead it in undesirable directions.

Managers generate alternatives on the basis of the definition given to the problem and their direct or remote experience with this type of problem. This experience may be personal or acquired through the observation of other people's actions. In the course of this process of distilling experience and applying it to the definition of alternatives, managers may encounter some obstacles: the tendency to rank different problems equally, the inefficient identification of alternatives, and the tendency to translate the solutions to problems experienced by the company at other times to the current problems.

Ranking different problems equally is an obstacle that consists of likening the nature of one situation to other analogous situations experienced by the company or by its managers in other contexts. Likening to other situations is valid when the objective circumstances permit this or the limits of the analogy are known and accepted. It ceases to be valid when it is a forced exercise; and when this exercise is carried out in such conditions, the alternative actions generated are of little use. As Neustadt and May (1986) point out, it is useful to use history to see the future. However, the parallelisms between the past and the future disappear when the contexts are different.

The inefficient identification of alternatives consists of a process by which managers observe what rivals are doing and try to imitate them. This is a dangerous exercise for two reasons. The first is that the observed company does not reveal to the observer the full reality of its actions but only a part, something akin to the tip of the iceberg. Thus, managers who observe other companies' practices see only a partial vision. If they then rashly describe the whole iceberg on the basis of its tip, they may suffer from a serious lack of realism. Secondly, this process may be pernicious because the alternatives that have been useful for one company may not be so for other companies. Each company has its own history, people, resources, and capabilities. Two companies in the same industry, with a similar size, may be as different as two companies competing in different industries. If a manager tries to generalize success stories or imitate decisions made by leading companies, without taking into account these complementary dimensions, the courses of action finally chosen may be totally inappropriate to the company.

Finally, the translation of solutions consists not only of identifying similar problems experienced at other times but also of choosing decisions that were successful and excluding those that did not work with problems experienced by the company in the past. In the same way that each company is unique, we can say that, at any given time, a company has an identity that is in part similar and in part dissimilar from that which it had in the past. The company's culture or management style may be the same, but the competitive realities and the type of capabilities needed have changed. Therefore, the mere transposition of solutions may be another factor precluding the generation of a sufficient number of solutions. The translation of solutions is, in part, a consequence of the two factors described above (ranking equally different problems and the inefficient identification of alternatives). It appears with a certain frequency in multinational companies. Thus, in these organizations, there is often a tendency—initially positive—to translate certain policies or solutions to certain problems that have been successful in one country. Consumer product companies such as L'Oréal or Heineken, or services companies such as Citibank or Carrefour, have an enormous experience in this practice and the problems they sometimes cause.

These three factors may raise obstacles to the efficient generation of alternatives, which is an essential step in any change process. These obstacles may manifest as hasty remedies for more or less identified problems or, worse still, a complete block of managers' creative ability to take a fresh look at the situation and address the problems and challenges with innovative solutions.

6.3. Inadequate organizational design

Organizational design is a basic factor in implementing a strategy, since it allows firms to pursue its activities efficiently and eventually to grow. The lack of coherence between a company's strategy and its organization is one of the causes of organizational paralysis. Many cases of disharmony between strategy and organizational design occur in fast-growth companies that start their expansion with a relatively simple organizational structure—for example, a functional one. The addition of new business units or new geographical areas imposes an additional restriction on the previous organization, which brings to light its difficulties in responding swiftly to what the market expects of it.

An extreme case of this disharmony is to be found in some internationalization decisions. Merloni, an Italian household appliances manufacturer, is a good example of this. During the 1970s and 1980s, Merloni embarked upon a very rapid international expansion, as a result of which an increasing percentage of its sales were made outside Italy. However, the manufacturing of household appliances continued to be concentrated in Italy. The strong pressure on the subsidiaries to achieve certain minimum sales targets was not supported by the production facilities, centralized in Italy, which failed to provide a prompt service to the subsidiaries. The system broke down when the Italian headquarters started to give preference to the export of large volumes to countries where there were no subsidiaries, to the detriment of the subsidiaries.

This contradiction shows, among other aspects, the importance of matching the organization to the strategy pursued. In the case of Merloni, its international growth strategy ended up being incompatible with a function-based organization centralized in Italy and a relatively low level of coordination between subsidiaries and the parent company. This disharmony led to a critical situation and, finally, to a complete reorganization of the company.

An additional aspect of this type of disharmony is to be found in the execution of some of the company's activities. The disharmony we have just described in Merloni between production and sales, or between design and production, is a classic example of a situation in the business world that hampers a firm's growth potential. This disharmony contrasts with the strategic harmony that some companies are capable of achieving in their operations and that constitutes a basic driver of corporate growth, as we have discussed in Chapter 6.

6.4. Organizational processes that hamper change

In Chapter 7 we pointed out that the company's resources and capabilities are not just an inventory: above all, they have a dynamic nature, as they are the outcome of people's professional experience over a relatively long period of time. Over the years people have learnt to use the firms' resources and deploy their capabilities in a particular way. This gives rise to the organizational processes a firm follows to address problems. Internal processes thus become a coordination mechanism of the company's resources and capabilities, and, as such, have a direct impact on the organization's growth (Nelson and Winter 1982).

Processes have a very significant effect on the company's evolution over time and on the deployment of resources and capabilities. Their specific mechanism of influence are the major and minor actions taken by the decision-makers at different times. These decisions are influenced by the company's internal and external context. One way of understanding these processes is to liken them to the software that a computer uses. Processes enable people to observe reality in a certain way and for resources and capabilities to be combined to respond to that reality. Sometimes, companies may have suitable resources and capabilities to respond to the pressures of change; however, they may lack the appropriate organizational processes that allow that change.

Internal processes and policies, together with resources and capabilities, influence the path that the company will follow in the future, inclining its decisions in one direction or another. This factor explains why the problems experienced by some companies in adapting to changes in their industry and fostering growth are not due so much to the absence of resources as to the existence of processes that contribute to perceiving problems under an inappropriate light and combining resources and capabilities inefficiently.

IBM's slow entry in the personal-computer industry in the early 1980s is a case in point. IBM's technological and marketing expertise—its approach to problem solving—favoured the mainframes and tended to belittle the personal computer. IBM's internal organizational processes and its way of solving problems, which had been successful for so many years, became an enormous obstacle that the company had to overcome before it could understand the changes that were taking place in the personal-computer industry and that effectively slowed down its adaptation.

This resistance to change caused by internal policies and processes, or by the way reality is understood, becomes markedly greater in industries such as software, semiconductors, or telecommunications, where there are increasing returns (Arthur 1994) that contribute to the tendency for leading companies to strengthen their leadership. These industries offer significant advantages to firms that are first to enter a market, such as achieving an efficient scale and gaining the experience that enables them to operate with lower costs. Furthermore, the rapid growth of a broad customer base may make switching costs from one product to another prohibitively high. Consequently, the competitive advantages of companies entering the market first tend to consolidate.

One should not overstate the role played by increasing returns. It is true that the high capital expenditures required by these industries, and the fact that customers are not inclined to change (both because of the high cost involved and because of the learning acquired about a particular product or technology), strengthen the leading companies' trend towards leadership. However, this trend is not absolute. Indeed, it could be argued that companies such as IBM or Digital were operating in such an industry in the 1970s and 1980s. However, their leadership was challenged by a new wave of innovations and newcomers— such as Microsoft, Compaq, or Dell—that made the products and services offered by the established companies obsolete. Thus, although the advantages of increasing returns are significant, they should not be valued for more than they are worth. If we did, we would be forgetting that, in the recent history of industries with increasing returns, there are already many examples of emerging companies that have challenged the leadership of established companies.

6.5. Inconsistency in the decision–making process

When choosing the decision to make from among the options available, managers may encounter a number of significant obstacles. First, the inconsistency in choosing the right option. Choosing options must be governed by a series of qualitative and quantitative criteria—for example, investment alternatives may be assessed using criteria such as return on investment, growth potential, new knowledge and learning that the investment would bring to the company, new jobs created, and growth options that the investment will generate in the future. The use of a large number of criteria is a sign of thoroughness in the choice process. However, at the same time, it requires greater rigour when comparing different options using the same criteria. A typical mistake is to compare different options with different criteria, excluding certain criteria in some cases so as to be able better to control the decision's complexity.

The second is the inconsistency between the elements comprising the decision itself. Thus, in the case of an investment decision, it is important that this decision contains more than a complete description of the quantitative assumptions on which the estimates are based. Much more important than this is to verify that the specific policies that will follow from this decision—policies affecting R&D, marketing, or manufacturing—are consistent with each other.

Innefficiency in the execution process of the decision is another problem. This type of inefficiency may have very different causes: lack of motivation of key people, inadequate incentives to favour change, the emergence of management coalitions with very different interests, or the lack of alignment between the appropriate organizational structure and the company's information, compensation, and control systems. These inefficiencies are not exclusive to growth processes. Generally speaking, they can be found in any company facing strategic change. They are particularly important in managing the company's growth process.

A final comment should be made here. Some of the factors that contribute to the inconsistency in the decision-making process are essential elements in the definition of the internal context, as we presented it in Chapter 4. An internal context with the right attributes is critical in endorsing the corporate growth process. On the contrary, an internal context that gives rise to some of the inconsistencies mentioned will block the growth process, either right from the start, or in its execution.

7. SOME FINAL REMARKS

In this chapter we have presented and developed the concept of strategic harmony, which is essential in understanding the limits and constraints of corporate growth. Strategic harmony is a natural extension of the business concept (introduced in Chapter 6) and has several dimensions: strategic harmony between the firm's strategy and the industry, between the firm's strategy and its resources and capabilities, and between the firm's strategy and its implementation. We have analysed some of the firm's external and internal factors that can give rise to disharmony and may eventually impede sustainable growth. Among them, we have highlighted the loss of value of resources and capabilities due to imitation and substitution, the lack of new initiatives, the tyranny of past success, the divergence between strategy and organization, and the inefficiency in managerial action.

The distinction between internal and external limits to corporate growth is a way of understanding reality that can be justified from a methodological viewpoint. However, this distinction must be used with caution, as both types of limit interact with each other. On the one hand, it is logical that the decisions made by a company to speed up growth (development of new products, implementation of certain technologies, pricing policies, etc.) will eventually have an impact on the industry in which the company operates. An increase in production capacity, for example, will affect the industry's level of aggregate capacity, perhaps influencing a future excess capacity. The introduction of new products may change the pattern of demand for the current products, both for the company itself and for other companies. Consequently, the company has a significant impact on the industry and its decisions may influence what we have called the company's external limits. However, these external factors may shape the internal limits to growth. Thus, demand patterns tend to favour certain customers or products over others. In other words, demand patterns force a company to improve certain capabilities. An industry leader's current customers may force the company to make certain decisions, which might not be exactly those that will guarantee sustained growth for the company in the future.

Internal and external limits to growth are closely interrelated. It could not be any other way, as the growth model and the growth process we have presented in this book show a continuous interplay. The internal context, the firm's resources and capabilities, its business concept, on the one hand, and the external context in which the company carries out its activities, on the other, are like two wings that help corporate growth fly or stop.

REFERENCES

ABELL, D. (1980), *Defining the Business* (Englewood Cliffs, NJ: Prentice-Hall).

ACKENHUSEN, M., and GHOSHAL, S. (1992), 'Canon: Competing on Capabilities', Case study, Insead, Fontainebleau.

ALLISON, G. T. (1971), *The Essence of Decision* (Boston: Little Brown).

AMIT, R., and SCHOEMAKER, P. J. H. (1993), 'Strategic Assets and Organizational Rent', *Strategic Management Journal*, 14 (19): 33–46.

ANDREWS, K. R. (1971), *The Concept of Corporate Strategy* (Homewood, Ill.: Irwin).

ANSOFF, I. (1965), *Corporate Strategy* (New York: McGraw-Hill).

ARORA, A., and GAMBARELLA, A. (1997), 'Domestic Markets and International Competitiveness: Generic and Product-Specific Competencies in the Engineering Sector', *Strategic Management Journal*, 18, Special Issue, (Summer): 53–74.

ARTHUR, B. (1994), *Increasing Returns and Path Dependency in the Economy* (Ann Arbor: University of Michigan Press).

ASHKENAS, R., ULRICH, D., JICK, T., and KERR, S. (1995), *The Boundaryless Organization* (San Francisco: Jossey Bass).

BADEN-FULLER, C., and STOPFORD, J. M. (1992), *Rejuvenating the Mature Business* (London: Routledge).

BAGHAI, M., COLEY, S. C., and WHITE, D. (1996), 'Staircases to Growth', *The McKinsey Quarterly*, 4: 39–61.

—— —— —— (1999), *The Alchemy of Growth* (London: Orion Business).

BARNARD, C. (1936), *The Functions of the Executive* (Cambridge, Mass.: Harvard University Press).

BARNEY, J. B. (1986), 'Organizational Culture: Can it be a Source of Competitive Advantage?', *Academy of Management Review*, 11 (3): 656–65.

—— (1995), 'Looking inside for competitive advantage', *Academy of Management Executive*, 9 (4) (Nov.): 49–61.

BARTLETT, C., and GHOSHAL, S. (1989), *Managing across Borders* (Boston: Harvard Business School Press).

—— and Nanda, A. (1990), 'Ingvar Kamprad and Ikea', Case no. 390-132, Harvard Business School, Boston.

BARTLETT, C. A., and RANGAN, U. S. (1985), 'Komatsu Limited', Case no. 389-089, Harvard Business School, Boston.

BAUMOL, W. (1962), 'On the Theory of the Expansion of the Firm', *American Economic Review*, 52: 1078–87.

BOUDEGUER, R. M., and BALLARÍN, E. (1993), 'Banco Popular Español', Case no. DG-1064-E, IESE, Barcelona.

BOURGEOIS, L. J., and EISENHARDT, K. M. (1988), 'Strategic Decision Processes in High Velocity Environments: Four Cases in the Microcomputer Industry', *Management Science*, 34: 816–35.

BOWER, J. (1970), *Managing the Resource Allocation Process* (Boston: Harvard Business School).

BOWER, J. and MATTHEWS, J. (1994), 'Marks & Spencer: Sir Richard Greenbury's Quiet Revolution', Case no. 395-454 (Boston: Harvard Business School).

BOWMAN, E. H., and HURRY, D. (1993), 'Strategy through the Options Lens: An Integrated View of Resource Investments and the Incremental-Choice Process', *Academy of Management Review*, 18 (4): 760–82.

BRANDENBURGER, A., and NALEBUFF, B. J. (1996), *Co-opetition* (New York: Currency/ Doubleday).

BREALEY, R., and MYERS, S. (1996), *Principles of Corporate Finance* (New York: McGraw-Hill).

BROWN, S., and EISENHARDT, K. M. (1998), *Competing on the Edge* (Boston: Harvard Business School Press).

BURGELMAN, R. A. (1983), 'A Model of the Interaction of Strategic Behavior, Corporate Context and the Concept of Strategy', *Academy of Management Review*, 3: 61–9.

—— and GROVE, A. S. (1996), 'Strategic Dissonance', *California Management Review*, 38 (2): 1–20.

—— and SAYLES, L. R. (1986), *Inside Corporate Innovation* (New York: Free Press).

CANALS, J. (1993*a*), *Competitive Strategies in European Banking* (Oxford: Oxford University Press).

—— (1993*b*), 'Banco Santander–Banco Popular (A)', Case no. ASE-240-E, IESE, Barcelona.

—— (1993*c*), 'Indo Internacional', Case no. ASE-300-E, IESE, Barcelona.

—— (1994), *La internacionalización de la empresa* (Madrid: McGraw-Hill).

—— (1997*a*), *Universal Banking* (Oxford: Oxford University Press).

—— (1997*b*), 'Excess Capacity and Global Competition: A Resource-Based Approach', in M. Thomas, D. O' Neal, and M. Ghertman (eds.), *Strategy, Structure and Style* (New York: John Wiley): 41–68.

—— (1998), 'Universal Banks: The need for Corporate Renewal', *European Management Journal*, 16 (5): 623–34.

—— (1999), 'The Spanish Banking Industry', IESE, Barcelona.

—— and BARDOLET, D. (1998), 'Glaxo: The Acquisition of Wellcome', Case no. ASE-386-E, IESE, Barcelona.

—— and DÁVILA, A. (1995), 'Seat in 1990', Case no. ASE-353-E, IESE, Barcelona.

—— and FERNÁNDEZ, A. (1995), 'Ficosa International', Case no. ASE-305-E, IESE, Barcelona.

—— and GIMENEZ, G. (1994), 'Volkswagen and the European Automobile Industry in 1993', Case no. ASE-336-E, IESE, Barcelona.

CHANDLER, A. (1962), *Strategy and Structure* (Cambridge, Mass.: MIT Press).

—— (1990), *Scale and Scope* (Cambridge, Mass.: Harvard University Press).

CHILD, J. (1972), 'Organization Structure, Environment and Performance: The Role of Strategic Choice', *Sociology*, 6: 2–22.

CHRISTENSEN, C. M. (1997), *The Innovator's Dilemma* (Boston: Harvard Business School Press).

—— and BOWER, J. L. (1996), 'Customer Power, Strategic Investment and the Failure of Leading Firms', *Strategic Management Journal*, 17 (3): 197–218.

CHRISTENSEN, C. R., ANDREWS, K., and BOWER, J. (1965), *Business Policy: Text and Cases* (Burr Ridge, Ill.: Irwin).

CLARK, K. B. and WHEELWRIGHT, S. C. (1993), *Managing New Product and Process Development* (New York: Free Press).

COASE, R. H. (1937), 'The Nature of the Firm', *Economica*, NS, 4: 386–405.

COLLINS, J. C. and PORRAS, J. I. (1994), *Built to Last* (New York: Harper Collins).

—— —— (1996), 'Building your Company's Vision', *Harvard Business Review* (Sept.–Oct.): 65–77.

COLLIS, D. J. (1987), 'Saatchi & Saatchi Company PLC', Case no. 387-170, Harvard Business School, Boston.

—— (1988), 'The Walt Disney Company', Case no. 388-147, Harvard Business School, Boston.

COLLIS, D. J. and MONTGOMERY, C. A. (1995), 'Competing on Resources', *Harvard Business Review* (July–Aug.): 118–28.

—— (1997), *Corporate Strategy* (Chicago: Irwin).

—— (1998), 'Creating Corporate Advantage', *Harvard Business Review* (May–June): 70–83.

DAY, G. (1990), *Market-Driven Strategy* (New York: Free Press).

DE GEUS, A. (1997), *The Living Company* (Boston: Harvard Business School Press).

DIERICKX, Y., and COOL, K. (1989), 'Asset Stock Accumulation and Sustainability of Competitive Advantage', *Management Science* (Dec.): 1.504–1.511.

DIXIT, A. K., and PINDYCK, R. S. (1995), 'The Options Approach to Capital Investment', *Harvard Business Review* (May–June): 105–18.

DONALDSON, G., and LORSCH, J. (1984), *Decision Making at the Top* (New York: Basic Books).

DOZ, Y. L. (1996), 'The Evolution of Cooperation in Strategic Alliances: Initial Conditions or Learning Processes?', *Strategic Management Journal*, Special Issue (Summer): 55–83.

DRUCKER, P. (1994), 'The Theory of Business', *Harvard Business Review* (Sept.–Oct.): 95–104.

EISENHARDT, K. M. and ZBARACKI, M. J. (1992), 'Strategic Decision Making', *Strategic Management Journal*, 13: 17–37.

ESTY, B. and GHEMAWAT, P. (1993), 'Gillette's Launch of Sensor', Case no. 792-028, Harvard Business School, Boston.

Europe's 500 (1998), *Europe's Most Dynamic Entrepreneurs* (Brussels).

GALBRAITH, J. (1977), *Organization Design* (Reading, Mass.: Addison-Wesley).

GARNSEY, E. (1998), 'A Theory of the Early Growth of the Firm', *Industrial and Corporate Change*, 7 (3): 523–56.

GEROSKI, P. and MACHIN, S. (1992), 'The Dynamics of Corporate Growth', (working paper, London Business School).

—— —— and WALTERS, C. F. (1996), 'Corporate Growth and Profitability, (discussion paper; CEPR).

GERTZ, D., and BAPTISTA, J. (1995), *Grow to be Great* (New York: Free Press).

GHEMAWAT, P. (1986), 'Sustainable Advantage', *Harvard Business Review*, 64 (Sept.–Oct.): 53–8.

—— (1987), 'Wal-Mart Stores' Discount Operations', Case no. 387-018, Harvard Business School, Boston.

—— (1991), *Commitment* (New York: Free Press).

—— and RICART, J. E. (1993), 'The Organizational Tension between Static and Dynamic Efficiency', *Strategic Management Journal*, 14, Special Issue (Winter): 59–74.

GHOSHAL, S., and BARTLETT, C. A. (1997), *The Individualized Corporation* (New York: HarperBusiness).

—— HAHN, M., and MORAN, P. (1997), 'Management Competence, Firm Growth and Economic Progress', (working paper; Insead, Fontainebleau, France).

—— MORAN, P., and DAGNINO, G. B. (1999), 'Toward an Integrative Theory of Firm Growth (mimeo; London Business School).

GOOLD, M. C., CAMPBELL, A., and ALEXANDER, M. (1994); *Corporate-Level Strategy* (New York: John Wiley & Sons).

GRANT, R. (1995), *Contemporary Strategy Analysis* (Oxford: Blackwell).

HALLOWELL, R. H., and HESKETT, J. L. (1995), 'Southwest Airlines: 1993 (A)', Case no. 694-023, Harvard Business School, Boston.

HAMEL, G. (1998), 'Strategy Innovation and the Quest for Value', *Sloan Management Review* (Winter): 7–14.

—— and PRAHALAD, C. K. (1989), 'Strategic Intent', *Harvard Business Review*, 67 (3): 63–76.

—— —— (1993), 'Strategy as Stretch and Leverage', *Harvard Business Review*, 71 (2): 75–84.

—— —— (1994), *Competing for the Future* (Boston: Harvard Business School Press).

HART, S. L. (1992), 'An Integrative Framework for Strategy-Making Processes', *Academy of Management Review*, 17 (2): 327–35.

HAX, A., and MAJLUFF, N. (1984), *Strategic Management: An Integrative Perspective* (Englewood Cliffs, NJ: Prentice-Hall).

—— —— (1991), *The Strategy Concept and Process* (Englewood Cliffs, NJ: Prentice-Hall).

HENDERSON, R., and MITCHELL, W. (1997), 'The Interactions of Organizational and Competitive Influences on Strategy and Performance', *Strategic Management Journal*, 18, Special Issue (Summer): 5–14.

HITT, M. A., and TYLER, B. B. (1991), 'Strategic Decision Models: Integrating Different Perspectives', *Strategic Management Journal*, 12: 327–51.

HOFFER, C. W., and SCHENDEL, D. (1978): *Strategy Formulation: Analytical Concepts* (New York: West Publishing Co.).

HUETE, L. M. (1993), 'Multiasistencia', Case no. P-830-E, IESE, Barcelona.

—— and SEGARRA, J. A. (1996), 'Port Aventura', Case no. P-891-E, IESE, Barcelona.

KAY, J. (1993), *Foundations of Corporate Success* (Oxford: Oxford University Press).

KHANNA, T., and PALEPU, K. (1997), 'Why Focused Strategies may be Wrong for Emerging Markets?', *Harvard Business Review* (July–Aug.): 41–51.

KIM, W. C., and MAUBORGNE, R. (1997), 'Value innovation', *Harvard Business Review*, (Jan.–Feb.): 102–12.

KIRZNER, I. M. (1973), *Competition and Entrepreneurship* (Chicago: University of Chicago Press).

KOTTER, J. P., and HESKETT, J. L. (1992), *Corporate Culture and Performance* (New York: Free Press).

KNIEF, C., GARCIA-PONT, C., and RICART, J. E. (1995), 'Internationalization of Telefonica España', Case no. DG-1136-E, IESE, Barcelona.

KREPS, D. (1990), 'Corporate Culture and Economic Theory', in J. Alt and K. Shepsle (eds.), *Perspectives on Positive Political Economy* (Cambridge: Cambridge University Press), 90–143.

LEONARD-BARTON, D. (1992), 'Core Capabilities and Core Rigidites: A Paradox in Managing New Product Development', *Strategic Management Journal*, 13 (1): 111–25.

—— (1995): *Wellsprings of Knowledge* (Boston: Harvard Business School Press).

LESSARD, D., ROMER, P., PERLMAN, L., SHIH, S., and VOLKENIA, M. (1998), 'Bank of America Round Table on the Soft Revolution: Achieving Growth by Managing Intangibles', *Journal of Applied Corporate Finance*, 11 (2): 8–27.

LEVINTHAL, D. A., and MARCH, J. G. (1993), 'The Myopia of Learning', *Strategic Management Journal*, 14, Special Issue (Winter): 95–112.

LIEBERMAN, M. B., and MONTGOMERY, D. B. (1988), 'First-Mover Advantages', *Strategic Management Journal*, 9, Special Issue (Summer): 41–58.

LIPPMAN, S. A., and RUMELT, R. P. (1982), 'Uncertain Imitability: An Analysis of Interfirm Differences in Efficiency under Competition', *Bell Journal of Economics*, 13: 418–38.

LUEHRMAN, T. (1998), 'Strategy as a Portfolio of Real Options', *Harvard Business Review* (Sept.–Oct.): 89–99.

McGAHAN, A. M., and PORTER, M. E. (1997), 'How Much Does Industry Matter, Really?', *Strategic Management Journal*, 18, Special Issue (Summer): 15–30.

McGRATH, R. G. (1997), 'A Real Options Logic for Initiating Technology Positioning Investments', *Academy of Management Review*, 22 (4): 974–96.

MARCH, J., and SIMON, H. (1958), *Organizations* (New York: John Wiley).

MARKIDES, C. (1997), 'Strategic Innovation', *Sloan Management Review* (Spring): 9–23.

MARRIS, R. (1963), 'A Model of the Managerial Enterprise', *Quarterly Journal of Economics*, 73: 185–209.

MILGROM, P., and ROBERTS, J. (1995), 'Complementarities and Fit: Strategy, Structure and Organizational Change in Manufacturing', *Journal of Accounting and Economics*, 19: 179–208.

MILES, R. E., and SNOW, C. (1994) *Fit, Failure and the Hall of Fame* (New York: Free Press).

MILLS, D. Q., and FRIESEN, G. B. (1996), *Broken Promises* (Boston: Harvard Business School Press).

MINTZBERG, H. (1979), *The Structuring of Organizations* (Englewood Cliffs, NJ: Prentice-Hall).

MONTGOMERY, C. A. (1994), 'Corporate Diversification', *Journal of Economic Perspectives* (Summer): 163–78.

NELSON, R., and WINTER, S. (1982), *An Evolutionary Theory of Economic Change* (Cambridge: Harvard University Press).

NEUSTADT, R. E., and MAY, E. R. (1986), *Thinking in Time* (New York: Free Press).

NICHOLS, N. A. (1994), 'Medicine, Management and Mergers: An Interview with Merck's P. Roy Vagelos', *Harvard Business Review* (Nov.–Dec.): 104–14.

NODA, T., and BOWER, J. L. (1996), 'Strategy Making as Iterated Processes of Resource Allocation', *Strategic Management Journal*, 17, Special Issue (Summer): 159–92.

NONAKA, I., and TAKEUCHI, H. (1995), *The Knowledge Creating Company* (Oxford: Oxford University Press).

NORMANN, R. (1977), *Management for Growth* (New York: John Wiley).

NORTH, D. C. (1990), *Institutions, Institutional Change and Economic Performance* (Cambridge: Cambridge University Press).

PAPADAKIS, V. M., LIOUKAS, S., and CHAMBERS, D. (1998), 'Strategic Decision-Making Processes', *Strategic Management Journal*, 19 (2): 115–47.

PENROSE, E. (1959), *The Theory of the Growth of the Firm* (New York: John Wiley).

PÉREZ LÓPEZ, J. A. (1993), *Fundamentos de Dirección de Empresas* (Madrid: Rialp).

PETERAF, M. A. (1993), 'The Cornerstones of Competitive Advantage', *Strategic Management Journal*, 14 (3): 179–92.

PORTER, M. E. (1980), *Competitive Strategy* (New York: Free Press).

—— (1985), *Competitive Advantage* (New York: Free Press).

—— (1996), 'What Is Strategy', *Harvard Business Review* (Nov.–Dec.): 61–78.

PRAHALAD, C. K., and HAMEL, G. (1990), 'The Core Competence of the Corporation', *Harvard Business Review*, 68 (3): 79–91.

RUMELT, R. P. (1974), *Strategy, Structure and Economic Performance* (Boston: Harvard Business School).

—— (1984), 'Towards a Strategic Theory of the Firm', in R. Lamb (ed.), *Competitive Strategic Management* (Englewood Cliffs, NJ: Prentice-Hall): 556–570.

RUMELT, R. P. (1991), 'How Much Does Industry Matter?', *Strategic Management Journal*, 12 (3): 167–85.

—— (1995), 'Inertia and Transformation', in C. A. Montgomery (ed.), *Resource-Based and Evolutionary Theories of the Firm* (Boston: Kluwer).

SALONER, G. (1991), 'Modeling Game Theory and Strategic Management', *Strategic Management Journal*, 12, Special Issue (Winter): 119–36.

SCHUMPETER, J. A. (1934), *The Theory of Economic Development* (Cambridge, Mass.: Harvard University Press).

SELZNICK, P. (1957), *Leadership in Administration* (New York: Harper & Row).

SHAPIRO, C. (1989), 'The Theory of Business Strategy', *Rand Journal of Economics*, 20: 125–37.

SIMON, H. (1993), 'Strategy and Organizational Evolution', *Strategic Management Journal*, 14, Special Issue (Winter): 131–42.

SIMONS, R. (1994), 'How New Top Managers Use Control Systems as Levers of Strategic Renewal', *Strategic Management Journal*, 15 (3): 169–89.

—— (1995), *Levers of Control* (Boston: Harvard Business School Press).

SLYWOTZKY, A. J. (1996), *Value Migration* (Boston: Harvard Business School).

SLYWOTZKY, A. J., MORRISON, D. J. and QUELLA, J. A. (1998), 'Achieving Sustained Shareholder Value Growth', *Mercer Management Journal*, 10: 9–22.

STALK, G. Jr., PECAUT, D. K. and BURNETT, B. (1996), 'Breaking Compromises', *Harvard Business Review* (Sept.–Oct.): 131.

STOPFORD, J. M., and BADEN-FULLER, C. (1994), 'Creating Corporate Entrepreneurship', *Strategic Management Journal*, 15 (7): 521–36.

TAYLOR, W. (1993), 'Message and Muscle: An Interview with Swatch Titan Nicolas Hayek', *Harvard Business Review*, 10 (Mar.–Apr.): 98–110.

TEECE, D. J., PISANO, G., and SHUEN, A. (1997), 'Dynamic Capabilities and Strategic Management', *Strategic Management Journal*, 18 (7): 509–33.

THOMAS, R. J. (1993), *New Product Development* (New York: John Wiley).

TRIPSAS, M. (1997), 'Unraveling the Process of Creative Destruction: Complementary Assets and Incumbent Survival in the Typesetter industry', *Strategic Management Journal*, 18, Special Issue (Summer): 119–42.

TUSHMAN, M., and O'REILLY, C. (1997), *Winning through Innovation* (Boston: Harvard Business School Press).

VAN DER HEIJDEN, K. (1996), *Scenarios: The Art of Strategic Conversation* (New York: John Wiley).

WACK, P. (1985), 'Scenarios: Uncharted Waters Ahead', *Harvard Business Review* (Sept.–Oct.): 72–89.

WERNERFELT, B. (1984), 'A Resource-Based View of the Firm', *Strategic Management Journal*, 5 (2): 171–80.

WILLIAMSON, O. (1975), *Markets and Hierarchies* (New York: Free Press).

INDEX